TREMORS
IN THE
BLOOD

TREMORS IN THE BLOOD

MURDER, OBSESSION, AND
THE BIRTH OF THE LIE DETECTOR

Amit Katwala

CROOKED
LANE

NEW YORK

Published in the United States by Crooked Lane Books, an imprint of The Quick Brown Fox & Company LLC.

Crooked Lane Books and its logo are trademarks of The Quick Brown Fox & Company LLC.

Library of Congress Catalog-in-Publication data available upon request.

ISBN (trade paperback): 978-1-63910-342-3
ISBN (ebook): 978-1-63910-343-0

Cover design by Sarah Brody
Cover photograph © Underwood Archives

Printed in the United States.

www.crookedlanebooks.com

Crooked Lane Books
34 West 27th St., 10th Floor
New York, NY 10001

First US Edition: March 2023
First published in the UK in 2022 by Mudlark

10 9 8 7 6 5 4 3 2 1

For Sara, my ground truth

CONTENTS

AUTHOR'S NOTE

This is the story of two murders and the machine that connects them: a near mythical box with the power to sort truth from lies.

Everything you're about to read really happened, and the account that follows is based on historical sources: thousands of newspaper and magazine articles, private letters, diaries, academic journals, photographs, court documents, prison records, books, physical artifacts, and interviews.

Anything between quotation marks comes from a written document or an interview—all dialogue attributed to people was said or written, or reportedly said or written, by those in question.

Where different accounts disagree on the exact wording, I've opted for clarity and concision. Where there are more significant disputes about what actually happened, I've noted these in the main text or in the notes and references at the end.

But this isn't a history book. The development of the lie detector is more relevant than ever, not only because the polygraph endures but because of what that reveals about our own attitudes toward science and technology, and our relationship with the truth.

In their pursuit of justice, the men who invented the lie detector unleashed a power they couldn't control. In turbulent times, they turned to science for answers—but it merely reflected their flaws and amplified their prejudice. They were in thrall to technology and buffeted by it—they constructed false idols and fell at their feet.

This is a book about science and psychology, yes, but it's also about people: their obsessions and rivalries, their dark impulses and violent passions. It is a true story.

"Guilt carries fear always about with it; there is a tremor in the blood of a thief."
—Daniel Defoe, 1730

PART ONE

PART ONE

THE SUNSET DISTRICT

A yellow car sped north, down out of the mountains, toward San Francisco. Its round headlights cut twin beams through the gathering mist. At the wheel, Henry Wilkens risked a glance in his rearview mirror. They were definitely being followed.

It was the evening of Tuesday, May 30, 1922—Decoration Day— and the nation had come to a halt to remember its dead and to decorate their graves. More than a hundred thousand Americans had perished in the Great War, and in the city it had been a solemn, gray occasion. Soldiers laid wreaths for the fallen, the silence broken only by the clamor of gulls circling in the bay and the great foghorn of Alcatraz Island booming in the distance.

But for most people, the public holiday (today known as Memorial Day) was already morphing into a leisure opportunity. It was the era of flapper girls and prohibition, and San Francisco was finally getting its swing back after the devastation of the 1906 earthquake and fire.

Each morning, commuters in sharp suits and hats rode ferries across the bay from Oakland and Berkeley, and piled onto busy streetcars. At night, women in fur coats approached unmarked doors with whispered passwords, hair curled and coiffed into elaborate bobs. But this wasn't the "Roaring Twenties" for everyone—unemployment had more than doubled after the war, and the national crime rate had shot up since the ban on alcohol.

Henry and his young family had spent the long weekend camping with friends at Felton Auto Park, near the San Lorenzo River in the foothills of the Santa Cruz mountains, about seventy miles south of San Francisco. Now, Henry—a thin-lipped thirty-six-year-old with intense brown eyes—was piloting the family's yellow Premier toward their little flat at 1540 Vallejo Street, on the slopes of the residential Russian Hill.

The car's gleaming wheel arches caught the fading light. Its soft roof was up, and the thick fabric rippled in the breeze. Henry's wife, Anna, sat beside him on the front bench seat. She was thirty-four, with jet-black hair, pale blue eyes, and a kind, nervous smile. Their children— eight-year-old Henry Jr. and three-year-old Helen—were asleep in the raised back seat of the vehicle. When he turned his head, Henry could just make out their golden hair poking out from under a blanket.

It had been a successful trip—certainly less explosive than some of the couple's previous weekends away. In court later, Henry described the four days at Felton as a kind of pastoral idyll. The men fished in the river and played horseshoes; the women sat and talked and sewed "with their eyes on the men folk." They swam and smoked and lay on blankets in the sun.

Each morning while Anna slept, Henry walked down to the river, with his daughter on his shoulders and his son by his side, to fetch water. He returned, swinging a bucket and singing. As his children frolicked around the camp stove, Henry boiled water for the coffee and fried eggs and bacon for breakfast. On the Sunday, he whipped up an eggnog and carried it into the tent for his wife.

A photo of the Wilkens family taken around this time shows a beaming Henry in a short-sleeved shirt, brown hair pushed back from his tanned face, and Anna's arm in his. Helen—who the family nick-named "Dot" or "Mousie"—is sitting on his knee, wearing a bow in her hair and the dangerous expression of a toddler whose patience is wearing thin. Sturdy little Henry Jr. stands grinning in the background, a small arm resting protectively on his mother's shoulder.

Henry and Anna were both born in what is now Germany, and came to the United States separately during waves of migration sparked by ongoing political unrest in Europe. California was a popular desti-nation, particularly after the gold rush of the 1850s, and by the early twentieth century more than one in five San Franciscans were German born or of German descent. They built churches, formed working men's clubs known as *vereins* and set up thriving businesses in the neighborhoods north of Market Street.

But the outbreak of the First World War had a drastic impact on their status in society. Although German Americans in San Francisco were not afflicted by the hysteria that swept other parts of the country, they found their hospitals and meeting halls renamed, and their community traditions quietly disappearing. Berlin Street became Brussels Street, and Hamburg Street changed to Ridgewood Avenue. Dachshunds became "liberty hounds," sauerkraut became "liberty cabbage," and German measles became "liberty measles." The frankfurter became the "hot dog."

By 1922, a third of the *vereins* had closed. "Some Germans continued to keep and maintain the old traditions after the war, but many of them, along with their children, used this period as an opportunity to fully assimilate into the American mainstream," writes Stefanie E. Williams in *The Argonaut.* The war forced Germans to choose between their ancestral homeland and their adopted country. Most chose America.

Henry first arrived in the United States in 1905—too late for him to shed his strong accent. He was born on July 25, 1885, to Heinrich Wicken and Anna Longuet from Travemünde, a beach town and ferry port on the Baltic Sea.

He initially settled in Bridgeport, Connecticut, where he worked as a machinist at the Locomobile car factory. After a year back in Germany in 1907, he moved to California in 1910 and had a string of jobs at factories and garages in and around San Francisco: Jenkins Machine Works, American Can Company, Pacific Telephone and Telegraph. At the Garford Truck Company, he worked his way up to shop foreman, managing up to fourteen people at a time.

By 1917, he had saved enough to start his own business, and he opened a garage on Cedar Avenue, making repairs and selling tires and other car accessories. It was a quick success, and soon Henry had to find bigger premises—eventually settling on an elegant building at 1837 Pacific Avenue, with a green-tiled facade and mosaic floor. He was proud to be able to fill it with top-of-the-line equipment: a Slather lathe, a Barnes drill press, a Burroughs adding machine.

On August 27, 1912, Henry married Anna Lange, who was also from Schleswig-Holstein, and who grew up in Elmshorn, around thirty kilometers north of Hamburg, where steamships departed, carrying thousands of emigrants across the Atlantic to the New World.

Anna was the third of six children born to Wilhelm Lange and Gesche Bornholdt, and was raised in a strict Lutheran household where the daughters were barred from going to parties or socializing with the opposite sex. When she arrived in America in 1905, it must have felt like her life had opened up into a million untold futures.

As she stepped off the boat, she carried a black prayer book decorated with a cross, with her name embossed on the front in small gold letters. Inside, there was a Bible quote in German, printed in neat type, Isaiah 41:10: "Do not fear, I am with you; do not recoil, for I am your God."

* * *

The other car had been trailing them for hours. The Wilkens family had left the Felton campground early that afternoon, forming a convoy with their friends Gus and Ethel Eckert, who had planned the trip and who were leading the way back to the city in their Overland car.

But as night drew in, Henry's attention was fixed on the vehicle behind. It was a large, dark blue Hudson touring car with a typical design for the early automobile era—like Henry's beloved Premier, it had a soft roof, big wheel arches, and round headlights mounted at the tip of its long nose. At times, it was obscured by the evening traffic; at others, it vanished entirely as the road twisted and turned. When the families stopped for ice cream in Saratoga, the Hudson seemed to have gone. It shot past as Henry parked the Premier, only to reappear as they passed through one of the little farming towns at the foot of the peninsula—Mountain View, he thought, or maybe Palo Alto.

As darkness fell over the Pacific and the mists closed in, the Hudson drew nearer.

When the convoy reached Colma, where the cramped cities of the Bay Area buried their dead in sprawling cemeteries, they ran into some light traffic, and the Eckerts decided to stop for fuel. Anna stretched a pale, gloved arm out of the window to wave goodbye to her friends. "Yoo-hoo," she called.

The air was turning cold, and Anna was keen to get home. Henry stepped on the gas and felt the engine purr in response as the yellow car accelerated toward forty miles an hour. They turned up the slope through Daly City, and then down onto Junipero Serra Boulevard toward San Francisco. The Premier's taillights flashed in the dark.

They reached the edge of the city at around seven thirty PM, and as they crested the hill at Nineteenth Avenue, it spread out before them: the distant lights of Fisherman's Wharf twinkled in the distance, and to the right the outline of Mount Sutro was a hulking presence in the gloom, obscuring the electric streetlamps of the Mission and the Financial District's glut of new, brick-faced skyscrapers.

To their left, the capillaries of the city's grid system were slowly edging out the remnants of Carville, where the down-at-the-heels lived in abandoned streetcars and old vehicles stacked and welded into improvised dwellings. Beyond that, sand dunes stretched out toward the sea, burnished gold by the setting sun. Waves crashed against an empty shore.

The summer fog was rolling in thick waves now, as cold ocean winds met warm California air. It condensed in heavy drops that slid down the Premier's windshield. Visibility was down to twenty-five feet, and as he reached the top of the hill, Henry slowed down, wary of the slippery conditions.

Then suddenly the dark blue Hudson was right behind them. Its bright lights dazzled Henry's vision, and as the cars roared down the hill toward the city, it gradually pulled alongside the Premier, as if trying to overtake it. Henry had been driving down the middle of the road, and he moved to the right to allow the Hudson to pass. But it didn't.

Instead, the chasing car edged closer, until the running boards along the sides of the vehicles were less than a foot apart. Henry looked across and saw two men sitting in the front seat. They had a gun. "I saw a shotgun, a sawed-off shotgun, or if it wasn't a shotgun, it was the biggest pistol I ever seen," he said afterward.

Looking past her husband out of the left window of the Premier, Anna glimpsed the silhouette of a man climbing out onto the running boards of the other car as it swerved closer, forcing Henry to steer toward the edge of the road. She cried out: "This is a holdup."

Moments later, Henry ran out of room, and the Premier slammed into the curb near the corner of Nineteenth Avenue and Moraga Street in the Sunset district. The engine spluttered and stopped, and the lights went out. The Hudson screeched to a halt as well, some twenty meters further down the hill.

For a few seconds, everything was still. Dogs barked and howled at the nearby McCormick Kennels. Anna turned to her children, stirring from sleep in the back seat. "Put your head under the blanket so they won't see you," she told them, blue eyes wide with alarm. "Pretend you are sick and we are going to a hospital."

When she looked up, there was a man standing at her window. He was about five foot ten, with green-gray eyes, Henry said later, and he was wearing a dark, slim suit and hat and had a blue handkerchief tied over his face as a mask. He was pointing a gun.

The man peered into the back seat and then turned his attention to the terrified couple. "Give me all the money you've got," he barked at Henry, who fumbled around in his pocket and handed over a wallet, which he later told police contained three $100 bills—the equivalent of almost $5,000 in cash today.

Then, Henry said, the man in the dark suit started to turn away. But his eyes caught the glint of Anna's jewelry, and he reached back into the vehicle and tried to roughly strip the rings from her fingers. This affront was too much for Henry, who was always quick tempered. "What's the matter with you?" he bellowed. "You've got enough, haven't you?" He reached for his own gun, which was stashed in the side compartment of the car. But he was too slow.

As Henry brought the revolver in his right hand into view, he said, the bandit raised his own weapon—a .38-caliber pistol—and fired. "Don't!" Anna screamed. She threw herself in front of the gun to shield her husband. The bullet hit her at an angle, piercing her right side and lodging underneath her heart. She cried out in pain. "My God! I'm shot."

The Hudson raced away with its lights off, swerving wildly around another car and disappearing into traffic. In the Premier, Henry put down his gun with shaking hands and turned his attention to his wife.

Anna's world was fading. Blood seeped from the wound in her side, and she was finding it difficult to keep her eyes open. Her breath was faint, and she couldn't move her legs. "I'm dying, I'm dying," she said. "Take me to the hospital."

Henry pushed the button to start the car and slammed it into gear. He was trying to remember how to get to the nearest hospital. Anna pointed weakly to a nearby house to try and get him to stop there, to get help. He ignored her.

Helen was crying in the back seat, and Henry Jr. came out from under the blanket and held his dying mother in place so she wouldn't slip to the floor of the car. "They clung to their mother," reported *The Call*. "They kissed her, and they sopped up with their hands and their grimy little handkerchiefs the blood that gushed from the wound in her breast while their father raced with death."

* * *

Further down Nineteenth Avenue, Jacob Gorfinkel was wondering whether to alert the police. The forty-seven-year-old attorney, who wore thick round glasses and combed his dark, receding hair artfully over his scalp, had been driving home with his family when two cars raced past him down Junipero Serra Boulevard. He'd heard loud voices as he'd passed them stopped by the side of the road. "It was such a foggy night that no companion car would have taken the chance of following so closely, so I made up my mind it was a pursuit," he said.

Gorfinkel's sixteen-year-old son, John, was obsessed with cars, and just after seven thirty PM he heard the distinctive sound of the Hudson as it raced past again with its lights off. A few minutes later, the yellow Premier pulled alongside Gorfinkel's car, and Henry flagged them down.

He was in a frantic state. His brown hair was in disarray, and there was blood on his hands and his clothes. He asked—begged—Gorfinkel to help him get Anna to the nearest hospital. "My wife has been shot!" he cried. She was running out of time.

Henry followed the attorney down Nineteenth Avenue to the edge of Golden Gate Park. "For God's sake, hurry!" he pleaded. The grim convoy turned east toward Park Emergency Hospital at 811 Stanyan Street, a modest sandstone and stucco building that was one of the first public emergency rooms built outside a city center.

When they finally arrived, Henry jumped out of the car to pry Anna away from their bloodstained children. "They huddled in each other's arms—alone in the death car—while the father carried the mother into the hospital," wrote *The Call*.

Inside, Anna was assessed by Dr. Thomas Burns, a twenty-five-year-old resident, fresh from medical school. Burns thought Henry was behaving strangely—he seemed to oscillate between nervous agitation and moments of eerie calm. Gorfinkel noticed something odd too. While his wife was being examined by the doctor, Henry seemed intent on pulling at her left hand. It looked like he was trying to take off her glove.

Burns soon realized he didn't have enough experience to do anything for Anna himself, and he quickly arranged a transfer to Mission Emergency on Potrero Avenue (now Zuckerberg General).

Anna was loaded into one of the hospital's new motorized ambulances, a dark van with "Emergency Hospitals San Francisco,

Department of Public Health" painted on the side, for the three-mile journey across the city. Henry followed in the Premier, driving as fast as he dared in the damp conditions.

The ambulance reached the hospital just before eight thirty PM, and Anna was on the operating table within five minutes. Doctors Frank Sheehy, a twenty-nine-year-old resident on secondment from Los Angeles, and H. L. Williamson, one of a handful of female doctors working in the city, raced to save her life. But it was already too late.

When Henry arrived three minutes later, screeching to a halt outside the red-brick building and charging through the doors of the emergency room, the doctors had to tell him that his wife was dead. He staggered like he'd been punched in the stomach. "My God, why couldn't they have killed me instead?" he wailed. "She tried to save me. They have taken everything I had." Then he collapsed.

* * *

The next morning, thick fog still lay over the city like a shroud. Anna's death was on the front pages of the major newspapers. "Woman Slain in Auto Hold Up," screamed *The Chronicle*. "Young Mother Gives Life to Save Husband."

The crime struck a chord with a populace that was already on edge. San Francisco in the 1920s was a slightly lawless place, being rebuilt at a rapid pace after the earthquake, which had killed three thousand people, leveled almost thirty thousand buildings, and left two hundred and twenty-five thousand homeless.

Between the gold rush and the port, the city had always had a seedier side, and the advent of prohibition in 1920 only strengthened the criminal element. The previous Friday, another couple—Arthur and Martha Herbst from Hillsborough—had been held up in a similar fashion just a few blocks away and robbed of $25,000 of jewelry and furs.

In a press conference, San Francisco's chief of police vowed to act. "Quick and concerted action is needed," said Daniel O'Brien, a deep-chested man in his late forties.

He joined the police in 1908 and had been promoted to chief in 1920, where one of his first major cases was the arrest of silent movie star Roscoe "Fatty" Arbuckle, who was accused of the rape and manslaughter of actress Virginia Rappe. Arbuckle, who was second in popularity only to Charlie Chaplin, was eventually acquitted after three trials, but the case propelled O'Brien into the public eye.

It was a role he enjoyed—he went on to play bit-part roles in several silent movies, and his son George became a popular film star in his own right. By the end of his career, O'Brien would serve as a city ambassador to the rich and famous: a photograph from this time shows him in full police garb—navy suit, badge pinned over the heart, peaked cap with "CHIEF" embroidered on the front—shaking hands with the film star Rudolph Valentino.

"The class of criminals responsible for the slaying of Mrs. Wilkens are absolutely devoid of any respect for human life," O'Brien told reporters. "Every effort must be put forth to drive the thug and holdup man from our midst."

But the officers who were searching for Anna's murderers were still largely untrained, low-paid, and poorly educated men for whom the job was their only legal shot at a lucrative career. Graft and corruption were rampant, as was the use of the notorious "third degree"—a euphemism for beating suspects to extract evidence or confessions. The chances of the law bringing anyone to justice were slim.

The police department and district attorney's office joined in a pledge to put an immediate halt to criminal activity in the city. Together, they set up a dragnet. Twelve carloads of men armed with sawed-off shotguns patrolled the roads heading out of the city, with a particular focus on the Sunset District where Anna had been shot. Other officers went door to door at rooming houses and hotels where criminals were known to congregate, hoping to find some trace of the bandits.

But they had very little to go on. By the time Detectives Henry McGrath and Michael Griffin arrived at the hospital on the night of the shooting, Henry had regained consciousness—but he was still shaky and his fractured, meager account didn't give them much detail to work with. He told them there had been three men sitting in the car, and that one had jumped out and taken $300 and two diamond rings, and then shot Anna when Henry reached for his gun.

Strangely, for someone who was an expert in cars—but perhaps understandably given the emotional strain he was under—Henry misidentified the vehicle that had been tailing him, even after a conversation at the hospital with Jacob Gorfinkel. The attorney was convinced it had been a dark-bodied Hudson touring car, but Henry told the detectives it was an old red Dodge.

The next morning, neighbors gathered in solemn groups outside Henry and Anna's flat on Vallejo Street, but the curtains were drawn and there was no one home. The kids were staying with Adolph Lange, Anna's uncle. Helen played with dolls and frolicked with the Lange's dachshund—the tears of the previous night seemingly forgotten. "Don't cry, Dot," her brother had told her. "God will take care of Mamma in heaven."

Henry was at his garage, moving around the workshop like a ghost, "his face tragic, his steps futile, for he hardly knows what he is doing," according to reporter Ernestine Black. "I couldn't stand it in the home where we have been so happy, so I came over here to the shop," he told her. A string of friends and well-wishers arrived bearing condolences—he silently shook each person's hand, but could barely muster the strength for conversation.

He was a broken man, haunted by what had happened and what he might have done differently: Should he have tried harder to get away? Had he made a mistake by drawing his own gun? His voice cracked and tears rolled down his face as he relayed the story to journalists and vowed to bring his wife's killers to justice. "I'll spend the rest of my life hunting for them," he said.

WRITTEN IN BLOOD

Milton Stout had a problem. It was Thursday, June 1—two days after Anna's murder—and Stout, the owner of a garage at 2765 Mission Street, had just been handed a $100 bill in payment for a $1.25 repair.

But the cash wasn't the issue. It was the identity of the men who'd given it to him. A hundred dollars was a huge amount at a time when the minimum wage in California was thirty-three cents an hour, and nothing in the pair's dress or demeanor suggested they'd come by the money legitimately. They were not the sort of men you wanted to pick a fight with. Everyone knew the Castor boys were trouble.

Walter Castor was twenty-seven, with a strong chin and light brown hair swept across a high forehead, above a face covered in scars: one on each eyebrow, another at the bridge of a nose that had been broken at least once. Old wounds marred the back of his right hand and wrist, and his left hand was missing its middle finger above the first joint. A tattoo of a woman and a flower wound its way up his left forearm.

Walter's blue eyes could sometimes look contemptuous, but mostly they carried a dull, almost stupid expression. He had been kicked in the head by a horse when he was seven, and he had never been quite the same. He suffered from terrible headaches and a constant ache at the base of his skull. His friends nicknamed him "Dizzy."

"Walter has never seemed to know the difference between right and wrong since his head was hurt," said his mother. "But he is lovable and wants to please the people he likes. He is like a child in some ways."

He was prone to violent outbursts and made erratic, impulsive, and dangerous decisions. It was his twenty-five-year-old brother, Arthur, who often had to rein him in. Arthur Castor was skinnier than Walter, with large blue eyes and the same brown hair. He had spent two years as a private in the Marines, serving mostly in Cuba, and was generally a calmer head—although he'd had his fair share of trouble with the law too.

There were six Castor brothers in all—Charlie, Walter, Robert, Arthur, Elmer, and Harold—the sons of city policeman Charles Castor and his Nebraska-born wife, Minnie.

The family were never model citizens—when he was fourteen, Arthur had been arrested for a late-night crime spree in which he and a friend smashed a jewelry store window with a brick to steal watches and revolvers, and ransacked a cigar stand for gum and chocolate.

But it was their father's sudden death later that year that really sent the whole family into a tailspin. In November 1911, Charles Castor was shot in the stomach while trying to apprehend a murder suspect outside the Ferry Building. His passing left the Castors in desperate straits.

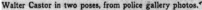

Walter Castor in two poses, from police gallery photos.

Arthur Castor

They had never been well off financially—at times they had relied on help from the Boys and Girls Aid Society to house their children—and now Minnie Castor was a widow with four kids under the age of eighteen.

Her oldest son held down jobs as a shipping clerk and a drayman, but the others turned to a life of drinking, fighting, and stealing. "Their history has been written in blood," wrote one newspaper.

At police headquarters in the Hall of Justice, former colleagues of the fallen officer muttered about his sons and shook their heads. "A good fellow, Charley Castor. Can't see where his boys got their bad ways."

* * *

Two years after his father's death, an eighteen-year-old Walter was arrested and fined $200 for an unprovoked attack on a sixteen-year-old Chinese school boy who was so brutally beaten that he was barely recognizable when he took the stand to give evidence. In December of the same year, 1913, Walter was convicted of manslaughter and sentenced to six years in San Quentin after shooting his neighbor in the stomach while hiding from police on his porch.

He was paroled in April 1917, but by January he was back in police custody again—accused of battery after hitting a pedestrian with a delivery truck, causing a fractured skull (on this occasion it seems to have been a genuine accident, and he did stop and drive the victim to hospital).

While his brother was in prison, Arthur was also sent away—to the Preston School of Industry, a notorious penal institution for teenagers in a mock medieval castle overlooking the town of Ione, California. New arrivals had their heads shaved and were dunked in a chemical bath before being shown to their dormitory, which had rows of thin mattresses and one lidless toilet. There were tennis courts and a library, but also brutal beatings and solitary confinement. While there, Arthur was accused of a sexual assault against a ten-year-old girl—although in court years later, he denied any knowledge of this.

By the time the brothers walked into Milton Stout's garage on June 1, 1922, Walter was actually on probation for yet another charge.

This time, he had been supplementing his living as a machinist with a scheme that *The Examiner* called a "novelty in the field of burglarious endeavor."

He and an associate were accused of stealing several hundred chickens on the western side of the Santa Clara Valley (which roughly corresponds to today's Silicon Valley). They'd been making weekly car trips, returning to the city each time to sell the "feathered loot." Walter was released on the promise that his younger sibling would keep an eye on him and help him find legitimate work—a few weeks earlier, Arthur had vouched for him in court.

Stout knew exactly whom he was dealing with. "Castor was a terror in the Mission district and had the reputation of being a troublemaker and a hoodlum," one paper had written of Walter.

As he counted out the brothers' change, the garage owner remembered the story he'd read in the newspapers the previous morning about Anna Wilkens's murder, and the fact that three $100 bills had been taken. After quietly waiting for the Castors to leave, Stout alerted the police.

* * *

The San Francisco Police Department had spent the previous two days chasing down dead ends. Chief O'Brien had allocated the case to Duncan Matheson, his captain of detectives.

Matheson was in his late fifties—born in Nova Scotia, he'd moved to the United States in 1883, and worked on the Southern Pacific railroad for thirteen years before joining the police in 1900. Two years later, he almost died during a pursuit when, while chasing a group of young troublemakers across the rooftops of Chinatown, he fell through an open skylight. The occupants of the house found him groaning with pain in a hallway thirty feet below.

He was a strait-laced, devout man of Scottish descent, with fair, receding hair and a neatly trimmed moustache. Matheson was a believer in "remolding" deviant young men through education and religious training, and in 1929 his reputation for thoroughness and integrity would see him elected city treasurer.

Matheson's team of fourteen detectives had conducted a citywide search, but with little to go on from Henry, they had turned up very few clues. A car dealer called C. W. White had reported being sideswiped by a Dodge near Tanforan, several miles south of the city, and police were trying to trace the car's owners.

They were also trying to find out the serial numbers of the bills that Henry Wilkens had handed over to the bandits. Matheson was working with police in Sacramento to trace a woman who, Henry said, had paid him the money in a business transaction. Meanwhile, The California State Automobile Association and the San Francisco Motor Car Dealers Association—two organizations with an interest in making sure people felt safe on the roads—were raising money toward a $5,000 reward for the capture and conviction of Anna's murderers.

But the tip from Stout was the best lead they had, so Matheson sent Detectives Leo Bunner, George Wall, and Henry McGrath to bring Walter and Arthur Castor in for questioning at the Hall of Justice.

"The Hall" was a five-story steel and granite structure with a sandstone and marble facade and arched windows, facing Portsmouth Square at the corner of Kearny and Washington. It was built in 1908 on the site of the old Hall of Justice, which was destroyed in the earthquake, and housed not only the police department but also the courtrooms, the morgue, and the county jail. Despite its elegant air, there was nothing refined about what went on inside.

On the afternoon of June 2, detectives led the Castor brothers, who were all too familiar with the building, to a wood-paneled room inside the police headquarters on the first floor.

When they were arrested, Walter had been carrying two more $100 bills, and the brothers were quizzed for hours on how they got the money and about their movements on the evening of Tuesday, May 30, when Anna Wilkens was killed.

Arthur told them he'd been out for a drive with his seventeen-year-old wife, Mary; his brother, Elmer; and Mary's father, Joseph Fortino. Walter, perhaps forgetting that he was out on parole for stealing chickens, gave his alibi as poultry dealer L. Hirschel, who he said he'd been towing a car for him on the night in question.

Afterward, the Castor brothers were led into a room with thirteen other young men, to take part in an identity parade in front of Henry Wilkens. He had been summoned to the Hall to look at the National car the Castors were driving when they were brought in to determine whether it was the same one that had followed him through the fog on Tuesday night.

He had said it wasn't, but it was difficult to trust him. Henry was an emotional wreck. He shuffled into the dingy lineup room with tear-reddened eyes, which he dabbed at periodically with a handkerchief. "That fellow can't see anything," Officer John Palmer remembered telling his colleagues. "He's goofy."

It seemed like most of the detective squad were in the room to watch the lineup, wrangling suspects or milling around with interest. Just before it started, a detective said something to Wilkens in German that triggered another burst of tears.

He was still weeping as the potential suspects filed out and arranged themselves against a wall. Walter and Arthur positioned themselves toward the far end of the line.

Henry shuffled slowly down the row, but his head was bowed, and he only seemed to throw the occasional sideways glance toward the men he was supposed to be identifying—the suspects who may have killed his wife. "He looked at the men, but I wouldn't say whether he saw them or not," said Detective George McLaughlin.

After going just a few feet down the line, Henry turned back, shaking his head. But the detectives insisted that he complete the lineup properly. He was still in tears, but the second time he did walk all the way to the end.

When he got to Arthur, he frowned and said, "No, this is not the man." In fact, Henry told the detectives, none of the men looked like his wife's killer—the man he remembered seeing was much older.

It was a frustrating afternoon for Duncan Matheson, the Captain of Detectives. He wanted to keep the Castors for further questioning, but given Henry's failure to identify either the brothers or their vehicle as being involved in the holdup, he was forced to release them. He kept the $100 bills, though—a photo from the following morning's *Call* shows Bunner and McLaughlin peering at one of the notes through a magnifying glass.

The next few days passed in a flurry of speculative inquiries. For the first time in the history of the San Francisco Police Department, radio stations were used to circulate a description of the bandits and their getaway vehicle over the airwaves. At the same time, telegrams were sent throughout southern California to garage owners, oil stations and repair shops.

The most promising tip came from R. P. McCabe, the owner of a drugstore on the corner of Fulton and Cole, about three miles from the crime scene. An hour or so after the shooting, around the same time Anna was dying on the operating table, he and his wife had seen a Dodge come tearing around the bend at high speed and smash into the curb. The three men inside shied away when McCabe shone a torch at them—but they seemed to match the description he'd heard on the radio.

Detectives also traced another car matching Henry's description to Burlingame, fifteen miles to the south in San Mateo County, but when they showed it to him he wasn't sure it was the right one either.

There was another lead from Mount Zion hospital—a man named Earl Young had come in with a head injury the morning after Anna's death and had been returning daily for treatment. Police trailed him from the hospital, and on Saturday, June 3, they arrested him and two other men—Thomas Lusk and John Gaynor. But this too was a dead end—Young was a boxer; Lusk was a friend who had been visiting him in the hospital; and Gaynor was the taxi driver who had taken him there. All three had watertight alibis and were released without charge.

As each new lead fizzled out, Matheson's thoughts kept returning to Walter and Arthur Castor—he knew their record, and the fact they'd had the money on them seemed damning. On the other hand, Henry hadn't recognized them, or their car—and they'd both given plausible alibis.

But Matheson's detectives had missed something. At the end of the police lineup, as the fifteen suspects filed slowly out of the room, Henry Wilkens had looked up at the Castor brothers, caught Arthur's eye, and winked.

ARGUMENTS AND ALIBIS

On Friday, June 3, 1922, eight-year-old Henry Wilkens Jr. paced solemnly down Valencia Street toward Wieboldt's Funeral Parlor. "He didn't cling closer to his aunt's hand nor burst into tears and hide his face in her skirts," wrote *The Call*'s Ernestine Black. "Instead, he manfully gulped down a sob, squared his shoulders and walked in."

Inside, his mother lay in an open casket, dressed in a blue silk dress she'd sewn herself. Anna's dark lashes stood out against pale skin, and her black hair was brushed back in soft waves. Henry Jr's little body "shook with sobs" when he saw her. He stood on his tiptoes and reached out a hand to touch her on the arm. "For the first time in eight years, his touch brought no loving response."

Henry Wilkens placed a bunch of red roses by his wife's body. His son took one and placed it carefully in his pocket with "cold, trembling fingers."

"He doesn't talk much, but he realizes what has happened," said Meta Lange, Anna's aunt. "Baby Helen doesn't realize it all and Henry [Jr.] seems to feel that he must help mother her."

At two PM, the funeral procession wound its way from Wieboldt's, through the busy streets of the Mission and south toward Colma, the so-called "City of the Silent," retracing in reverse the fateful pursuit through the fog just three days earlier.

A mild breeze was blowing in from the west as the mourners arrived at Cypress Lawn, a crematorium and cemetery set in acres of rolling greenery, dotted with spruce trees. The children were spared the trauma of attending the service itself, but Anna's aunt and uncle were there, as was her sister, Helen Lange, a pretty twenty-two-year-old who had recently spent six weeks living with the Wilkens family after arriving from Germany in February 1922.

Henry was wearing a blue serge suit, bought new for the occasion, and a dark tie. He had a black mourning band around his arm, and his eyes were red from tears and lack of sleep. He struggled to control his emotions during the service and again when his wife's coffin was fed into the incinerator. According to the newspapers, both Henry and Helen Lange collapsed during the service.

From the pulpit, the Reverend K. C. Struckmeier had raged against the perceived weaknesses of the justice system in both English and German. "It is time to end this outrageous sentimentality over criminals," he said. "We have had enough of light sentences and easy judges. A brave and self-sacrificing woman was shot down brutally and cold-bloodedly. Justice demands a life for a life."

Those words may have been ringing in Henry's ears as he left Anna's uncle's house early the following morning. It had been four days since his wife's death, and he had been the picture of the grief-stricken husband—a victim whose blissful home life was torn apart by the random cruelty of an unknown gunman. But on Saturday, June 3, the day after the funeral, a more complicated picture began to emerge in the newspapers.

On May 8, just three weeks before her death, Anna Wilkens had visited an attorney and filed a suit for separate maintenance. She wanted a divorce. She accused Henry of extreme cruelty, drunkenness, and infidelity, and applied for temporary alimony of $150 a month and custody of the children. The suit shed light on a marriage that was far from happy. Henry and Anna both had vicious tempers, and when one or both had been drinking, things could descend into blazing rows in German. "When they had an argument, it was an argument," said one attorney later.

Henry would disappear for booze-filled business lunches—Anna accused him of seeing other women. "My sister and her husband did not get along well together," said Anna's sister Helen, who was with the family through much of March and April of 1922. "She was imaginative and jealous every time he spoke to another woman." Anna would gossip with the neighbors about how Henry was taking other women out in his car. That made him angry. "He had a quick temper when he drank and would fly into rages," Helen said.

The relationship deteriorated in the year leading up to Anna's death. She was drinking more than ever, and Henry was getting more violent. Anna's lawsuit described two drunken beatings, one of which left her with a black eye, and there were several more she didn't mention.

When the Wilkens family visited Anna's aunt and uncle at their ranch outside Petaluma in July 1921, Anna's face, arms, and shoulders were badly bruised—shocking black and blue marks against her pale skin. "He admitted that he had beaten her, declaring that she had falsely accused him of intimacy with another woman," said her aunt. "He expressed himself as contrite and promised me he would not do it again."

Over Easter, in April 1922, the family took a weekend trip to Napa Valley, where Henry knocked out one of Anna's teeth during a fierce argument. He had been "drinking heavily of claret," and the couple got into a fight when Henry and Helen said they were going to pick up Henry Jr. from a family friend's house, but returned without the boy.

The couple shouted at each other in German, and then Henry hit Anna twice in the face, leaving her with a bloody mouth and a darkening bruise over one eye that had only just faded when she died.

"Why should my husband beat me like this?" Anna cried. Henry's response was chilling. "Well, nobody saw me do it."

Helen started crying when she came into the room and saw her sister's injured face. Henry jumped to his feet to console his sister-in-law, who was leaning against a doorframe in floods of tears. He told her Anna had hit her head on a windowsill. They called a doctor, who examined Anna and said, "There doesn't seem to be as much wrong with the woman as the man."

That night, when the unhappy trio finally did go to their friend's house to pick up Henry Jr., Henry told the friend, Gertrude Stirness, that his wife had been "telling lies" and that he had beaten her for it.

Another verbal fight ensued, and at some point Henry scooped up his daughter in his arms and ran out of the house. "Stop him," shouted Helen Lange. "He's going to kill himself!"

Stirness ran after Henry and caught him in the middle of the street. "In the argument that followed, he collapsed in the road," reported *The Call*. "But before doing so," Helen said, he showed her a pistol he was carrying. "He said he was going to kill himself and "take his little girl with him."

Later, Henry would claim that he was ashamed by what he had done and that he had sworn never to lay a hand on his wife again. But when he was confronted by the press the morning after Anna's funeral, he denied the allegations entirely and said the suit was "all a mistake." "My wife and I never were separated, and she never left our home," he said. "There were no hard feelings between us nor any lack of love. We had our little differences, but everything had been patched up."

* * *

These revelations stirred the city's newspaper editors into a frenzy. But the police department continued its investigation along the same lines as before. Detective McGrath told reporters that he'd known about the Wilkens' marital strife since the day after Anna's death, but that after questioning Henry Jr., he was satisfied with Henry's account of the killing. Captain of Detectives Duncan Matheson said there was "no doubt" in his mind that robbery was the only motive. But elsewhere in the Hall of Justice, suspicions were starting to mount.

On Sunday, June 4, San Francisco's district attorney, Matthew Brady, announced his intention to launch an independent probe and to bring Henry Wilkens back in for questioning following the news about his marriage.

Brady was in his mid-forties but looked much older—he was a stout man with white hair, a paunch, and a taste for the public eye. District attorneys were elected, so visibility was vitally important for Brady, who was "part prosecutor, part politician—an intelligent attorney with career ambition," as Kate Winkler Dawson puts it in *American Sherlock*.

He won office for the first time in 1919 and propelled himself into the papers during the multiple trials of Fatty Arbuckle in 1921, during which he pushed the pace of prosecution to what some argued was an irresponsible degree, resulting in Arbuckle eventually being acquitted.

Brady was out of town when he first heard about the Arbuckle case, and had rushed back to the city to take over personally, "granting interviews, making pronouncements, and outlining the strategy of the prosecution."

Here, he sniffed another opportunity to have a defining impact on a well-publicized case. "I have decided to summon Mr. Wilkens before me because of conflicting reports regarding the death of his wife," Brady told reporters. "I intend to conduct a thorough inquiry into all circumstances of the case in order to be fortified for future developments. I will ask Mr. Wilkens to tell me the whole story surrounding his wife's death and their domestic troubles, and then decide what further action, if any, to take."

On Monday, June 5, a grand jury met to rule on the cause of Anna's death. Henry repeated the woeful tale of the chase, the shooting, the frantic dash to the hospital. Henry Jr. perched on a chair next to the coroner, who adopted a kindly expression as the tearful child relayed how he'd hidden under a blanket while his mother tussled with the bandit.

But the most consequential evidence came from Jacob Gorfinkel, the attorney who had helped Henry get Anna to hospital on the night of the shooting. He testified that the car that had pursued the family was definitely not a Dodge, contradicting what Henry had told police.

That was the main topic of conversation the following morning when Matheson gathered his detectives to discuss their next move. It had been a week since Anna's death, and they were starting to doubt Henry's interpretation of events.

After the meeting, one group of detectives started exploring whether Henry might have been wrong about the make and model of the car that had chased him. They took a thorough description from Jacob Gorfinkel and then took him on a trip to see the Castors' National touring car, to determine whether it was the one involved in the shooting.

But the National wasn't at the Castor house, and neither were the brothers. The remaining occupants told detectives the car had been taken in for repairs to a garage on Golden Gate Avenue.

When they got there, Gorfinkel looked closely at the National, but he didn't think it was the same car he'd seen pursuing the Wilkens family either. Then, almost offhandedly, one of the detectives asked garage owner Walter Brownlee whether the Castors ever rented cars from him. "Yes," he said. "Walter Castor has rented automobiles from me on several occasions. Why, he even had a machine that was returned about twenty-five minutes after Mrs. Wilkens was killed."

The detectives were stunned. Brownlee told them that on May 29, the day before the murder, Walter had rented an old Hudson touring car for the day. But he didn't return it until eight thirty PM the following day—about an hour after the shooting.

Gorfinkel looked at the Hudson, and he was almost certain it was the vehicle he'd seen. His wife and car-mad son agreed, which meant that Duncan Matheson urgently needed to speak to Walter and Arthur Castor again. "I am assuming that this identification is correct, as the Gorfinkels were absolutely positive that it was the machine used by the robbers," said Matheson, who was under fire for releasing the brothers so quickly. "But there was nothing on which I could hold the Castors, and they have been released. I have not been looking for them and had no evidence to warrant their arrest."

That quickly changed. Over the following days, the Castors' alibis fell apart. The poultry dealer Walter said he'd been helping at the time of the shooting told the inquest that those events had actually been two days prior. Arthur's father-in-law denied seeing him on the evening of May 30, while his sister-in-law said he'd left the house early that morning and hadn't returned until late at night.

The police seemed to be closing in on the truth. In the identity parade, Henry had claimed not to recognize either Walter or Arthur Castor, but on Thursday, June 8, police discovered that, in fact, Henry and Walter had worked together for several months in 1918, when Henry was the foreman at the Garford Truck Company. He had been Walter's boss.

Reporters called at Henry's home and work, confronting him with this new information. He feigned ignorance. "I don't know the Castors," he said. "I never knew them. I never even saw or heard of them before. They are total strangers to me. What are you getting at anyway—has something new come up about them?" But two witnesses had Walter and Henry working there concurrently, and a check of the company records revealed that both men were listed on the payroll for June 1918.

In the space of a few days, the investigation had completely flipped around, Matheson admitted to reporters. Henry Wilkens was now a key suspect in his own wife's murder.

To make matters worse for the detective, Arthur and Walter Castor seemed to have completely disappeared from the city. There was no sign of them at their homes or at their mother's house on Kansas Street, where their brother Elmer said they'd gone in search of manual labor on the roads—one to Arizona, the other to southern California.

Matheson's two main suspects were missing, and he was dealing with a grieving husband who may have deliberately lied to the police. With growing pressure from all sides, and Henry still refusing to change his story, Matheson and Chief O'Brien looked across the bay to Berkeley.

There, a visionary police chief, a rookie cop, and a teenage magician had been developing a machine with the power to sort truth from fiction.

It had already been used to investigate robberies and murders across the Bay Area, and was building a fearsome reputation in the speakeasies and cells of San Francisco. The detectives were sure it could help them solve the Wilkens case.

PART TWO

PART TWO

THE TOWN MARSHAL

By 1922, the basement of Berkeley's City Hall was the center of a national revolution. The open space that housed the Berkeley Police Department was laid out with rows of dark filing cabinets, holding data on the skull measurements and fingerprints of convicted criminals so that repeat offenders could be more easily identified.

Maps and charts hung on the walls, detailing the frequency and location of robberies in the town. And in a makeshift forensic lab, the country's first, scientists from the University of California pored over microscopic fibers and analyzed blood stains and explosives.

At the heart of it all, at an oak desk stacked neatly with journals and books, sat August Vollmer—a tall, gray-haired man in his mid-forties, with piercing blue-gray eyes and round, rimless glasses. Berkeley's chief of police was already developing the legendary status that would see him dubbed "the father of modern policing."

He was, one biographer wrote, "a truly complete man"—in his spare time he hunted rabbits in the Berkeley hills, and every day he went for a three-mile swim in the bay. He "had the physique and coordination of a top athlete" and was an expert at a swimming stroke called the "Australian crawl."

"Vollmer is an iron-gray man, with iron in his face and gray in his hair," wrote a *Collier's* magazine profile in November 1924—an issue with a brand-new Sherlock Holmes story from Sir Arthur Conan Doyle on the cover. "He somehow gives the impression that his mind is as disciplined as his body."

He chased down violent criminals, defused angry mobs, and on two separate occasions he leaped into the water to save young women from drowning. It was a similar act of heroism involving a runaway train that first set him on the journey from friendly neighborhood mailman to world-renowned police chief.

Gus, as his friends called him, was born in New Orleans in the early hours of March 7, 1876, to John and Philippine Vollmer, who had come over from Germany in the summer of 1869, fleeing rising tensions in Europe.

One hot afternoon when Vollmer was eight, he came home with a bloody nose after being punched in the face by an older boy. His father was furious at him for not fighting back, and the next morning he enrolled his son in boxing lessons—a twice-a-week practice that helped instill a discipline and athleticism that would become the backbone of Vollmer's life, especially after his father's sudden death from a heart attack just three months later.

In a way, the tragedy—John was only forty-six—robbed Vollmer; his younger brother, Edward; and his adopted sister, Josie, of both parents, because their mother now had to spend six long days a week keeping the family's grocery business afloat. The children passed their time wandering the streets of New Orleans—ambling down to the docks to watch the boats being unloaded, hiking along the Mississippi, or swimming in Lake Pontchartrain.

Philippine was struggling to manage the business and three kids, however, and in 1886 she moved the family back to her hometown in Bavaria. When they returned to Louisiana two years later, they found a changed city. Crime was on the rise, and a string of brothels and opium dens had sprung up, bringing gangs and violence with them.

So, in 1891, when Vollmer was fourteen, the family moved to the West Coast. By then, he had finished two years of education—courses in bookkeeping, typing, and shorthand. He wanted to be a stenographer.

In San Francisco, he found work delivering packages and messages for a furniture store while his mother worked as a nurse. Later that year, she moved the family again—across the glittering bay to Berkeley, a growing town of steep hills and stunning views, with cheaper rent than the big city. But it was a decision that tore the family apart.

Initially, Vollmer stayed in San Francisco. He'd found a job he enjoyed as a shipping clerk, and a group to go hiking, hunting, and swimming with. He had taken up the guitar, and in the evenings he and his friends would strum and sing around a roaring fire.

His older sister, Josie, didn't make the move either. When Philippine told her they were moving again, she locked herself in her room, and when the family woke up the next morning, she was gone. They searched the city and sent word back to New Orleans in case she had decided to return there. But she was never seen or heard from again.

* * *

In 1894, Vollmer moved back in with his mother and brother, in Berkeley. It was a small, simple town, typical of turn-of-the-century America. Most citizens got around in horse-drawn buggies, which made their way along dirt tracks that wound into the hills. Older men wore bushy beards and drooping moustaches; women with powdered faces strolled along the wooden sidewalks in large hats decorated with artificial flowers. The population was under fifteen thousand—split between the warehouses and saloons of the commercial district, and the gleaming university campus nestled into the base of the Contra Costa hills, with their stunning views over the Golden Gate.

Vollmer built a happy life full of laughter and home-cooked meals. He followed in his father's footsteps by going into business, with a coal and feed store. In his spare time, he set up the North Berkeley Volunteer Fire Station to provide emergency coverage to a previously unprotected area of the town, and could have happily whiled away his years between running the store and serving the community.

But the course of Vollmer's life changed on April 25, 1898, when America declared war on Spain. The conflict began with the explosion of the USS *Maine* in the harbor of Havana, and those sparks were fanned into an inferno by the clamoring of the newspapers for retribution.

Vollmer was twenty-two years old and like more than a million other men, he felt compelled to enlist. "I promised Father I'd never run from a fight, and our country needs volunteers," he told his worried mother. He sold his share of the business and boarded a ferry to San Francisco to sign up. He was one of only 13 percent of applicants who were selected.

After a month of training at the Presidio, the military fort at the northern tip of the city, Vollmer boarded the USS *Ohio* as part of the Third Artillery Division of the Eighth Army Corps and set sail for the Philippines, a Spanish colony that had become a key front in the war.

The tropical conditions were a nightmare—unrelenting heat mixed with torrential downpour—but Vollmer distinguished himself during his service. He fought in dozens of battles and spent weeks manning the guns on a steamer called the *Laguna de Bay* as it patrolled up and down the Pasig River, standing on a raised platform with only a flimsy improvised turret to shield him from sniper fire.

Sometimes the men had to leave the vessel entirely to push the boat around tight bends. "The trick to maneuver was to dodge the bullets coming from the jungle thickets," Vollmer said. "There seemed to be a Filipino hidden behind every tree." Between February 5 and May 17, 1899, he was in action almost every day. "Men died, they were replaced by other men, and the fight went on," he wrote.

For one daring mission in the summer of 1899, Vollmer and a fellow soldier crawled into the bottom of a casco boat—a square-bottomed barge—which was then loaded with nipa grass, a local crop. The plan, which Vollmer had devised himself, was to sneak through enemy territory to make contact with the Macabebes, a potentially friendly group who had been cut off from the fighting in what was now a war between American soldiers and Filipino insurgents.

They'd hired local men to pilot the boat in the hope of passing through without suspicion, but Vollmer knew that if they were caught, he was likely to be tortured and killed. "Don't let them take you alive," their captain had said. "Save the last bullet for yourself."

The midday sun was stifling as the boat made its slow way upriver, and lying under the dry grass, Vollmer was starting to let his guard down, when he heard sudden gunshots ringing out overhead. Armed rebels had seen the boat and ordered it to pull up to the bank to be searched. Vollmer knew this could be fatal—the rebels might find them, and there was a distinct possibility that the locals they'd hired would give up the Americans to save themselves.

There were raised voices—an argument—and then silence. Then the rebels began jabbing their long rifles into the nipa grass, prodding to see if anything was hidden underneath. Vollmer gripped his pistol and held his breath. After what felt like hours, he heard a barked order, and felt the boat pushing off from the bank. They had escaped, and they managed to make contact with the Macabebes and complete the mission.

The war also gave Vollmer his first taste of policing. In the lull between the taking of Manila from the Spanish and the rebel uprising, US soldiers were instructed to keep the peace in the capital. Vollmer worked twelve-hour shifts patrolling the city, with instructions to try and avoid arresting people, wherever possible, because Manila's jails were overflowing. He stopped troublemakers from congregating, organized groups to clean up the rubbish piling up in the streets, and got a first look at the basics of police administration.

When he returned to America in August 1899, Vollmer found himself at something of a loose end. His previous dreams seemed small, and although he considered going back into business for himself, he could never settle on what kind of enterprise he wanted to run. So, in the meantime, he returned to his mother's home in Berkeley and found a job as a mail carrier.

Vollmer's role was to cover for the other postmen when they were absent because of sickness, so the job took him all over town, and he became a familiar and popular sight—long legs striding up and down Berkeley's hills—up winding roads that were once cow trails, past the hill homes with their lush lawns dotted with redwood and eucalyptus, and Japanese plum trees that added bursts of pink blossom in the spring.

It was only meant to be a temporary position, but he enjoyed the social aspects of the job and working outdoors, and it provided a

comfortable living. He was still doing it four years later, when his life
changed forever.

* * *

It was just before noon on January 16, 1904. Vollmer was heading
downhill toward Berkeley station, to finish his morning mail route,
when he noticed a commotion in the middle of the street. A railway
flatcar loaded with building supplies had come uncoupled and was rolling dangerously toward the station, four blocks further down the slope.

It was a chilly Saturday, and the surrounding streets were busy
with shoppers shrouded in winter coats and armed with umbrellas
against the drizzle that was sure to come sweeping in. Workmen were
frantically trying to slow the car down by throwing bricks onto the
rails, but it was still picking up speed.

A passenger train was due in at midday, and Vollmer knew that
people tended to hang around the trackside waiting for it—the situation had the potential to be a disaster. He dropped his bag of mail and
began racing down the hill, pumping his arms and legs until he pulled
alongside the runaway flatcar. He leaped onto it from behind, grabbed
the slats and hauled himself on board. But the brake was at the front,
so now he needed to pick his way past the piles of bricks on the flatcar,
which was still accelerating.

If he'd looked up, Vollmer would have seen a horrifying sight—
white steam billowing from the engine of the midday train arriving
from San Francisco, on a track perpendicular to the one he was now
hurtling down. If he didn't manage to stop in time, he would collide
square-on with the side of the train and surely be killed.

Vollmer made his way toward the front of the car as quickly as
he dared. Finally, he grabbed the brake wheel and twisted it with all
his strength, and after a brief moment of panic when he thought he'd
turned it the wrong way, the flatcar came to a screeching halt just short
of the station.

The incident made Vollmer a minor celebrity. He was already well
liked across town by those who knew him from his postal routes, and
now his picture was in *The Berkeley Daily Gazette*, where he was being

lauded for his bravery. The newspaper's editor, Friend Richardson, (a prominent Quaker who would go on to become governor of California) was among those impressed. In January 1905—a year later—he telephoned Vollmer and asked him to come down to the newsroom for a chat.

Vollmer had no idea why a newspaper editor wanted to speak to him—after all, he barely had any formal education—and he entered Richardson's second-floor office with a degree of trepidation.

"I've got a proposition to make, and I didn't want to talk about it over the telephone," said the editor, a portly man with a moustache and a receding hairline, who had been scribbling furiously with a yellow pencil when Vollmer walked in. "I've been talking to several of my friends, and we want you to run for marshal at the election in April. The idea may come as a surprise to you, but we feel you are the man for the job."

The title of town marshal was a Wild West relic for an important role—that of enforcing law and order across Berkeley. "To tell the truth, such an idea never occurred to me," Vollmer said. "I've been thinking lately that I don't want to be a mail carrier all my life, but what I'd like to do is go into business."

"You could go into business later, but right now we need you," Richardson replied. "This town is full of dope dens and gambling joints, and crooks are coming here too fast."

He thought the experience Vollmer had collected in the Philippines, combined with the bravery he'd shown in the flatcar incident, made him the perfect man for the job. "You act quick, and you are not afraid, and that is what we want: a man who can clean up Berkeley and make it safe for our citizens."

Vollmer was unconvinced, not least because of what his family considered the "social disgrace" of being a policeman. At the turn of the century, the rate of violent crime was between four and ten times higher in America than in Europe, and policing was tainted by corruption. Officers employed violent tactics and took money to look the other way. In the 1890s, the Lexow Committee, an investigation into police corruption in New York, found that the profession had become "pay to play," with bribes of up to five times an officer's salary required to move up through the ranks. Years later, Vollmer himself described it as an "era of incivility, ignorance, brutality, and graft."

But despite his misgivings, he decided to run for election as town marshal. Two days after the meeting, his candidacy was announced in *The Gazette*. "Gus Vollmer is a man of mental acumen and sagacity," Richardson wrote. "His service in the army has particularly fitted him for the job of hunting down and apprehending criminals."

The election was scheduled for April 1905, and another dramatic and remarkably similar act of bravery did no damage to Vollmer's chances. On the morning of Saturday, March 25, 1905, he was scanning the headlines at a newspaper stand on Shattuck Avenue in downtown Berkeley when a group of runaway horses came charging around the corner with a Wells-Fargo delivery wagon in tow.

Again, Vollmer rushed to help. He seized the reins and was dragged along the ground for some distance, emerging with lacerated hands and torn clothing, but with catastrophe again averted. The incident cemented his position as a local hero, and he won the election in a three-to-one landslide—aided by Richardson's support and political connections, and a whirlwind of dinners and drinks receptions with Berkeley's upper classes.

Vollmer was sworn in on April 15 and given his badge—a seven-pointed tin star stamped with the words "Marshal of Berkeley." He immediately began making changes, drawing heavily on his brief policing experience in the Philippines. He appointed two new deputy marshals and lobbied the town's trustees for the money to hire more men and for pay rises and uniforms—blue coats with brass buttons and a helmet-shaped hat, modeled on the one used by London's Metropolitan police.

Over the next few months, Vollmer and his deputies started fulfilling one of his key election promises by conducting raids on the opium dens and illicit casinos that were popular among Berkeley's Chinese community.

Even those who had mocked the twenty-nine-year-old "Boy Marshal" were impressed. He was reelected in 1907, running again on the Republican ticket, and when Berkeley officially adopted a city charter in 1909, Vollmer went from elected town marshal to appointed chief of police.

That meant he no longer had to dabble in politics every two years, and it gave him the freedom to introduce some of the new ideas that would become his hallmark over the next four decades.

Vollmer was the first police chief in America to buy bicycles for his deputies to get around—he calculated that it would enable them to cover three times as much ground as someone on foot.

By the end of 1914, he had created the first fleet of police cars, with the purchase of a small Model T Ford for each officer (although he never learned to drive himself).

He installed a signaling system that let him contact officers more quickly, to improve response times. Red lights were strung between telephone poles across the city, and twenty small call boxes with phones placed at regular intervals. A master switch at police headquarters could trigger the lights, which could either signal an officer to go to the nearest call box or flash out a message in Morse code.

But perhaps Vollmer's biggest innovation was his compassion. If you were picked up for drunkenness, you would be brought in to sleep it off and released the next morning without charge. Anyone could come in and ask for a night's lodgings, and they'd be given two clean blankets, a shower, and a "good ham-and-egg breakfast" in the morning. "The chief was a humanitarian," said one of his officers.

Vollmer loved children, although he was sterile and couldn't have any of his own. He kept a bowl of sweets on his desk for young visitors, who called him "Uncle Gus." Despite grumbling from some of the older officers, he reserved room in the police department for a Children's Room, which acted as an informal youth club that kept troubled kids off the streets. It was filled with toys, animals, and the sound of music—it was not uncommon to hear yodeling or the twang of a ukulele. "Show them that the law is their friend and not their enemy" was Vollmer's frequent refrain.

He abhorred physical violence on the part of his officers, and the beatings that were routinely handed out to noncompliant suspects during interrogations (although early in his career he did dole out the occasional spanking and once "mildly" whipped three youths for stealing). Vollmer's overwhelming emphasis was on prevention, not punishment. "I'm not judging you on arrests," he would tell new recruits. "I'm judging you on how many people you keep from doing something wrong."

COLLEGE COPS

In 1907, a milkman on his rounds came across the body of a young man in a Berkeley garden, clutching a glass bottle labeled "Poison," the contents of which were later revealed to be deadly potassium cyanide.

Suicide was the obvious conclusion, but after a visit from a friend of the deceased, Police Chief Gus Vollmer consulted with physiologist Dr. Jacques Loeb, who told him that if the man had really killed himself with cyanide, the toxin would have relaxed all his muscles, and he couldn't have still been grasping the bottle. "It must have been placed there by the murderer to make it look like suicide," Loeb said.

Vollmer and his men quickly identified a potential suspect, who had been seen arguing with the dead man, and the case went before a grand jury, where the testimony hinged on whether the bottle had actually been in the victim's hand or not. Vollmer's officers swore it had been in his grip, but the milkman and several others said it had been lying on the ground a few inches away. No one had taken a photograph. The jury ruled it death by suicide, and the man Vollmer had accused of murder filed charges against him for false arrest.

The case had a profound impact on Vollmer's attitude toward policing. Although he'd thrown himself into the role of chief, in the back of his mind he still considered it something of a stopgap before a return to the business world. But this case made him realize how much more he had to learn—and how much of a difference he could make. "We were just dumb cops, trying to get along in the old routine way, and falling down badly when something happened that required a little knowledge and real skill," he told a reporter years later. "I decided then to stay in the police game until I could do something to overcome these vital deficiencies."

From that moment on, Vollmer became a voracious reader. He pressed his friend Loeb for book recommendations and devoured tomes on criminal psychology. Every two weeks, he'd visit a police department elsewhere in the Bay Area to meet its leaders and learn about their methods. In San Francisco, Chief Jere Dinan taught him how to set up a detective bureau for investigating more complex crimes.

Vollmer implemented stringent procedures for collecting evidence and keeping records, which he knew would be key to gaining convictions. He hired a statistician, C. D. Lee, to develop a method for classifying facts and evidence; working with a counterpart in Oakland, Lee created a system for collecting data from pawnshops and keeping track of stolen bicycles.

Vollmer also began collating what officers called the "morgue book"—pictures of dead bodies in varying states of decomposition, as well as images of knives, guns, burned-out houses, and wrecked cars that might prove useful in future investigations.

To share his new knowledge, Vollmer set up weekly "crab sessions" on Friday afternoons, where officers could raise any issues with no recriminations. He brought in speakers, ranging from experts in science (and sometimes pseudoscience), to ex-convicts and drug addicts.

Vollmer steered the Berkeley Police Department through all manner of tricky situations. After the earthquake of 1906 struck the Bay Area in only his second year in office, he helped Berkeley house an influx of tens of thousands of refugees—maintaining order and clamping down on looting with his usual blend of firmness and fairness, even as the population more than doubled.

When the town banned the sale of alcohol within its city limits in January 1907, Vollmer and his deputies spent weeks shutting down speakeasies hidden in cigar shops and behind grocery storefronts. And during the influenza pandemic of 1918, he helped maintain public health by strictly enforcing guidelines on wearing masks—he arrested a hundred and seventy-five "mask slackers" in the space of a few days.

His focus on work sometimes came at a personal cost. In 1911, he married Lydia Sturtevant, a blue-eyed, red-haired opera singer whom he'd known since he was a teenager. But he was more committed to his job than to his marriage—he worked long hours on evenings and weekends, and even when he was home, he was reading about or thinking about policing. On their honeymoon in Los Angeles, Vollmer ditched his new bride to help defuse an angry mob. By 1915, they were living apart, and in 1920, Sturtevant was granted a divorce on grounds of "desertion."

* * *

If his personal life was faltering, professionally Vollmer was going from strength to strength. Crime in Berkeley was falling—burglaries had declined 50 percent even as the town's population had increased—and he was soon gaining national attention.

In June 1917, the San Diego City Council invited Vollmer to conduct a survey of the local police department and suggest potential improvements—the first of dozens of such reports he'd conduct throughout his life, from Detroit to Havana.

He once spent three days in San Diego posing as a homeless person, walking the streets in a dirty hat and coat, and sleeping in empty railroad cars to see law enforcement from a different perspective. On the fourth day, he went to a hotel. "He took off his dirty clothes, shaved off the stubble, took a bath, and dressed in a neat gray suit, a white shirt, and a red necktie," wrote Alfred E. Parker in *The Berkeley Police Story*. "He looked in the mirror again and laughed."

But despite his success, Vollmer was growing frustrated with some of his men and their reluctance or inability to follow instructions. Over time, he became convinced that police officers needed more education than his weekly sessions could provide. He became one of the first people in the world to push for formal education for police, and he instituted a new program set up specifically for new officers.

It began in the summer of 1907, teaching police methods, fingerprinting, criminal law, photography, public health, psychiatry, and more. "Ordinary policemen began to learn things they had never dreamed of," wrote Robert Shaw in a biography of Vollmer that was serialized in *The Oakland Call*. "They began to peer through microscopes, to learn the essentials of law and evidence, to delve into some of the strange recesses of the human mind."

Vollmer gave his officers detection techniques that could have come from the pages of Sherlock Holmes. He taught them how to tell from a man's footprints if he was walking or running, and tested them on their powers of observation: Did they notice a person's height, or the color of his eyes? He implored them not to overlay their own narrative onto the evidence in front of them and to accept only the facts.

But he was still being forced to discipline and fire his officers on a regular basis, for everything from taking bribes to beating suspects. "Strangely enough, some men just do not possess the ability to become police officers," he reflected. "They have neither the intelligence, the initiative, the leadership, nor the tact to handle police problems."

Vollmer was pondering this dilemma one morning when Officer Frank Waterbury came into his office and dropped a stack of the morning's papers on his desk. As he flicked through the *Daily Californian*, the university newspaper, he noticed a number of job ads targeted toward college students.

He wanted educated, intelligent men for the police force, and he suddenly thought the University of California in Berkeley might be the perfect place to find them. "The policeman's job is the highest calling in the world," he said later. "The men who do that job should be the finest men. They should be the best educated. They should be college graduates."

The advert ran in all caps:

COLLEGE MEN WANTED FOR POLICE FORCE. INTERESTING
EXPERIENCE. LEARN A NEW PROFESSION. SERVE ON THE
BERKELEY POLICE FORCE WHILE YOU GO TO COLLEGE.
CONTACT AUGUST VOLLMER, CHIEF OF POLICE.

To his surprise, Vollmer was inundated with more than a hundred applications—it helped that the pay was good—and he borrowed intelligence and psychiatric screening tests from the army to help sift through them. Until that point, the force had generally only hired people over the age of twenty-five, and Vollmer's plan to recruit fresh-faced students was—like a lot of his ideas—initially met with ridicule in the press and resistance from his more experienced men. (They may have felt slightly threatened—at the time, most police officers had no more than an eighth-grade education, and Vollmer had even less.)

But his "college cops" quickly proved themselves to be perceptive, diligent, and just as tough as the hardened detectives on the squad. They went on to prestigious roles in policing, politics, and academia. Walter Gordon, the first Black officer in Berkeley and one of the first college cops, overcame appalling racism from both citizens and colleagues and became the Governor of the US Virgin Islands. William Dean was awarded the Medal of Honor after evading capture for thirty-six days behind enemy lines during the Korean War and spending two years in a prisoner-of-war camp. Frank Waterbury, who had been skeptical of the plan from the outset, was won over when a college cop called O. W. Wilson apprehended Kid Bennet, an escaped convict and "the toughest thug in these parts in many a day."

Their legal and scientific expertise helped propel Berkeley to the cutting edge of criminology. The department led the way on communication—it was one of the first to use two-way radios—and statistical analysis, including the mapping of crime hotspots. It was also a pioneer in the new field of forensics.

Vollmer was heavily influenced by the work of the German criminologist Hans Gross, who'd written that, "In a certain sense, a large part of the criminalist's work is nothing more than a battle against lies. He has to discover the truth and fight the opposite. He meets the opposite at every step."

The chief wanted to do more than just catch criminals. He wanted to end untruth, unmask liars, and beat back the scourge of deception. Soon, he had a plan—and he pinned his hopes on one of his most gifted college cops.

THE ROOKIE

John Larson crouched in the dark outside a house on McKinley Avenue in downtown Berkeley, waiting for a damn rooster to crow. It was just before three AM on a cold January morning in 1921, and the police department's unluckiest officer was on another thankless assignment.

It wasn't meant to be like this, Larson may have reflected as he waited on the street, with the dim glow of the full moon on his dark, crumpled uniform and his untidy light-brown hair, which he tried vainly to control by fairly plastering it to his scalp.

He'd been on the force since October, one of a new breed of college-educated officers brought in by Chief Vollmer. Like his fellow college cops, Larson had seen the advertisements in the student newspaper and decided to apply—unlike them, he was drawn by more than just good pay. He wanted to further his research in criminology.

Of course, he hadn't expected to be given the best assignments right away, but he would have liked a little more recognition for his efforts, and for the unique experience he brought to the role. He was the only police officer in America with a PhD—the nation's first "doctoral cop."

But he quickly found that his degrees and titles in physiology and psychology were of little use in the cut and thrust of precinct life. As a rookie cop, the twenty-eight-year-old Larson was at the same level as men several years his junior, trudging the same eight-hour beat, night after night, around Berkeley's steep hills: investigating robberies, shutting down speakeasies, and trying to clamp down on the continued opium problem in the city.

Patrolmen in Berkeley worked one of three 8-hour shifts: like the other college cops, Larson usually took the four PM to midnight slot so he could fit in his commitments at the university.

A typical working day began with roll call at quarter to four, followed by eight hours on patrol with a short break to eat. Vollmer had divided the town into sections, and officers were expected to cover their whole section several times during a shift, according to a formula that the chief had worked out, as well as to respond to any calls that might come through via the signaling system. At midnight, Larson had to return to the station to write up reports: half an hour was allotted for this, but often there were so many to do that he had to work overtime.

Tonight, Larson was following up on a routine noise complaint. A woman on Grove Street, not far from police headquarters in the basement of City Hall, had complained that she kept being woken in the night by the crowing of her neighbor's rooster. But the owner denied it, and Larson was dispatched to investigate. "I think the bird does crow," he'd written in his report earlier that day—the owner's wife had admitted hearing the rooster.

But to settle the case definitively, Larson needed evidence. He was sent on what *The Oakland Tribune* mockingly dubbed a "special investigation" to listen out for the bird at the appropriate hour. He had a habit of drawing the short straw.

As he tried to keep warm in the overnight chill, Larson was reminded of the cold East Coast winters of his youth. He had been born in Nova Scotia, Canada, in December 1892, to Scandinavian parents. His father, Lars, earned a meager living cutting stones in a quarry. When Larson was a child, Lars moved the family to New Hampshire, chasing work in one of the new factories that were springing up to make textiles and machinery. But not long afterward, his parents separated, and the bookish, slightly awkward boy and his mother were pitched into financial peril.

But Larson worked hard, and a dizzying array of odd jobs helped pay for a place at Boston University, where he studied biology and languages. He collected dishes at a restaurant, delivered newspapers, operated elevators, and cut stones in a quarry, like his father before him. In term time, he tutored some of the wealthier students. Although his relative poverty meant he felt out of place among his peers, his education and manner made it difficult for him to find friends elsewhere.

Part of the problem, Larson thought as he glanced at his watch and willed morning to come, was that he was too honest. Most officers given the job of listening out for a bird would have taken refuge in an all-night diner or dozed off in one of the squad cars Chief Vollmer had equipped them with. Larson was different.

When he'd worked as a conductor on a trolley line in Quincy during the summers, his colleagues—who typically stole one in every three fares—mocked him for his scruples. They thought he was a fool. But Larson had been raised to believe in being truthful at all costs— and it would cost him frequently throughout his life. He believed strongly in doing the right thing—and that's why he wanted to become a criminologist.

In 1915, he'd written his master's thesis on fingerprint identification, which had just become admissible in court. He'd developed a way of tracing people based on just the swirls of a single digit rather than the ten that were commonly required at the time.

But his ambitions hadn't stopped there. He was irresistibly drawn toward unsolved problems. His motivation wasn't just to try and catch criminals—like Vollmer, Larson wanted to predict crimes and stop them before they happened. He thought that, as well as helping identify the culprits, fingerprints could determine whether someone was likely to commit crimes in future—he believed there were hidden patterns in the whorls that held clues to temperament and morality.

The dream of predictive psychology took Larson to Berkeley, where he embarked on a PhD at the University of California, investigating whether thyroid deficiencies could predict criminal behavior and emotional deficits. For his thesis, he experimented on hundreds of rats to see if transplants and selectively "feeding" certain areas of the brain could change their behavior.

Although this rooster assignment was boring, it did at least offer some respite from the hectic schedule Larson had been maintaining since joining the force. He'd been conducting thyroid experiments in the lab, running courses in psychiatry, and writing a book about his fingerprinting work, all while pounding the streets of Berkeley as a beat cop several evenings a week. He often missed meals, and there were holes in his shoes because he never had time to get them resoled.

Although his academic career was thriving, the night job was a different matter. He was "hardworking but impulsive, physically vigorous but clumsy, compulsively honest but self-conscious," writes the historian Ken Alder in *The Lie Detectors*.

Larson was easily the worst shot in the department, not helped by the fact that he was almost blind in his right eye. While learning to drive one of the department's Model T Fords, he had managed to get in two car accidents in one evening, to the delight of the local papers, which had already been mocking the flowery language of his police reports.

Once, while driving Vollmer to a dinner engagement high in the Berkeley hills, the chief became so alarmed at Larson's driving that he held the door of the car open, ready to jump out.

Larson wasn't really getting on with his fellow officers either, especially the ones more tuned into the old ways. His rigidity, combined with his almost complete lack of tact, did nothing to endear him to the veterans who were already suspicious of the new breed of college cops.

Officer Henry Villa, a tall, handsome Italian who thought of himself as the department's ace detective, delighted in prodding at Larson, trying to get a rise out of him. But he soon discovered steel under the meek exterior.

When Larson returned, shaken, from dropping Vollmer off at his dinner, he found Villa had taken temporary charge of the station as acting sergeant. Larson was in a foul mood—he'd been waiting in vain to hear from a woman he'd been seeing—and just wanted to be left alone to work on his fingerprint files.

It was a quiet evening, and most of the men were out on their beats, but Villa hung around the record room where Larson was peering through a lens at fingerprint records. "There had not yet been an open showdown except constant insults and being pushed around by the boisterous Villa," Larson wrote.

This time, when Villa reached down and ruffled up his colleague's hair, Larson "blew his top." He jumped up, grabbed Villa, and threw him out of his office in an embrace "so forceful that he nearly broke Villa's back, tearing his coat and smashing his watch."

Things quieted down until close to midnight, when the desk sergeant returned. Larson heard excited voices from the squad room, and he was called outside just as the midnight shift returned to the station. Looking around, Larson saw few friendly faces. But he didn't care. He was itching for a fight.

The officers cleared a circle on the concrete floor, and Larson and Villa placed their guns, clubs, and handcuffs out of reach on a table. There was an unspoken signal, and Villa rushed at him with a "bull-like roar." Larson ducked out of the way and then seized the other officer in a headlock and dragged them both to the floor. "Just before the nasal cartilages were broken, Villa screamed, tears coming, and the round was over."

Despite the trials of life on the force, Larson stuck with it and took on more hours after being awarded his doctorate. He wanted to experience the frontline of law enforcement before moving into criminology—to have some real-world examples to draw on in his quest to predict crime before it happened.

The boorishness of some of his colleagues only deepened Larson's resolve. He hated the way they worked—how they'd pull over vehicles to extract bribes, confiscate prohibited alcohol to drink themselves, and dole out painful "third-degree" beatings instead of getting to the truth through interviews and evidence. Despite Vollmer's efforts to modernize the force, this kind of behavior was still rampant. In 1924, Berkeley's own Henry Villa was expelled from the police and sentenced to five years in prison for taking bribes.

Like Vollmer, Larson believed officers could change if they were given better tools than just their fists and nightsticks. When he wasn't on patrol; or lecturing; or shivering in the dark, waiting for a rooster to crow, Larson was in a lab at the university, developing new ways to use science in the fight against crime. And as he stood there in the cold, ruing his latest dud assignment, he was only weeks away from a breakthrough that would change his life forever.

THE APPARATUS

G us Vollmer was lost in thought. It was February 1921, and the chief was sitting at his desk at police headquarters, sun-wrinkled face creased into a frown of concentration. He jotted notes on a yellow pad in his looping handwriting.

He'd spent the morning flicking through the latest issue of the *Journal of the American Institute of Criminal Law and Criminology*, which had finally published a paper he'd submitted, more than six months earlier, about his plans to build a policing school in Berkeley. But something else had caught his eye.

Sandwiched between Vollmer's article and one debating the benefits of hanging the mentally ill was a paper by a psychologist and lawyer called William Moulton Marston. Six years earlier, as a Harvard psychology undergraduate, Marston had conducted an experiment in which he claimed to be able to detect whether someone was telling the truth.

Inspired by an observation from his wife, Elizabeth—also a psychology student—who'd noticed how her blood pressure seemed to spike when she was upset or angry, Marston asked his fellow students to tell either a true story, written down on a card in front of them, or a false one that they'd made up themselves a few minutes earlier. He discovered that he could tell, based on blood pressure readings alone, which of his peers were lying.

Marston and his course mates were used to this kind of psychological prodding. Their tutor was Hugo Munsterberg, a German experimental psychologist who had pioneered the systematic use of physiological measurements as a proxy for studying emotion. In his Harvard lab, Munsterberg examined scores of students using word association games, measuring their reaction times and their bodily responses to thoughts of joy, horror, and patriotism.

The idea that the actions of the body could betray the mind has been around for centuries. In ancient China, suspects were made to chew uncooked rice: the grains were thought to stick in the dry, nervous mouths of the guilty. In 1730, the English author Daniel Defoe suggested that the racing pulse of potential pickpockets would give them away. "Guilt carries fear always about with it," he wrote. "There is a tremor in the blood of a thief."

Scientific investigations into this idea began in the 1850s. The Swiss psychiatrist Carl Jung used a galvanometer to track emotional changes in his patients, recording how the electrical conductance across the sweaty surface of the skin changed over time. In Russia, neuropsychologist Alexander Luria measured the reaction time and chattering fingertips of criminals under investigation.

In the late nineteenth century, the Italian criminologist Cesare Lombroso interrogated suspects using an air-filled glove to measure blood pressure. Another contraption required the subject to plunge their forearm into a tank of water—the more the level of the liquid fluctuated as they spoke, the greater the chance they were lying. Lombroso's student Angelo Mosso designed a carefully balanced bed that would tip to one side as blood rushed to a suspect's face in the course of a lie (although it was never built).

Marston's insight about blood pressure and deception built on this work. Over the next few years, he conducted a handful of small-scale experiments—first with applicants to the army and then with German prisoners in the aftermath of the First World War. But on both occasions, his superiors were left disappointed. Although Marston generally seemed to get the right answers, the manner of this precocious, handsome young man made them doubt his reliability.

The general impression they were left with was that the results had more to do with Marston as an individual than any scientific breakthrough he'd made. And he never seemed too interested in the hard work required to turn his discovery from an interesting observation into a practical, scientific tool.

It took him two years to even publish the results of his first experiments. Over forty pages, he described in fine detail the blood pressure rise and fall in each of his subjects, and outlined what he saw as the telltale signs of deception. "The sudden sharp, short rises of blood pressure betray these substantial lies in an otherwise true story," he wrote.

Vollmer read Marston's latest article with growing interest. He'd heard about previous attempts to detect lying in the work of Hans Gross—things like chewing rice—and "decided they were crude, amateurish, and impractical for his use." But if blood pressure rises during lying, he thought, couldn't that be registered on a machine? He turned the idea over in his head for a few minutes. Then he put down his notepad and reached for the telephone to call the desk sergeant, grasping the stick in one hand and pressing the bulb of the receiver to his ear with the other. "Send John Larson in to see me as soon as he reports for duty," he said.

* * *

That afternoon, Larson dressed in his dark patrolman's uniform with the star over the heart and made his way into work for what he thought would be a standard evening on the downtown beat.

The sun was low in the sky when he arrived at City Hall, a sparkling three-story building built in 1909 and styled on the grand Hotel de Ville in the French town of Tours, with elegant white carvings and a clock tower that had been demanded by Berkeley's discerning cultural elite. The budget didn't quite stretch to a clock, though—even today, passers-by who glance up looking for the hour are met with a blank white circle. It's timeless, in every sense.

Larson crossed the manicured lawn and ignored the city employees making their way up the grand main staircase. Instead, he walked around the left-hand side of the building to the south wing, opened a discreet side door, and descended a flight of stairs into the basement headquarters of the Berkeley Police Department.

It was filled with the musty smell of sweat and old books. Exposed pipes ran along the ceiling, and windows at ground level filtered in a meager amount of daylight. Dozens of officers worked under naked bulbs that hung from the ceiling.

Larson checked in with the desk sergeant and was ordered to report straight to the chief—not usually a good sign. For a moment, he stood frozen in something like panic. He thought he was in trouble.

About six weeks earlier, around the end of 1920, Larson had been on duty on the four PM to midnight shift. Vollmer had worked out detailed route maps for each of his officers, but after making a few rounds of the "interwoven meshwork of dirty alleys," most of them simply parked their car at a convenient intersection and watched the signal light.

Despite his usual diligence, Larson was no different. He was "loafing" and watching the light when his old foe Henry Villa pulled up in his car and surprised Larson by suggesting they drive up to Barney's Diner together for a malted milk.

They returned to their beats at about eleven forty-five PM and were back at the station by midnight to write their reports on a quiet night. But it hadn't been a quiet night—at about ten thirty PM, the Sunset Hardware Store in Larson's territory had been cleaned out by a gang who smashed in the back window. He'd completely missed it, and Vollmer had seemed off with him ever since.

Larson picked his way past desks piled with equipment: one had ink pads for taking fingerprints; at another, police photographers diligently worked their way through rolls of film at trays of developing fluid.

Next, he passed through the open area where the officers shared desks, sitting at wide tables on chairs with wooden rollers. Eventually, he reached the chief's office and his big flat-topped desk, which was neat and tidy save for a telephone, a reading lamp, a stack of books and journals, and a bowl of sweets for the children that Vollmer so adored. The walls were decorated with paintings of California landscapes.

Vollmer looked up and smiled when Larson entered. The chief favored gray suits that matched the steeliness of his eyes, and his body was still lithe and strong. He had a way of holding himself that made him seem even taller than he actually was.

He had been following the rookie's work on fingerprinting and hormones closely, and thought Larson would be the perfect man for the job he had in mind. "Sit down," he said in his deep, strong voice. "I'm playing with an idea. I need your help. John, have you ever studied anything about detecting lies?"

The question set Larson's mind racing—he'd never looked into the research on deception, but he was definitely intrigued, as well as relieved he wasn't about to be disciplined. "That would be a tough assignment," he said when Vollmer explained what he wanted to do. "Yes it will be," the chief replied. "I'd like to do some experimenting."

Vollmer handed Larson a book by Cesare Lombroso, the Italian criminologist, and the journal with Marston's article in it. The paper described a series of blood pressure tests conducted by Marston on nineteen people in Boston—sixteen women and three men—whose crimes ranged from shoplifting to fornication, to being a "stubborn child."

The first case was of a forty-two-year-old White woman (each entry had the race neatly listed in brackets after the gender) and recovering drug user who was arrested after a hypodermic kit was found in her room. There was a brief record of the case given to Marston before the deception test ("Defendant claims she is not now using drugs"), followed by his verdict based on the blood pressure readings ("Innocent. Woman is not now using drugs") and a follow-up explaining why he'd gotten it right ("Medical examination showed increased weight, better all-round health, etc., which could not have existed were defendant now using drugs").

Larson turned the pages with growing interest. He was captivated. Here was a discovery that could help solve the cases where there wasn't enough physical evidence to bring anyone to justice, even with the new techniques Vollmer was pioneering. It could end some of the brutal tactics he'd encountered in his five months on the force and bring honesty and justice into policing.

He thought he could do better than Marston, though. The physiology lab at Berkeley was full of measurement equipment he could use to get a more accurate view of deception. By the time he left Vollmer's office that day, Larson had devised a plan for the experiments he could run, and—even better—Vollmer had reassigned him to work on the idea full-time. He would be a fully paid-up police officer, working solely in the lab—it was his dream role. No more late nights, no more hazing, no more roosters. "Remember, John," Vollmer had said, as he sent the delighted rookie on his way, "I want to be the first one tested."

* * *

Over the next few weeks, Larson quickly set to work on improving Marston's method—turning it from a fleeting measure on the dial of a blood pressure monitor into something more objective, which could potentially be used as evidence in court.

He combined Marston's paper with a couple of books Vollmer had recommended—including one by Vittorio Benussi, an Austrian psychologist who had achieved 75 percent accuracy in detecting deception by measuring people's breathing rates.

Dr. Robert Gesell, a physiology professor at Berkeley, had already developed a modified blood pressure cuff for tracking changes in flow and volume over time. Vollmer suggested that it might be adapted to detect lying. Larson used Gesell's device as his base.

He spent long hours in the lab, attaching friends and a rotating cast of college students to various pieces of equipment, trying to determine whether the readings from each instrument correlated with lying. Larson confirmed Marston's finding that when people lied, their breathing rate and pulse seemed to change in intensity and quicken. But to go further, he needed a way to record the body's reactions so that they could be properly assessed after the fact.

In 1906, Dr. James Mackenzie, a British cardiologist, had devised a machine that tracked blood pressure at the wrist and neck and translated it into two continuous lines drawn onto paper by pens that moved in concert with the subject's body. Larson borrowed this idea for his own device, and he corralled the mechanic at the city garage into building a prototype—a grab bag of medical equipment attached to a wooden breadboard.

The machine had an ordinary blood pressure cuff that was wrapped around the upper arm, with a tube leading to a heavy rubber bulb inside a larger glass one. As blood pumped through a subject's veins, their arteries swelled, inflating the rubber bulb and changing the volume of air inside the glass one. A connected tube transferred this change to a delicate rubber tambour, which translated it into the movement of a thin stylus scratching a thin path on a slow-moving drum of smoked paper, white lines against black.

Larson added a pneumograph—two bands of elastic that wrapped around the chest to measure lung capacity and breathing rate, which were also recorded on the paper via a similar system of tubes and actuators. The finished machine was a mess—a Frankenstein device that was a mixture of all the research that had come before.

It looked, a reporter for *The Examiner* wrote later, like "a combination of a radio set, a stethoscope, a dentist's drill, a gas stove, an aneroid barometer, a time ball, a wind gauge, and an Ingersoll watch." But it provided, for the first time ever, a fixed record of a person's blood pressure and the beat of their heart.

It was rough around the edges, Larson thought, but it ought to work. In public, he called it the "cardio-pneumo-psychograph"—a label as unwieldy as that first prototype. Eventually, it would get a different name—the same moniker Mackenzie had given his cardiology device, a term derived from the Greek for "many writing." Privately, Larson always thought of it as "the apparatus." Everyone else called it the polygraph.

While the mechanic was tinkering with the machinery, Larson worked on the "software" of lie detector tests from his "magpie den" of an office. When Marston tested subjects, he had no way of taking continuous measurements of blood pressure, so he took readings once a minute while they told their stories. That was fine—but it made scientific validation of the results almost impossible.

Larson decided to reverse the procedure. In the experiment he devised, his "cardio-pneumo-psychograph" would take continuous measurements from the body while the investigator asked specific, direct questions. That way, the answer to a certain query could be matched to its exact physiological response.

*   *   *

A month after his meeting with Vollmer, Larson was ready to show the apparatus to his boss. He'd promised the chief he'd be the first person to be tested, and in March 1921 he arranged a demonstration of the device at police headquarters.

He set up the lie detector in a small office in the basement. It had a square wooden block, like a chopping board, with a large iron column rising from it that held two thin styluses. These interacted with a horizontal scroll of charcoal-blackened paper, about a foot and a half long, which slowly rotated from right to left, propelled by two spinning drums. As it turned, the moving pens scratched away the black dust, leaving bone-white lines. Rubber tubes snaked away from the device toward an empty wooden chair, like the tentacles of some strange beast probing in the dark for its first victim.

Vollmer walked into the room with a group of skeptical officers in tow, including department veteran Jack Fisher—an intimidating presence who had served with the intelligence division in Siberia during the war. They were eager to see what the college boy had come up with.

Larson watched nervously as they scrutinized his work—the tangled mass of tubing and wires, the glass bulbs and rubber appendages. "It isn't much to look at," he laughed. "But let's see what it can do."

But something wasn't right. Vollmer had a playful look in his blue-gray eyes, and the beginnings of a smirk. Instead of taking the test as planned, the chief ordered Larson to strap himself into his own machine.

Once the rookie was hooked up, Vollmer—who was familiar with the basic premise of the test—started asking him questions, beginning with very simple ones. As Larson answered, the gathered officers peered over his shoulder at the lines on the chart.

Larson knew what was coming. Vollmer hadn't brought up the theft at the hardware store, but the chief had ways of finding out what his officers got up to. Larson suspected Villa might have squealed.

So, when the question finally came—"Were you off your beat the night of the Sunset Hardware Store burglary?"—he didn't even have to answer. Larson's body betrayed him before he could even speak; his physiological response so extreme that the needles of the machine shot off the piece of paper entirely. There was a stunned silence. "You don't have to answer," crowed the chief. "We've got you hoisted by your own petard."

Fisher, the veteran officer, went pale and offered to resign rather than be attached to "that God-damn thing." Vollmer laughed. "I don't need the machine for you."

Next, it was Vollmer's turn to be hooked to the device. Larson passed the cables around his chest and waist to measure his breathing, fitted the blood pressure cuff around his arm, and pumped it up to the correct tightness with a rubber hand bulb. The strangeness of the situation amused him. "I never thought I'd ever try to catch you lying," he said.

"I hope you do, John," replied Vollmer. "Just go ahead. See if you can catch me."

For the first time, Larson ran through the preamble to the test that would become second nature over the decades to come. "Remember to answer 'yes' or 'no' to all questions," he told Vollmer. "No comments."

Vollmer smiled. "The comments will come later."

Larson started the test with simple questions to try and establish a baseline: "Did you eat lunch today?" he asked.

"Do you like to swim? Do you like ice cream?"

Vollmer answered "yes" to each of these questions, and each time the pens on the polygraph traced a steady course—going up and down with the beat of his heart.

Larson continued, firing more questions at his boss. On two occasions—once, when he asked when Vollmer had gone to sleep, and again when he asked whether he liked roast beef—the needles made slightly more dramatic movements. The second time this happened, Vollmer stopped the test.

"It works, John," he said. "I lied two times, about the time I went to bed and my not liking roast beef, and every time the needle shot up."

He was ecstatic—he ordered Larson to test every officer in the department who could spare the time.

"I really think, John, we are on the right track," he said. "But we've got to move slow. We've got to prove this machine works on an actual case."

SECRETS OF THE SOUL

For months in the spring of 1921, College Hall—a women's-only private dorm at the university in Berkeley—had been at the center of a crime wave. The residence, located on the northeastern corner of campus, where Hearst Avenue began to climb into the hills, was home to ninety young women—eighteen- and nineteen-year-olds from good families who had found their possessions disappearing.

It started small—silk undergarments, books, registered letters—items whose absence could be attributed to carelessness. At first, the housemother was reluctant to involve the authorities. She brought all the girls together for a meeting, where she compelled the thief to come forward. When that didn't work, she launched her own investigation—but got no further than noting that the robberies seemed to be concentrated in one corner of the dorm.

Things came to a head on the night of March 30, 1921, when Ethel McCutcheon—a sophomore from Bakersfield—returned to her room to find her evening dresses had been removed from her closet and spread out on the bed. A textbook with $45 tucked inside had been taken, and her bureau had been ransacked too. McCutcheon alerted the other students, who had also been hit: Rita Benedict, a freshman from Lodi, had more than $100 in jewelry and money go missing. And Margaret Taylor, a first-year student from San Diego, couldn't find her diamond ring, valued at $400. She had no choice but to contact the police.

"I am really doing what all of the ninety girls in our dormitory didn't want anyone to do," Taylor told the desk sergeant at City Hall. She seemed embarrassed to have to ask. "We do not want publicity, but this thing really can't go on."

Vollmer assigned the case to seasoned veteran Jack Fisher and Bill Wiltberger, a college cop who had joined the force the previous November. Wiltberger toured Berkeley and Oakland's secondhand stores, old bookshops, and pawnshops in search of the missing items. Meanwhile, Fisher questioned the young women, and although they were mostly from affluent families with no need to steal, he found no shortage of suspects.

As the investigation dragged on, the housemother began to worry that the repeated visits from the police—conspicuous in their sharp uniforms—might start to tarnish the reputation of College Hall, which had been set up as an experiment in women's education and was the first residence of its kind at Berkeley.

Fisher was growing impatient with the rumors and jealous barbs and contradictory accusations being fired between the young women. He wanted to wrap the case up quickly—and he thought John Larson and the strange device he'd been building might be able to help.

Larson was running daily tests of his invention on his colleagues, as well as controlled experiments on university undergraduates. With each examination, he sharpened his technique and became better at telling when subjects were lying. But he knew that a real-world test, where he tried to root out a motivated and unknown liar, would be the only way to properly validate the technology.

"Aside from a few experimental tests, no real cases had been run, that is, cases in which the suspect repressed the truth through fear of the consequences," Larson wrote. So he was pleased when Vollmer called him in one day.

"John, I think we've got a real case to work on," said the chief, his deep voice brimming with excitement. He outlined Fisher's struggles so far and suggested Larson take his apparatus to the dormitory and test all ninety residents. "It's a great opportunity to see what the machine can really do."

Larson was slightly wary of the assignment—he'd been hoping for something a little more straightforward. But he knew the College Hall case would be the "acid test" of lie detection, and he approached it with care. Unlike Marston, whose experimental procedure included a large dose of improvisation, Larson was a meticulous planner.

After securing permission from the housemother, he called all the girls together and asked them to vote on whether they'd be willing to be tested on the machine. They unanimously agreed—although refusing to take part would have seemed like a clear indication of guilt, so they really had no choice.

Larson's experimental method—largely the same as the one used by polygraph examiners today—involved comparing the body's response to innocuous control questions with how it reacted to target questions relating to the crime or subject being investigated.

"The questions should be simple and not too involved," Larson wrote—each one was designed to be answered just "yes" or "no," to minimize differences between individuals. This was meant to be an examination, not an interrogation—a scientific test, not a fishing expedition.

On April 19, 1921, the lie detector was finally ready for its grand debut in a criminal case. Fourteen young women from the dorm were asked to come to the physiology lab.

They waited in an antechamber outside and were summoned one by one. First up was Margaret Taylor, the woman whose diamond ring had gone missing. She wasn't really considered a suspect—in fact, she'd been helping Fisher with his inquiries—but it was worth ruling out the possibility that the complaints had been faked.

Larson called the twenty-year-old Taylor into the lab. It was a pivotal moment in his life, for more than one reason. As she took a seat, her bright blue eyes took in the strange contraption on the table next to her. Larson's took in her pretty face and the golden ringlets cascading down to her shoulders.

Fisher loomed moodily in the background, and Vollmer stood at the back of the room too, eager to see how the machine performed in the real world. Larson wrapped a blood pressure cuff around Taylor's bare arm and pumped it up until it pinched tightly against her pale skin.

He wound a rubber hose around her chest to measure her breathing—he could feel it rising and falling with her breath—and told her to hold still as he switched on all the instruments. "The drums began to revolve, the black recording paper turned, and the long rubber hoses swelled and subsided to the rhythm of her body's organs, while a pair of long sharp needles scratched out her body's message against the black recording paper, as if tracing a silhouette of her thoughts," writes Ken Alder.

It was an odd situation, and Larson could perhaps sense Taylor's tension. He broke the ice, according to *Reader's Digest*, with some "charming conversation." Per this possibly slightly exaggerated account, Larson quickly forgot the control questions he'd planned to ask. They talked about her favorite books and music, and her parents.

She asked about his work—he told her about his interest in finger-printing and criminology, how he wanted to prevent crimes instead of solving them. "He found her intelligent and witty, as well as lovely . . . She told him he was wonderful to be doing so much and to be so ambitious."

Despite the nine-year age gap, Larson thought Taylor was "one of the most fascinating girls he had ever met—vivacious and intelligent, deeply interested in many subjects."

Eventually, as if snapping out of a kind of trance, Larson remembered that he was supposed to be conducting a police investigation. "Now," he said, with a smile, "shall we get down to business?"

Over the next six minutes or so—any longer and the blood pressure cuff started to hurt—Larson worked his way through a list of eight questions, starting with the innocuous ("Do you like college?" "Are you interested in this test?") and progressing to the targets ("Did you steal the money?"). The drums spun, the pens scratched, and Margaret Taylor's inner life was etched forever onto a roll of black paper. At the end of the test, Larson paused to examine the records—he'd have a closer look later—scanning the waving lines for swings in blood pressure and heart rate that might indicate deceit.

For the rest of the day, as a light drizzle slicked the paths and parks of Berkeley, Larson moved down the list of women. "The more he conversed with different students, the more he regretted that he was not still talking to Margaret Taylor." Then he came to Helen Graham.

She was slightly older than most of the other residents of College Hall and had trained as a nurse. In her yearbook photo, she's turned away from the camera, looking back at the lens with a smirk—dark hair cut into a flapper bob. Graham was from a modest Kansas family, but her roommate told Detective Fisher that she spent money at a rate that seemed out of step with her background—she wore a diamond ring and a pendant with big stones. She was one of his main suspects.

Graham showed no emotion as Larson worked his way through the list of questions, until he reached one about the missing diamond ring. After she answered, he glanced at the chart.

"The test shows you stole it," he said flatly.

The woman seemed to stop breathing. She glared at Larson. "I think all these questions are an insult," she said. "Just because I'm excited and mad at being asked all these questions, the needle jumps, and you think I'm lying."

Her eyes burned with rage. She started shouting. "It's the third degree, that's what it is. The needle shoots up and I'm a liar!"

"No one has said you are a liar," Larson said in a low voice, trying to defuse the situation.

"You're trying to make me out a thief— that's what you're doing. I won't stand for it, I tell you."

As Larson leaned forward to take a blood pressure reading, Graham burst out of the chair. She charged over to the spinning drums of the polygraph, which were still tracing her body's increasingly violent movements. Larson and Fisher jumped up and had to forcibly prevent her from destroying the equipment as she railed against the men and their machine. Her blood pressure and heart rate were still going up as she tore the cuff off her arm.

"Are you through with this crazy stunt?" she spat.

"Yes, we're through," Larson replied.

But Graham was already charging out of the room. Outside, she told one of the other women she had wanted to tear up the charts and that if she hadn't been restrained by the equipment she would have "smashed Officer Fisher in the face."

Inside, Larson and Vollmer exchanged glances. "That isn't the girl the housemother suspected, but I'm betting she's the one," Larson said.

"I don't think there is any doubt of it, but we have no confession," Vollmer said. "I'll have the girl watched. Maybe we'll get some real evidence."

Overnight, Larson found out more about Graham from the other women in the dorm. She'd passed a preliminary test he had conducted because she'd been up late the night before playing cards, smoking cigarettes, and drinking strong coffee in the hope of fooling the machine.

Her dorm mates told Larson and Fisher that Graham had been entangled in several passionate affairs and that she'd once induced an abortion by taking the anti-malaria drug quinine—hardly relevant to the case, but a cause for suspicion by the attitudes of the time.

The day after the lie detector test, Graham turned up at the police department, demanding to speak to Larson and asking to see the chart. He and Fisher then interrogated her for twelve hours while she continued to maintain her innocence. Eventually, though, she broke into "an attack of sobbing"—agreeing that it was possible she might have taken the items in her sleep.

She offered to replace the missing ring and the money if it meant the police would stop investigating her. Larson was always inclined to pursue the truth at whatever cost, and told her if she was genuinely innocent, she shouldn't make that offer. Fisher, by contrast, said if she was guilty, she'd be prosecuted whether she replaced the items or not.

They sent her home, but she turned up at the police station every day that week, begging to be seen. It was only when she threatened to hurt herself that Larson finally relented. "During the interview she threatened suicide unless the case was cleared up at once," Larson wrote, also remarking on Graham's "very unstable personality."

But by April 30, Graham still hadn't confessed. She was still being followed by the police, and she'd tried twice to offer Taylor a replacement for the ring.

Larson arranged another interrogation, where he and Fisher supplemented the lie detector with a more traditional interview technique.

"Officer Fisher played the role of 'hard-boiled cop' with his usual adroitness, and I was her friend," Larson remembered.

The interview revealed Graham's traumatic life story: she'd been sexually abused as a child and felt intensely guilty about an affair she'd had with a married medical student before coming to California.

After several hours of this, Fisher rose suddenly to his feet and stormed out—threatening Graham with the prospect of imprisonment in San Quentin, which still housed women until 1933. The ploy worked. While Fisher was out of the room, Larson finally managed to extract a confession from Graham. She admitted to taking the money and the ring as well as some items of clothing—but not the underwear. In exchange for admitting to the theft, she wanted guaranteed immunity from prosecution and to avoid being named in any publicity.

When Fisher returned, Graham signed a written confession. It had taken some time and a bit of help, but the lie detector had solved its first case. Vollmer was delighted. The machine worked! He was eager to roll it out on more hardened criminals.

"The problem of lying, the bane of the human race for hundreds of years, could now be dealt with," is how one biographer summarized his thoughts at the time. But for Graham, it was a devastating blow. She dropped out of university and moved out of College Hall into a hotel in the city while she prepared to return to her parents' farm.

Larson had mixed feelings about the case. Yes, Graham had eventually confessed, but only after a month of being ostracized by her peers and hounded by the police. When she got back to Kansas, she wrote him a letter recanting her statement, "saying that she had been told that she was a fool for confessing," Larson recalled. "She even denied her guilt and intimated that she had been tricked into a confession."

As Larson worked on more cases that year—many involving sororities and college students—he started to realize that the inner rumblings of the body were more complicated than they seemed; that a change in blood pressure was not necessarily a telltale sign of deceit. A lie detector test was inherently stressful—being asked about a theft or a murder weapon could cause an emotional response whether you were guilty or not.

And Larson often found himself investigating people who, like Heather Graham, felt desperately guilty—just not of the crime he happened to be investigating. In the course of his work, he "unmasked midnight poker games, petty shoplifters, pregnancies, and attempted abortions, often without solving the original crime itself," writes Alder. Larson began to wonder whether Graham really was guilty or if she'd simply been made to feel that way. "Indeed, the evidence strongly suggests that Helen Graham was singled out mainly for her sexual transgressions," Alder argues—her dormmates had gossiped to Fisher about promiscuity and rumors of an abortion.

Although he was largely responsible for her confession, Larson began to sympathize with the young woman—starting a pattern he'd repeat throughout his career. "I am very sorry that you have been feeling blue and wish that I could do something to make you feel better," he wrote to her in May 1921.

In his experiments, he'd been trying to rule out external factors that might be influencing the tests, and he was starting to suspect that in some cases it might be the questioner and not the questions that was eliciting an emotional response (perhaps unsurprisingly, considering most of the subjects in that first year were young women).

To test this theory, he asked Margaret Taylor to come back to the lab for a follow-up experiment. It was perhaps the boldest thing he'd ever done.

"I thought you'd told me that I had passed," she said when she arrived. "Now what's wrong?"

"Nothing," he said. "But I've got a new question here that's not on the list I first prepared."

Seating Taylor in front of the lie detector again, he went through the preamble of the experiment—stealing glances at her golden hair, the perfect blue of her bright eyes. They ran through the test fairly quickly: he asked her to lie to him on purpose, he tried to tell when she was doing it. They had a light, easy rapport.

Before he let her go, there was one more thing he wanted to know. "There's a special question that I want you to be sure to answer truthfully," he said, according to *Reader's Digest* (Larson later dismissed this account as "pure hooey").

His voice had acquired a strange quality. "It's here on the list. Go ahead, please." Taylor took the piece of paper from the detective. Her eyes widened imperceptibly as she read the four words written there in Larson's spidery handwriting. She could feel the blood rushing to her face.

Larson had discovered during his experiments that short, basic queries were the best, and the question he had written down for Taylor could not have been more simple: "Do you love me?"

"No," she said quickly—but Larson didn't need a machine to tell that she was lying. For a moment, she looked across at the rookie detective, his eyes fixed on hers. Then her gaze flicked over to the rolling drums of the apparatus and the black paper that had opened a window to her heart. "The wings of the 'lie detector' trembled, fluttered, waved a frantic SOS," wrote *The Examiner*—retelling the story sixteen months later, on the day of Larson and Taylor's wedding.

In time, Larson would remember this moment fondly. He marveled at the possibilities of the device—not only could it solve crimes, but it could shine a light on the deepest secrets of the soul, uncover hidden longings and dark impulses. But while his romance with Taylor blossomed, his relationship with the machine that brought them together quickly turned sour. And as far as Larson was concerned, there was only one man to blame for that.

THE MAGICIAN

It was a slow evening at Berkeley police headquarters in the hot, dry summer of 1921. Most of the daytime staff had gone home, and the night shift was out on patrol. A scattering of detectives worked by electric light, writing up case files or manning the chief's signaling system from a mahogany cabinet studded with dials and switches.

A sudden burst of laughter pierced the studious atmosphere. In a small lab at one end of the basement, seventeen-year-old Leonarde Keeler was holding court. His wide-set hazel eyes sparkled, and a small group of teenage boys and girls sat in rapt attention as he talked. There were always young people coming and going in those days—part of August Vollmer's unique approach to policing—but Keeler's gangly frame and thick blond hair had become a particularly familiar sight in the preceding months. He was obsessed with the lie detector—and it was about to consume his life.

Keeler was born on October 30, 1903, into Berkeley's cultural elite. His father, Charles, was a poet, spiritualist, and all-round eccentric—tall, thin, and handsome, he made a dramatic sight striding around Berkeley in his black cape, with a gold-topped cane and his dark hair falling in long curtains (Leonarde found this deeply embarrassing).

Charles moved in rarefied circles with artists, naturalists, and architects, and supplemented his writing income by chipping away at a sizeable inheritance. In the early 1920s, he founded his own faith—the "Cosmic Religion"—which aimed to unite people of all creeds through the universal principles of "love, truth and beauty."

In 1893, the year he turned twenty-three, Charles married Louise Mapes Bunnell, a student of one of his artist friends, the landscape painter William Keith. The couple lived on a wooded slope overlooking the university, in an elegant redwood house designed by renowned architect and family friend Bernard Maybeck and festooned with Persian rugs, Chinese lanterns, and other artifacts from Charles's travels across the South Pacific and beyond. It nestled among the trees like a fairy-tale cottage. They had a happy, creative life. Louise illustrated her husband's poems with artful woodcuts and painted portraits of him posing in Athenian robes, a crown of flowers in his hair.

The Keelers had high hopes for their middle child, their only son. They wanted him to become a painter or an inventor, "one of the great contributors to the thought of this wonderful generation in which we live." They named him after Leonardo da Vinci, but he preferred the more prosaic nickname "Nard."

A cozy life of ideas, books, and cocktail parties beckoned, until the early hours of April 18, 1906, when the earthquake struck the bay and changed the course of Leonarde Keeler's life. At just after five that morning, the family woke to a huge bang, as the brick chimney of their house came crashing down onto the outside porch where the children were sleeping. Charles snatched his son to safety just in time.

As active members of Berkeley's civic life, the Keelers worked tirelessly to help the city deal with the influx of refugees from San Francisco. But the effort took its toll on Louise, and she fell ill and died within a year. Charles never really got over it.

In 1907, he moved his three children out of their home and in with his mother-in-law on the other side of Berkeley, swapping its high ceilings for a brown shingle house that was barely big enough to hold them all. Then in 1909, when Leonarde Keeler was six, his father departed on an around-the-world speaking and poetry tour. He was gone for three years.

Their older sister, Merodine, had gone to college, so Keeler and his younger sister, Eloise, were left to roam free with the neighborhood kids, chasing each other over fences, playing cops and robbers, and clambering over the beams and rafters of partly built houses in the rapidly expanding city.

With limited supervision from his ailing grandmother, Keeler soon fell in with a bad crowd. It seemed that every time Charles returned from a trip, his son was in trouble again, but he had no idea what to do about it.

Keeler was caught stealing money from his grandma's purse to buy candy for his friends, and—after he nearly lost his sight when one of the gang hit him in the face with a hard rubber ball—his exasperated father turned to hypnosis for a solution. For nights at a time, Charles sat by his son's bedside as he slept, repeating a mantra that he hoped would provide the resilience to stand up to peer pressure. "Leonarde, you hear me speak," he whispered. "You are brave, you have great courage. You are independent. You make your own plans and work them out for yourself."

By 1916, demand for Charles's fantastical poetry had slumped amid the bloodshed of the First World War, and the inheritance money was running out. After a brief stint in New York, where Leonarde bounced between private boarding and state school, depending on the state of his father's finances, the family settled back in California, where they lived in a secluded canyon in the Berkeley hills.

It was just one big studio room with a small kitchen, no electricity and no heating save for a fireplace. They slept on outdoor porches. But it was here that Keeler came into his own. The modest dwelling was set in an acre of lush forest with a stream babbling through it. There was a shed behind the house that the teenage Keeler claimed as his den—he spent many happy hours tinkering with a crystal radio set and tending to a growing menagerie of animals: "lizards, snakes, rats, mice, and even a tarantula."

He matured into an athletic and self-assured young man with an impressive array of hobbies, from photography to mountain climbing. Quiet but charismatic, Keeler had a way of dominating a room without saying much. "He drew people to him like a magnet," wrote one friend. "He seemed constantly in search of adventure," wrote his sister Eloise. "Danger exhilarated him."

Keeler went on expeditions with the Boy Scouts along the Russian River and played the flute in the school orchestra. He was on the track team, and in his final year of high school he was elected student body president. On Saturdays, he took dancing lessons. American choreographer Agnes de Mille, a long-time friend, said he was the best dance partner that she ever had.

"He was spare and stringy and tough, muscles like a countryman, like a farmer or a hunter," she wrote. "His face was not handsome, but very strong, the smile sardonic, the eyes of a steely gray looked at you with great intensity from narrow lids and sliding sideways to make his points or study your reactions to every nuance of a situation."

At school carnivals, Keeler put on spectacular magic shows involving sleight-of-hand card tricks; snake charming; and on one occasion, a pistol loaded with blanks. He got his first taste of a police interrogation when he and his friend Warren Olney were spotted pulling up outside a shop in Oakland's Chinatown, carrying a gun—they'd borrowed it from Olney's father and said they'd gone there to buy blank rounds and incense for their magic show.

However, Keeler's outgoing nature was undercut by serious health issues. In 1918, as the influenza pandemic raged worldwide and killed an estimated fifty million people, he was struck down by a severe streptococcus infection that developed into blood poisoning, affecting the lining of his brain and the valves of his heart.

In the hospital, he overheard the nurses talking about how he might die. Charles brought in a faith healer, who compelled the stricken teenager to rise again, which he did—but the illness left him prone to fainting spells for the rest of his life.

In early 1921, Keeler was on an expedition in the California mountains with the John Muir conservation club when he felt a sharp pain in his abdomen. He had acute appendicitis and underwent urgent surgery to remove his gall bladder and appendix. He spent two weeks in the hospital recovering, and doctors advised him not to return to school until the beginning of the following academic year.

That left Keeler with eight months to kill. He'd already exhausted much of the entertainment on offer during his first illness, when he spent the recovery period practicing wildlife photography and tending to his snakes—and he was soon bored out of his mind and getting into trouble again. So, just as he had when Keeler's behavior had caused him difficulties in the past, Charles asked an old friend for advice.

Charles Keeler had known August Vollmer since Gus's days as a Berkeley mailman, when he would push his two-wheeled cart up the steep hill to the Keeler home, sometimes stopping to give the infant Leonarde a ride around in it. Since then, Charles had observed Vollmer's rise to influential police chief with interest.

Their paths had intertwined when—in an effort to make some extra money—the poet took up a position at the Berkeley Chamber of Commerce. Charles had used his influence there to help Vollmer block a proposed merger with Oakland that threatened to unwind much of the progress he'd made with the Berkeley Police Department. So, the chief owed him a favor.

On one of Charles's visits to the basement of City Hall, Vollmer showed his friend a psychological chart he had been preparing—possibly one of the first polygraph records.

"I wish Leonarde could see that chart," Charles said, remembering that his son had expressed an interest in psychology. "I think it would interest him."

"Send him in and I'll show it to him," said Vollmer.

A couple of days later, Leonarde Keeler arrived at the police department for the first time. Vollmer hadn't seen much of him since he was a young boy, and he was impressed by Keeler's "personality and alertness." In time, the chief would come to regard Keeler "with the affection that a father would a son."

For Keeler, what started as a mild diversion—"I intended merely to pass the time until I should return to school"—soon became an obsession. Until that point, his knowledge of criminology had come from the stories of Sherlock Holmes, whose new adventures were still being published regularly in *The Strand* magazine. "I had developed a lively curiosity to see a real system of crime prevention and detection in action," he wrote.

He started to spend most of his days at the department, hanging around outside Vollmer's office, learning about the fingerprint system and other branches of detective work that were coming into existence for the first time in Berkeley. Keeler's intelligence, curiosity, and charm soon endeared him to the older officers. At first, he spent most of his time in the darkroom, helping the police photographer develop pictures of crime scenes—which Vollmer had become an enthusiastic supporter of following the very Holmesian "case of the poison vial."

One of Keeler's tasks in the photography department was to take pictures of the charts being pulled from a "mysterious contrivance being used to detect the lies of criminals." The lie detector immediately sparked his interest—how could it not? "I wondered about this machine, and of course was sure "it couldn't be done," he wrote.

Before long, Vollmer introduced Keeler to his other young protégé—John Larson. It was a moment that changed both of their lives forever—and a preface to what became a toxic relationship. Keeler, pumped up with teenage bravado, told Larson he thought he could easily fool the device. "Well come on in and try your luck," Larson said, motioning for the skinny youth to enter the little office that served as his interrogation room.

Keeler stepped in, took off his coat and rolled up his right shirt sleeve. He took a seat, craning his neck to peer more closely at the instruments as Larson taped a new roll of smoked paper around the drums and set them spinning. Larson asked Keeler to come up with a list of ten questions he wanted to be interrogated on, which he did—although he couldn't resist one more cocky jab at the apparatus. Admittedly, the idea that the bizarre contraption in front of him could dig into the depths of the human mind must have seemed ridiculous. "I don't care what you ask," Keeler said. "That machine can't detect lies."

He was still confident when Larson started asking the questions. Keeler told the truth on nine out of the ten questions but lied on the fourth one. "I knew Dr. Larson could never tell where I had lied, for I had been sitting quietly without becoming the least excited," he said. But he was wrong.

At the end of the test, Larson looked up at the confident boy in front of him with a grin and a short, sharp laugh. "Ha! You're an easy one," he said. "Lied on the fourth question, didn't you?"

Keeler was amazed. His skepticism fell away as Larson talked him through the chart, pointing out how his blood pressure had suddenly risen when he'd lied on the fourth question, and how imperceptible clues from his body had translated to lines on the paper.

"You can't beat it!" Larson said. "You may tell a lie with perfect ease, but your whole system will revolt, and consequently your heart action will change; and look at your breathing curve—even that changed."

Keeler's fascination with the machine grew after he watched Larson using it to extract a confession from a burglary suspect. "From the moment that Nard saw the work of Larson in 1921, his life took on new meaning, and his mind and body seemed to be charged with energy," wrote Vollmer.

He spent the next four months learning everything he could about the machine. When he wasn't in the lab, watching Larson conducting tests, he was studying the charts or photographing them. He helped prepare the blackened paper by coating it in soot—although as much ended up on his hands and face as on the charts themselves. He even wrote about the lie detector in a composition for his English class.

Soon, Keeler was acting as Larson's assistant—helping the detective assemble and dismantle the heavy equipment when it needed to be transported to tests at prisons and state hospitals. They drove all over California together in an old Ford touring car loaded with coils and smoked drums, Larson nervously clutching the wheel, and Keeler in the passenger seat, holding the more delicate parts of the apparatus on his knees. Together, they attached the lie detector to gamblers, thieves, and murderers; to the insane and feeble minded; and with great amusement, to Larson's dog.

Vollmer also gave Keeler "free rein" to experiment with the device himself. He took delight in showing off to his classmates night after night at City Hall. "He'd get them to lie about their ages, report cards, dates—anything he could dream up," remembered his sister Eloise (who fainted the first time he tested her). Keeler was quiet, but he was a showman at heart, and sometimes police officers even dropped what they were doing to see him work his magic.

On this particular evening, in the summer of 1921, a group of teens from the local high school had gathered to watch another demonstration, crowding into the small room where the machine was set up. A high window let in the evening light from outside, and there were shelves stacked with rolls of completed records. The apparatus was set up on a dark wooden table that had been pushed into the corner.

Frances Chick, a friend of Keeler's sister, was sitting in a chair with the blood pressure cuff on her arm and the rubber tubing wrapped around her chest. Keeler flicked the switch and then, keeping his voice quiet and low, started the interrogation, aping the method he'd watched Larson using but playing to the crowd with dramatic pauses and arched eyebrows as the needles traced their path.

"Do you love Harry?" he asked.

"No."

"Do you love Ralph?"

"No."

"Do you love Curtis?"

"No'

"Do you love Charlie?"

"No."

On the last question, the lines suddenly jumped, and the group burst out laughing. "It's true," admitted a red-faced Frances Chick. "I do have kind of a crush on Charlie. But I never dreamed anybody would find out."

* * *

Keeler soon found that Larson's apparatus had many drawbacks. It took half an hour to set up, a fiddly business that involved carefully taping the soot-blackened graph paper to the rolling drums without marking it.

The record, once it was made, was extremely fragile—any contact with it would erase the lines, so the rolls of paper had to be cautiously removed from the machine and then shellacked, using a preparation that Inspector Frank Waterbury referred to as a mixture of turpentine and "jackass whiskey." This preserved the charts but made them brittle, and they had to be rolled away for storage, which took up an inordinate amount of space.

So, over the next few years—at Vollmer's suggestion—Larson and Keeler began to split their labor. While Larson ran controlled experiments to try and validate the lie detector scientifically, Keeler began tinkering with the machinery—trying to make the device more reliable and more portable, all while honing his own skills as an examiner in an unofficial capacity.

But where Larson was patient and methodical, Keeler was headstrong and brash, and his attitude would become a constant source of tension between the two men. The machine brought them together, and it would tear them apart. It would make them famous and ruin their lives. But that all lay in the future. Across the bay, a strange disappearance was about to catapult the lie detector irrevocably into the public eye.

THE BAKER AND THE PRIEST

In the tiny town of Colma, the dead have always outnumbered the living. In 1914, San Francisco authorities began digging up the gold rush graveyards that were occupying prime real estate in the heart of the city. They established a streetcar route running ten miles south from Mission Street, to ferry the exhumed caskets of former residents to their new final resting place on repurposed farmland. For $10, your loved one's remains could be relocated—and you could even ride along with them on the "cemeteries line"; otherwise, they would be dumped in a mass grave.

The dark carriages were a grim but familiar sight to the residents of Colma, whose livelihoods were tied up with death: florists and stonemasons and clergymen. "The electric streetcars emerged daily from the fog like props from a gothic novel," writes Kate Winkler Dawson.

On August 2, 1921, a chilly Tuesday night, something else came sliding out of the mist. It was a small, light-colored Ford with a strange character at the wheel. His features were almost hidden by a wide-brimmed cloth hat, and he was wearing dark driving goggles, old-fashioned even then.

The car turned onto San Pedro Road in Colma and pulled up opposite the Holy Angels Catholic Church. The fog swirled around the driver as he crossed the road to the wood-framed church, which was attached to a large concrete building where the priest, Father Patrick Heslin, lived with his housekeeper Marie Wendel. As he walked toward the front door of the dwelling, the man turned up the collar of his heavy coat, shielding his face. He rang the bell.

Heslin was fifty-eight years old and had only been in Colma for ten days. He had just moved to his new parish from a church in Turlock, about a hundred miles east, where he offered a "kind but authoritative" voice for the community. He was tall and handsome, with dark, thinning hair and an accent that traced him back to County Longford in Ireland. The priest was sitting in his study when he heard the doorbell ring. There was a short pause, then loud knocking and a frantic pounding. He heard his housekeeper unlock the door and swing it open.

The stranger was tall and thin, with a high, curving forehead. He had a thick accent, Wendel said later, and seemed twitchy—he refused to come inside. "I'm in a hurry," he told her. She called up to Heslin. "There's a man who wants you to minister to a dying friend." Her voice sounded strained.

When Heslin came downstairs, the man in the dark goggles explained that he had someone nearby who was dying of tuberculosis and needed a priest to deliver his last rites. The contagious disease was the leading cause of death in the United States in the early twentieth century, but despite the dangers Heslin agreed to go. "I will be back as soon as possible," he told Wendel.

He put on his coat and went next door to the church to grab a leather case containing the bread and wine of the sacrament, as the stranger swung the Ford around to face the highway. The priest climbed in, and Wendel peered through the curtains as the car drove south, slipping back into the evening mist. It was the last time anyone saw Heslin alive.

* * *

The church bells were silent the next morning—it was Father Heslin's job to ring in the dawn. When she found his bedroom empty and his bed untouched, his housekeeper—who had stayed up past midnight, worrying and waiting—telephoned the office of Edward Hanna, the Archbishop of San Francisco. He left with "a small, dark man, probably a foreigner," she told the clerk.

Hanna was not overly concerned until later that day, when the clerk walked into his office, holding a ransom note. It had arrived by special delivery, and the rambling and incoherent text inside read like it had been written by two different people: the typewritten sections were tidy and well phrased, but jarred with manic handwriting, confusing and peppered with spelling mistakes.

Act with caution, for I have Father _____ (of Colma) in a bootleg cellar, where a lighted candle is left burning when I leave, and at the bottom of the candle are all the chemicals necessary to generate enough poison gas to kill a dozen men.

This was typewritten, and the writer had left a large gap after the word "Father" as if he was unsure exactly which priest he was going to kidnap and had filled it in afterward. The note ended with a pencil scrawl: *"Had to HITT him four times and he is unconscious from pressure on brain. So better hurry and no fooling. TONIGHT at 9 o'clock."*

The note said Heslin was tied up with chains, and the author threatened to leave him for dead if he was bothered by the police. *"If the door is opened to this cellar by anyone except myself, it will ignite a bunch of matches and upset a can of gasoline on top of him and the entire police force,"* it said. The writer boasted of having a military background and claimed to have shot thousands of men in the Argonne. *"Killing men is no novelty to me,"* it read.

The note demanded $6,500 in small bills to be delivered in a sealed package to a location whose details would be specified in a separate message later that night. *"Get out with the money, leave the car and follow the string that is attached to the white strip until you come to the end of the string. Then put down the package and go back to town."*

But the message with the rest of the delivery instructions never arrived. The San Francisco police were baffled. They probed the case from every possible angle. Chief Dan O'Brien organized an aerial search for wrecked vehicles along the Pacific Coast to the south of the city, the route the stranger's car had taken.

The road, which snaked from Colma through the Pedro Valley to Half Moon Bay, was treacherous—fringed by steep ravines and fog-cloaked bends. Hundreds of volunteers fanned out across the area.

The papers spread fake news—*The Oakland Tribune* speculated that the priest had been kidnapped by a couple to perform a clandestine wedding ceremony, and reporters descended on the town of Colma like flies, buzzing around the housekeeper, Marie Wendel, and accusing her of being an accomplice.

The ransom note was the only solid piece of evidence, so detectives hired three document experts, including Oscar Heinrich, a forensics pioneer dubbed the "American Sherlock." He predicted, based on the way the writer formed his A's, H's, T's and U's, that he was a baker. "That's the style bakers use in writing on cakes," he said. "Look at the frosted lettering on your next birthday cake."

The police had their own theories. O'Brien was convinced there was a mob connection—that Heslin had been called to administer the last rites to a foreign gangster, who had then confessed to a murder in front of the priest, requiring a snipping of loose ends. Silvio Landini, Colma's rotund constable, thought money might be the motive—Heslin was said to have invested heavily in war bonds.

Detective Duncan Matheson was in charge of the investigation, and his men combed the sparsely populated coastline for signs of the priest, searching isolated mountain shacks and trudging through the devil grass and black soil of the artichoke farms. Hundreds of local stores closed so the proprietors could join in the search, and in the orange groves further south, fruit pickers laid down their baskets to hunt for the priest. The San Francisco diocese offered a $5,000 reward for finding Heslin—dead or alive.

Mistaken sightings of Heslin came in from all over California—he was seen in a car near Fremont, speeding south; and struggling with two men on the road to Los Angeles, still dressed in his priestly garb.

But there were no real breakthroughs until Wednesday, August 10—eight days after Heslin's disappearance. The archbishop arose to discover that a second note had been slipped under the door of his mansion on Fulton Street during the night. *"Fate made me do this,"* it read. *"Sickness, misery, has compelled my action. I must have money."* The priest was alive and well, the author promised—but the ransom demand had also been upped to $15,000.

That afternoon, George Lynn—a smart young reporter for *The Examiner*—went to the archbishop's house to investigate rumors that there had been a third note delivered (there hadn't). When he got there, there was a peculiar man ascending the stone steps leading up to the house. He was wearing a cream outfit and a straw hat—clothing more suited to Florida than San Francisco.

When Lynn was admitted to the residence by Archbishop Hanna's Filipino servant, the man followed him inside. "I don't know this man," the reporter said quickly. "He just walked in with me. I'm not responsible for him."

"I came to see the archbishop too," the stranger snapped. "I think I know where the missing priest is."

* * *

The man's name was William Hightower. He was tall and balding, with a fringe of sparse graying hair that made him look older than his forty-three years. He was from near Waco, Texas, where he'd spent his youth working on the cotton plantations, and he told his story in a high-pitched southern drawl.

It went like this: A few days earlier, Hightower had bumped into a young woman called Dolly Mason, whom he knew from his time living in Salt Lake City. She told him about a man she'd met the previous night—a foreign bootlegger who had drunkenly professed his hatred of the Catholic Church and shown her a revolver. "You do right to be afraid of that gun," he'd said. "It has taken human life."

The case had been all over the newspapers, which had stoked up a xenophobic storm—everyone in the city knew a priest was missing and that a foreigner was to blame. Mason asked the man—who she thought might be Greek—where the victim was buried. "He isn't alone," the foreigner replied. "I've a man watching him all the time—a man who sits and cooks flapjacks."

Hightower—who told Lynn he was an out-of-work baker—said Mason's story had reminded him of something. There was a billboard by the side of the Pedro Valley Road near Salada Beach—an advert for Albers Brothers' flour. It had an illustration of a man frying flapjacks. "It might not be a real man who is watching that body," Hightower told himself. "It might be a picture on a signboard."

The next day, Hightower found the billboard, which stood between the road and the cliffs some twenty miles south of the city, within the area that had been extensively combed by search parties. When he peered over the edge of the cliff, which fell away 150 feet down to the beach, something caught his eye. There was a black scarf fluttering in the breeze about ten feet below the lip, pinned to the sandy surface by the breeze.

He clambered down and found an area where a section of the cliff had fallen away, leaving a level bench cut into the slope, nearly invisible from the road. There, among the sand and the devil grass, he found a revolver with some spent cartridges, and a bloody rag.

"Maybe it's that missing priest," he told police later. "That's what I've been thinking. The ground's loose too. Seems to me that's worth looking into, don't you agree?"

* * *

Archbishop Hanna had been sifting through nonsense leads all week, and he was not impressed by Hightower's tall tale. "If you will return tomorrow about ten in the morning, I'll send a couple of investigators with you," he told him. George Lynn, on the other hand, knew a good story when he heard one—even if it didn't end up having anything to do with the missing priest. As they left, he hailed a cab and asked Hightower to accompany him to *The Examiner*'s offices, where he repeated his story to Bill Hines, the city editor.

Hines authorized a search party to visit the site Hightower had described—bringing the police on board on the strict condition that they keep whatever they found secret from the city's other newspapers until *The Examiner*'s scoop hit the streets.

That night, a group of men climbed into Chief O'Brien's squad car—stopping at his house to pick up shovels, and in Colma to fetch Constable Landini, who had become a local hero since prohibition by providing advance warning of planned raids. He squeezed onto the front bench seat.

As O'Brien drove through the fog, stopping regularly to wipe the windscreen clear, Hightower entertained Hines; Lynn; *The Examiner*'s star writer, Ernest Hopkins; and the newspaper photographer with stories, including one about how he'd shot a policeman's hat off once in Texas. It can't have landed well given the company he was in.

It was eleven PM by the time they reached the cliffside above Salada Beach. The lights of the squad car illuminated a giant billboard advertising Albers Brothers' flour, just as Hightower had said. On the other side of the road, the search party could see the dark silhouette of the so-called "Mystery Castle," a mock medieval mansion that operated as an illegal abortion clinic until the proprietor was sent to San Quentin in 1920.

Hightower led as the group picked their way down a rocky trail toward the beach, a dramatic scene lit only by the flickering glow of matches and the "dim phosphorescence of the sea"—they'd departed in such haste that they'd forgotten to bring lanterns.

They could hear waves crashing against the shore below them, and the mist dampened their clothes. "The gale dashed sand in the eyes and blew speech away before it could be heard," wrote Hopkins. "Through stunted black gorse that blotched the shadowy sand, it sang like a murderer's wailing laughter."

When he got to the right spot, Hightower hopped over a rocky outcrop and down out of sight. The others followed more carefully and found Hightower on his hands and knees, tugging a piece of black cloth out of the sand. "There it is," he shouted. "That's the spot."

Lynn and one of the officers grabbed their shovels and began digging in the soft ground. Hightower joined in too, flinging sand with the zeal of an 1850s prospector. Landini took a step back to avoid the bombardment. "If the body is in here, you ought to be a little easy with that shovel," he warned Hightower. "You might strike the face and mar it, and we don't want to do that." Hightower paused and glanced up. "Don't worry," he said. "I'm digging at the feet."

Before the others could process the implications of that statement, Lynn felt his shovel strike a hard object under the sand. "Something's here," he called. He slowly lifted it up. It was a hand.

Father Heslin's face had been smashed in with a blunt object, and he had been shot in the back of the head at point-blank range. Parts of his skull were missing. He was still wearing his sacred vestments, and there was a small picture of Christ buried alongside him. The men stared solemnly at the corpse by the glow of lanterns that Landini had borrowed from a nearby farm.

"Human life is a funny thing," Hightower whispered to O'Brien, who glared back at him. The man who had led them to the body was now the prime suspect. "Let's go," the police chief shouted, and dragged Hightower back up the cliff to his waiting squad car.

THE INFERNAL MACHINE

The Examiner had the scoop of the decade. Thanks to George Lynn's diligent work, Father Heslin's body had been found and a prime suspect identified, and their rivals had no idea. The doors of the newspaper's offices were locked, and no one was allowed to enter or leave until the morning edition hit the streets—and the city's other papers were left scrambling to catch up.

Over the next week, police officers and reporters raced—often against each other—to uncover the next clue in a case that had gripped the nation. Reporters hired experts to match the ransom note to the typewriter found in Hightower's cheap lodgings. Police found a revolver matching the bullets that had killed the priest. Oscar Heinrich, the forensics expert, matched sand from a hat in Hightower's room to grains from the beach where Heslin's body was found.

Journalists found tent pegs and bits of string at the grave site and matched them to a canvas tent in Hightower's room, which had the word "TUBERCULOSIS" scrawled on it in a large-print version of Hightower's baker's handwriting. It was a clever ploy to keep prying eyes away.

There were bloodstained pieces of burlap and spent .45 cartridges, a butcher's knife, and a selection of newspapers with stories about the case. There were rambling poems that Hightower had composed himself. And there was what Hightower called his "infernal machine"—a homemade weapon improvised from some short lengths of pipe plastered to a wooden frame. The user could pull a long string to simultaneously fire ten shells loaded with buckshot, spraying shrapnel across a wide area at waist height. It was, wrote *The Chronicle*, "diabolical in its ingenuity and one of the most deadly things ever conceived"—police figured that Hightower had planned to use it after collecting his ransom to prevent any attempt at a pursuit.

On the day of Heslin's funeral, after three days of heavy questioning, Hightower was formally charged with murder. Police doubted his tale about Dolly Mason and the bootlegger, but they searched for her anyway, and Hightower was adamant that she would exonerate him. "You've got a funny way of showing your gratitude when I solved your case for you," he complained.

Despite all the evidence against him, Hightower refused to confess. In fact, he didn't seem remorseful at all. He acted horrified that the detectives thought he would do something as awful as murdering a priest. It was, those who interviewed him agreed, as if he truly believed that he was innocent.

There were two months to go until the trial, but the newspapers were still hungry for exclusives, and Eugene Block, the enterprising city editor of *The San Francisco Call*, had thought of the perfect way to move the story on and get one over on *The Examiner*. He phoned August Vollmer to arrange a lie detector test.

The Berkeley police chief was a good friend of Block, and he listened to the editor's proposal with interest. He was eager to give John Larson's apparatus a crack at something more serious than sorority scandal. "It would increase interest in the instrument and the technique," he said. "You'll be hearing from John Larson within the hour."

Block spent three days planning. He secured permission from Hightower's attorney ("They'll find out he's telling the truth," he boasted) and from the district attorney, Franklin Swart. Block's bosses were keen but cautious. "Go ahead if you can," they told him. "But you'll have to carry the ball yourself."

The operation would need to be carried out in utmost secrecy to keep the other papers off the scent. It wouldn't be easy—the jail was "swarming with reporters who kept a day and night vigil" on Hightower in case he decided to confess, or perhaps to take his own life. "Anything could happen."

On the night of August 16, John Larson and an assistant, Phillips Edson, met Block and veteran reporter Elford Eddy at *The Call*'s offices. They drove to Redwood City and the home of the paper's circulation manager, John Grey, where they had a "quick dinner that seemed endless" while they waited for the competing journalists to leave.

Finally, at two AM, they piled into the car and made the short journey to the jail where Hightower was being held in Redwood City. It was a brilliant moonlit night, and the quartet made a strange sight as they lugged the heavy equipment into the jail on Broadway Avenue.

Larson and Edson set up the lie detector—attaching the rollers to the wooden base and fixing the roll of smoked paper, connecting the various tubes that would be fixed to the suspect's body. Hightower was roused from sleep and led downstairs from his second-floor cell. He had cheerfully agreed to take part in the test, but now he seemed hesitant. He paused outside the room for a few minutes, making idle conversation, delaying the inevitable.

Finally, he stepped inside. He was wearing prison overalls and a heavy white shirt, and he shot quick, piercing glances at the people inside: John Larson, looking serious and professional in his dark suit, with his hair cut short and shaved down to the scalp at the sides; his assistant, Edson, a young man with chubby cheeks and a dark skinny tie; and the district attorney, Franklin Swart, who would be asking the questions. Elford Eddy from *The Call* was in the room with a photographer, but the other papers had been denied entry— there were, bragged the next day's paper, a dozen or more now outside clamoring for entry.

Hightower's gaze passed over the scales for measuring a criminal's limbs and digits, and the ink and paper set out on the fingerprinting table. It quickly settled on the apparatus, laid out in the middle of the room. The man fancied himself an inventor, and he might have recognized the aesthetic—if not the intent—of his "infernal machine" in the lie detector's slapdash construction. His breath seemed to quicken, although his face was an implacable mask. "I don't want to be photographed again," he said. "When people see my picture in the paper, it makes them think they have seen me before."

The test began with almost complete silence. No one in the room stirred or spoke for nearly ten minutes. There was just the sound of Hightower's breathing and the rhythmic click of the pens. "It was like a dentist preparing to pull a hard tooth," wrote Eddy. "He does not take his forceps, get a stranglehold on the tooth and yank until something gives. He fusses around for a considerable time, treating the gums, getting things settled and quiet for the big jerk."

With a baseline reading secured, and Hightower's breathing and blood pressure starting to settle, Edson changed the drum of paper for a fresh one, and Swart started asking questions. "Have you ever had dizzy spells?" he asked. "Have you ever had fits, convulsions, or spasms? Have you a fiery temper?"

Hightower answered "no" to each question—sticking to one-word answers as Larson had requested. Swart continued. "Have you ever had a nervous breakdown?"

"No."

"Has anyone got it in for you?"

"No."

Sometimes, he elaborated. When asked, "Do you think you are getting a square deal in life?"

Hightower replied, "No. I don't think any man who has not been a success thinks so." Larson noted that down as a significant response.

Before the next section of the test, Edson changed the paper again, and Larson gave the preamble that he'd been sharpening over the month that had passed since the College Hall case. "Remember, that if you lie to us on a single question, we will detect it," he said. At this, Hightower seemed to stiffen—and the chart showed a slight increase in his blood pressure and breathing rate.

"Did you murder Father Heslin?" Swart asked. Hightower paused, and although his face was still, the lines on the chart shot up and down like the waves of an angry sea. "No!" he said finally. But his emotions had betrayed him.

Swart had many more questions. He asked about the murder weapon and the burial site. He asked about Hightower's infernal machine. The suspect denied everything—but the recordings showed the telltale changes, even if his face gave nothing away.

At the end of the test, Hightower stood up. He didn't ask about his results, and Larson offered no comment. He was led back upstairs to his cell. "Now we had a scoop," wrote Block.

Larson's exclusive ran the next morning. "An analysis of the test on Hightower affords the conclusion that the suspect was covering up important facts on every crucial question he was asked," he wrote. "He certainly has explanations to make as to his reactions and the causes for them."

He was very careful in his phrasing—he knew better than anyone that a failed lie detector test wasn't a sure sign of guilt. There were all sorts of reasons a person's blood pressure or heart rate might spike under interrogation. But the rest of the coverage was not so cautious.

"Science Indicates Hightower's Guilt" blared the front-page head-line above Larson's piece, cuing up several pages of analysis. There were even excerpts from the charts themselves, annotated to highlight the peaks and troughs that were as good as a confession in the eyes of the reporters—the body's own smoking gun.

"There is no question in my mind but that the blood pressure records of William Hightower's reactions prove his guilt beyond a doubt," wrote Vollmer, who had also been asked to analyze the charts. "The tracings are conclusive, and the changes are too great to bring about any other conclusion than that Hightower is guilty."

A few weeks later, after a trial centered on forensic evidence and housekeeper Marie Wendel's belated identification of Hightower as the stranger at the door that night, Father Heslin's murderer was sentenced to life in San Quentin. (He was released on May 20, 1965, aged eighty-six. "The past is past," he said. "I am looking forward to the future. I've got a lot of living to do.")

The Hightower case should have been a triumph for John Larson. But afterward, the breathless tone of the media coverage annoyed him. He knew the work to scientifically validate the device was far from over, and he was anxious that it not be seen as a gimmick. He was a scientist, and he wanted the respect of his peers—not just for the machine he had developed, but also for himself.

It was still bothering him ten years later. "This write-up is an excellent example of the type of article which the average newspaper man considers of great help to a scientist in presenting his materials to the public, but which is actually a decided hindrance, since it tends to prejudice scientific minds against any test given this sort of publicity," he wrote in his 1932 book *Lying and Its Detection*. In the hands of the papers, Larson's device took on a shape and form that he couldn't control. The cardio-pneumo-psychograph became "the lie detector."

But in truth, both he and Vollmer had helped fan the flames. Whatever their private concerns, their public comments around this time were always effusive. Even in his cautious analysis of Hightower's case, Larson claimed his technique was "100 percent accurate."

Vollmer went further. "The guilt or innocence of an individual is no longer a debatable question," he wrote. "The old cry of having been 'railroaded' to the penitentiary will avail nothing, for the reason that a mechanical instrument of the future will prove, beyond a question of doubt, the guilt or innocence of the accused." Could you blame the press for getting carried away?

"Nothing could have been more dramatic, more dispassionately heartless than the manner in which science dissected Hightower, felt his heart beats, his pulse, examined his breathing, looked beneath the flesh for indications," wrote Eddy in *The Call*. "And nothing could have been fairer."

In fact, nothing could have been further from the truth. It may have proven Hightower guilty, but the lie detector was not infallible, not objective, and ultimately not scientific. It amplified and reflected the flaws in society and the scars of the men who built it—and the Henry Wilkens case would soon shake Larson's faith in his own invention to the core.

PART THREE

PACIFIC HEIGHTS

At six AM on Friday, June 9, 1922, Henry Wilkens kissed his sleeping children goodbye, slipped out of the house, and disappeared. It had been a tense night in the Vallejo Street flat—he'd slept fitfully, breaking often into "hysterical weeping" and leaving his sister-in-law, Helen Lange, concerned he might kill himself.

"I am afraid he is not coming back," she sobbed. "During the night Henry was in a terrible state. He was sick and nervous, pacing the floor, and I watched him closely every instant for I feared that he would attempt to do himself an injury."

The grieving mechanic was weighed down by sorrow or guilt over his wife's death, worn out by the incessant inquiries of reporters, who had been calling at home and work, and by police, who had new questions about his relationship with Arthur and Walter Castor and wanted to know why he hadn't identified them during the lineup.

It had been a week since the brothers' release from the Hall of Justice without charge, and there was still no sign of them. Lead detective Duncan Matheson was getting hammered in the press for letting them go. "The police pulled a boner of 100 percent ivory and they know it," sneered *The Hanford Sentinel*. Matheson was determined not to let Henry slip through his grasp too, and when Lange called saying she was worried about him, he ordered his men to track him down.

Henry went from the flat to his garage at 1837 Pacific, where he took his car and left without telling his staff where he was going. Then he went to see a friend, real estate broker William McNevin, possibly to arrange the sale of his workshop. A few weeks later, on June 25, an advert appeared in *The Chronicle*, listing it for $3,500: "This business has had years of continuous prosperity; owner is selling at great sacrifice only on account of death in family and intention of leaving San Francisco," it read.

By mid-morning, McNevin had convinced Henry to go to police headquarters. He took him there himself. Henry was clearly agitated and threatened to take his own life. "I cannot stand it any longer," he told Matheson. "I am nervous, excited, and anxious. My telephone bell never stopped ringing until three o'clock this morning. I can't rest. I can't sleep. I feel in torture."

Henry knew that public opinion was starting to turn against him. Some newspapers had dubbed Henry "a second Carl Wanderer," in reference to a double murder in Chicago the previous June that had gained national prominence. Wanderer had been given the death penalty for staging the murder of his wife by a "ragged stranger" when in reality he'd killed them both. Henry would have been well aware that execution was a distinct possibility for whoever was found guilty of Anna's murder. It didn't look good.

Matheson did his best to calm Henry down and arranged to meet him for lunch. In the meantime, he asked Detective Leo Bunner to accompany him around the city. "It is feared that he might carry out his threat," reported *The Oakland Tribune*. At the same time, Matheson got Henry to agree to be tested on a new machine that had been gaining traction in Berkeley, and which promised to clear up the mess he was in—if he was telling the truth.

* * *

Later that day, John Larson dismantled the lie detector, packed its components into a large case, and caught a ferry across the bay toward the Hall of Justice. It was another cloudy day in a city cloaked in perpetual fog, and a warm westerly breeze rippled the waters as Larson crossed, with two other officers to help him carry the equipment. He was in civilian clothes—it had been a long time since he'd worn a uniform—and was wearing a dark suit, with a high-collared white shirt and glasses with small, round frames.

He reached the Hall of Justice, with its imposing granite face, and made his way to the SFPD headquarters on the first floor. Inside Chief

O'Brien's office, Larson and his assistants set up the apparatus on a dark wooden bureau.

When they were done, Henry—who was cooperative but moody after being kept under guard all afternoon—was led into the room. It was packed with reporters, photographers, and curious police officers, but had the quiet solemnity of a church service. Matheson was a notable absentee—reporters were told that Henry had taken such a strong dislike to the captain of detectives that his presence might interfere with the test.

Henry was wearing dark trousers and a waistcoat, a light pinstripe shirt, and a black tie. The outfit made his body seem strangely small, as if he'd physically shrunk in stature in the days since his wife's death. His brown hair was short and neat, but he looked tired—bags were starting to form under his eyes.

He took off his coat and sat down in the chair next to the machine, facing away from the window, and looked at the contraption with interest as the flashbulbs of the photographers popped. "His general manner, however, is sullen," reported *The Examiner*. "His black eyes are gloomy, and their look is accentuated by the darkness of his skin."

Larson took the seat opposite. They faced each other in the center of the audience like boxers in a ring.

Henry rolled up his sleeves. His arms were tanned and hairy, and surprisingly muscular compared to his slight frame. The apparatus was to his left, with the iron rod connecting the equipment sitting behind his left shoulder—a slender stem that branched into valves and dials at the top like some strange tree. The paper scroll of the chart ran alongside him—it was about a foot high and the width of a man's torso—and looped around two rotating drums fixed to the baseboard. Vine-like appendages hung from the "trunk" of the lie detector.

Larson wound a thick rubber tube around Henry's waist. It rested around his diaphragm, between the second and third buttons of his waistcoat. He pushed up Henry's left shirt sleeve and attached a blood pressure cuff to his arm, just above the elbow, securing it with three small buckles. Then he used a handheld pump to bring it up to the correct pressure. To Henry, it felt uncomfortably tight, and by the end of the test his arm was aching.

When he turned his head, he could see his body's deepest murmurs spooling out like the rumblings of an incoming earthquake, "in hieroglyphics that resemble the charting of a transatlantic cable message," as *The Examiner* described.

Larson had come to think of his machine as measuring two quite different things. His theory was that blood pressure and pulse readings tapped into the autonomic nervous system—that involuntary and uncontrollable fear of being caught, the rising sense of panic you felt in your throat and at the tips of your fingers, the "tremor in the blood," as Daniel Defoe put it. On the other hand, in Larson's view, breathing betrayed something more conscious: the considered lie, the deliberate deception. He thought a change in respiration could signify "conscious preparation to tell an untruth."

Larson placed a large, square cushion next to the machine for Henry to rest his left arm on. The suspect kept his right hand in his lap, the fingers tightly clenched. The room was silent—already the lie detector had developed an almost sacred air, with its own rituals and rites. Larson picked up a pen and a small stopwatch from the bureau. He knew that the next few hours would be tense, and perhaps dramatic. But it was time for the truth to come out.

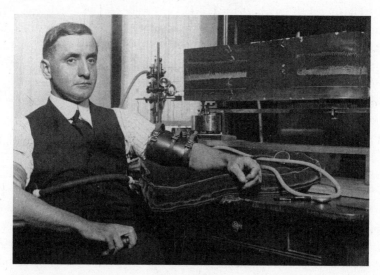

Henry Wilkens.

"You are being subjected to a test," Larson began, quiet and serious, like a judge reading a prisoner their sentence. "If you lie in answer to any of these questions it will be instantly recorded. Answer all questions by "yes" or "no" if possible. Think carefully and answer truthfully."

Henry's eyes flicked around the room between the faces of his interrogators. He agreed to follow the instructions.

"Do you object to the test?" Larson asked.

"No," Henry replied in his accented English.

"Do you like the movies?"

"No."

"Have you ever had a nervous breakdown?"

"Yes."

As he asked each question, Larson marked the scrolling chart with a flick of his pen and started the stopwatch—counting down a full minute before moving on to the next.

"Do you drink to excess?"

"No."

"Do you smoke?"

"No."

"Have you ever seen visions?"

"No."

In the long pauses, the only sounds in the room were the ticking of Larson's watch, Henry's slow breathing, and the scratching of the pens as they translated it onto the smoked paper of the polygraph chart.

The start of the test went badly. Henry's blood pressure was high, and he kept closing his eyes and fidgeting in his chair. He blamed his grief and the strangeness of the situation. Three times, the test had to be stopped because the readings were so erratic. Henry complained of feeling weak and said he hadn't eaten all day.

But as Larson moved down his list of control questions ("Do you enjoy outdoor sports?" "Yes"; "Are you fond of books?" "No") Henry became noticeably calmer, and the lines began to steady—sharp peaks and crevasses flattened into rolling hills. Fifteen minutes in, his blood pressure had dropped twenty points, and his heartbeat and breathing had settled down into a regular pattern.

Larson glanced at O'Brien, who gave him the signal to move on to the second list of questions—the ones that would determine whether Henry was an innocent victim or a devious criminal. There were the same number of questions as in the control section, but this time they were all related to the night of Anna's death. In the minute of silence that followed each prompt, Larson peered at the paper scroll, looking for clues: Marston had identified a drop of fifteen millimeters of mercury as one clear sign of deception, Larson was developing his own methods for reading the charts too.

"Did you know in advance anything about the holdup?"

"No."

The pens continued their slow dance.

"Did you lie on this question?"

"Yes."

The room held its breath—everyone except Henry, that is, who seemed totally oblivious that he'd just admitted to lying on the test. Larson gave O'Brien a sharp look but continued—there was a rhythm to these things that it was important to stick to.

"Did Mrs. Wilkens wear gloves at the time of the murder?"

"No."

"Did you hire any person to commit this murder?"

"No."

With each question, Henry denied any knowledge of the crime. The chart rolled on.

"Do you know Arthur or Walter Castor?"

"One of them."

"Which one, and how long have you known him?"

"Walter—five or six months."

"Did you have any agreement with the Castor brothers about this murder?"

"No."

"Do you know anything about the third man?"

"No."

"When did you first see the Dodge car?"

"When it was first alongside of me."

"Were the holdup men young?"

"Yes."

"Could you identify them?"

"I think I could."

"Did you ever have a .38 caliber gun?"

"No."

"Have you lied about any of these questions?"

"No."

"Do you wish to change your answers?"

"No."

* * *

After the initial flurry of tension, Henry's blood pressure stayed low throughout the test. His heart rate and breathing were steady, only spiking right at the end when O'Brien asked him if he'd meant to admit to lying on the first question. Henry looked surprised and his pulse quickened, before he explained that no, of course he hadn't lied; he had simply misunderstood the question.

At the end of the test, Larson loosened the cuff on Henry's arm, and the pair posed for photographs before the detective was swamped by reporters who wanted his verdict. "Wilkens is of a very nervous temperament," he told them. "He was a willing subject, and I am convinced after checking up his score that he told the truth. There was not a single break in his chart. His answers were made promptly." It looked, at first glance, like Henry was telling the truth.

That was good enough for the papers, which trumpeted the result on their front pages. "Wilkens Faces Science and Science Says He Tells The Truth," announced *The Examiner* above a column from Larson, explaining the result.

"Crucial questions which, if answered in the affirmative, would have implicated Wilkens in the murder had no more effect than the indifferent questions," he wrote. "From a hasty examination of the records and the brief time the subject was under observation the findings in the record do not seem significant enough to implicate Wilkens in the crime being investigated." Others said Henry had given the lie detector "a run for its money and emerged with flying colors."

But when Larson looked at the full polygraph chart later that evening, he considered it "doubtful." Back in Berkeley, he showed it to Leonarde Keeler and Gus Vollmer, who both "independently felt that Wilkens might be guilty" too, although Vollmer had already told *The Gazette* he was convinced Henry was innocent.

The extreme agitation Henry had shown at the beginning of the test was a concern, and Larson felt there had been too many spectators, too many cameras. "His record showed a mass type of reaction with many disturbances, and an interpretation was difficult," Larson wrote in his book. But he kept these doubts to himself for now. It was a prominent case, and he wanted the lie detector to succeed.

In the years that followed, lie detector tests would become a useful tool for extracting confessions from recalcitrant suspects. But Henry's record was not decisive, and with the Castors still in the wind and little hard evidence available, O'Brien and Matheson had no grounds to arrest him. "I did not witness Wilkens's examination on the "lie detector.'" Matheson told reporters, "but from what Dr. Larson tells me, the man told the absolute truth in answering questions propounded to him regarding the murder. The machine would appear to clear him of any suspicion."

Privately, Matheson was not ready to give up on his new prime suspect. He'd been pilloried in the press for letting the Castors go without charge, and he wasn't about to let Henry slip through his fingers, regardless of what some machine said. The district attorney's office was starting to draw a net around Henry as well—the ambitious Matthew Brady sensed there was a high-profile success on the cards if they could link the garage owner to his wife's death.

When Henry finally left the Hall of Justice that evening, arm still throbbing from the apparatus, it felt like a weight had been lifted from his shoulders. But he was being followed.

* * *

A few minutes before eight PM, Henry left his garage on Pacific Avenue and began walking west, heading away from home. Milton Cohen, an investigator from the DA's office, had followed him there from the

Hall of Justice—tasked with trailing him to see where he went, who he met, and whether good old-fashioned detective work could succeed where the lie detector had apparently failed.

Cohen had already followed Henry to a bar, back home, out shopping, and then to his garage. Now he fell into step a safe distance behind as Henry walked up Pacific Avenue for a couple of blocks, until the road began to climb. A few minutes later, he boarded a rickety streetcar to carry him further up the hill. Cohen flagged down a taxi and ordered it to follow the streetcar as it rose slowly west toward Pacific Heights and the Presidio.

At the end of the line, on the corner of Pacific and Broderick, Henry stepped down from the car. The electric streetlights were starting to come on, but the pools of brightness were interspersed with patches of twilight gloom. The taxi pulled up a discreet distance away. Cohen kept his eyes fixed on Henry, who stood under a streetlight, glancing up and down the road at the vehicles rolling past.

Soon afterward, a mud-splattered Ford pulled up. Its curtains were drawn across the rear windows, and the vehicle was so covered in grime that the license plate was illegible. It slowed down without stopping, and someone jumped out of the passenger side. The car pulled away to circle around the block, and the thin, fair-haired man who had left it approached Henry. Cohen stared in shock. It was Robert Castor—the brother of the fugitives, Arthur and Walter, who had a significant rap sheet of his own.

In September 1918, Robert—who was two years older than Walter and four years older than Arthur—had been charged with manslaughter. For five months, he had been living with a married woman, a Mrs. Hazel Powers, whose husband was a bugler in a machine gun battalion in France.

One morning, the illicit couple got into a fight at the house they were sharing on Tenth Avenue. One of the neighbors thought it might have been over money, or maybe driven by jealousy—Walter had been living with the couple at first too, but Robert sent his brother away because he was paying too much attention to Powers.

The neighbor heard shouting—and then gunshots. Robert had shot Powers in the head. She was found unconscious in the corner of a room, a bullet wound in her right temple. Clothes were strewn around—it looked like Robert had been packing his suitcases. After shooting Powers, Robert turned the gun on himself. He staggered out of the front door with a hole in his chest. "Never mind me," he told a fireman who had heard the gunfire. "I have shot my wife." Incredibly, Robert survived the gunshot wound and—even more incredibly—was immediately released on probation after his trial.

Together, Robert Castor and Henry Wilkens ambled halfway up the block, heading west toward Baker Street, and paused under another lamppost. Milton Cohen crept forward to observe them. In the glow of the electric light, Cohen saw Henry pulling something from his pocket and handing it to Robert.

If he'd been able to get close enough to listen, he'd have heard them talking about the murder case, and Henry telling Robert about his interesting experience on the lie detector that afternoon—boasting about how he'd managed to pass the test.

Henry and Robert talked for a little longer, and then Henry suddenly turned and walked quickly back toward the streetcar stop on Broderick Street, looking over his shoulder as he went. "I told him that there was a sedan car there that looked suspicious, and I thought it was following us," Robert explained later. "He ran for the Pacific Avenue car and went away."

Cohen scribbled down some notes. Clearly, there was more to this story than Henry had admitted to. For days, he'd denied ever having met Walter and Arthur Castor, but now he appeared to be having a clandestine meeting with their brother.

John Larson and his lie detector had failed to tease out the truth, and it was a failure that would soon have terrible consequences. For now, there was nothing Cohen could do but report back to Brady at the DA's office and wait for more developments in the hunt for the Castor brothers. It was almost dark, and as Cohen pulled away in the taxi to deliver his findings to the Hall of Justice, he caught one last glimpse of Henry pacing down the hill toward the streetcar line, his dark shape casting a long, soft shadow in the fading light.

SAP AND SAWDUST

In the gold-rush town of Eureka, three hundred miles north of San Francisco, on the verdant shores of Humboldt Bay, Arthur and Walter Castor were trying to make a fresh start.

As soon as they'd left the Hall of Justice on June 1, after Henry Wilkens's failure to identify them in the police lineup, they'd started making plans to flee the city. Walter wanted to go straight away, but Arthur thought it would be safer to wait until morning, and there was someone they needed to see before they left.

It was still dark on the morning of June 2, when the brothers arrived at Henry's house—not yet six AM, according to Arthur's testimony at trial. It was the day of Anna's funeral, and at *The Examiner*'s offices in the Hearst Building, first editions were rolling off the presses, with news of the Castor interrogation front and center. The Castors needed to get out of San Francisco before suspicion shone on them again—but first they needed a getaway vehicle that the police wouldn't recognize. And they wanted Henry to pay for it.

After a terse conversation on the doorstep, a bleary-eyed Henry—who was still in his pajamas—handed Walter some money, and the brothers drove to their brother Robert's house to pick up a Ford that he'd been trying to sell. They left their National car parked there and drove back to Henry's, where they negotiated a price of $250 for the Ford. Robert took $50 from Walter, and Henry promised to pay the remaining $200 at a later date (this money is what Milton Cohen would see Henry handing over after his lie detector test on June 9).

With their business concluded, Henry went back inside to prepare for his wife's funeral. Walter and Arthur embarked on a complicated escape from the city, involving a taxi, the car they'd just bought, and a sailboat to Sausalito, up the coast and through the Golden Gate— the mile-wide inlet that separates San Francisco from Marin to the north.

Their brother Robert visited each of their houses in the Ford, to collect their belongings and pick up Arthur's young wife, Mary Fortino, and then took the ferry to Sausalito to hand over the car.

From there, Arthur, Walter, and Mary drove north, the landscape slowly shifting from rolling farmland to dense stands of redwoods as they left the city behind. Their route took them up the coast, along what is now Highway 101—via Ukiah, Willits, and Fort Bragg, before winding uphill through the forests, where gold prospectors once panned in the rivers and where lumberjacks now wielded their saws.

On Sunday, June 4, they arrived in Eureka, where they rented a flat and started looking for work. Arthur had his wife with him already, and Walter was soon joined by a surprising female companion—his brother Robert's wife. Annie Downs was in her late twenties, with a delicate nose, wide eyes, and a round face. She had been romantically entangled with the Castor brothers for a long time—first with Robert, then with Walter. "Walter lost to Bob in the first round," wrote *The Sacramento Bee*. "But the marriage was not a particularly happy one, and Annie finally left Bob and went to live with Walter."

For a week or so, the quartet enjoyed a semblance of normal life. They rented an apartment in the center of Eureka, a block from the county jail at Fourth Street and J, and within walking distance of the green-blue waters of Arcata Bay, where wrens and blackbirds flitted through the reeds, and the wharf, where felled redwoods were carved up and shipped south, and the smell of sap and sawdust filled the air.

The men looked for work under the fake name Fowler and tried to build a new life for themselves away from the prying eyes of the San Francisco Police Department. But it wasn't long before local law enforcement was on their case.

The papers blamed Annie Downs, who they said had been recklessly discussing the Wilkens case with strangers in Eureka. But actually, the brothers gave themselves away when they tried to sell the Ford at a local garage on Monday, June 12.

Although they'd both been living under the name Fowler, the deed of ownership on the car—which Robert had signed over to Walter and posted to them—still read "Castor." The garage manager recognized that name from press coverage of the Wilkens case, and after giving them a $10 down payment on the car and asking them to come back the next day, he informed Arthur Ross, the local sheriff.

Ross made inquiries and learned that although the Castor brothers weren't officially wanted in connection with Anna's murder, there was an existing warrant out for Arthur Castor's arrest. He'd been accused of passing bad checks at a string of butchers' shops in San Francisco the previous winter, signing them under the name C. Fowler. (It's not entirely clear why he wasn't arrested for this when he was in police custody the previous week. It's possible that Duncan Matheson reinstated the search as a way to get him brought back to the city for questioning in the Wilkens case, or simply that the SFPD wasn't organized enough to make the connection sooner.)

When the brothers returned to the garage the next morning, Arthur was arrested. Ross telephoned Matheson in San Francisco, who immediately dispatched Detective Charles Maher to Eureka to bring Arthur back to the city for questioning in the Wilkens case.

But Walter managed to slip away. Later that day, he visited Arthur at the county jail, and then he and Annie were seen leaving town in the Ford—fugitive and lover driving north through the redwood forests, leaving everything behind.

* * *

On the morning of Monday, June 19, 1922, August Vollmer stood in front of a crowd in the Colonial Room of the St. Francis Hotel on Union Square, feeling unusually nervous.

The hotel was the hangout of San Francisco's wealthy elite—a meeting place for rail tycoons, oil barons, and silent film stars. It was here, nine months earlier, that the actress Virginia Rappe had met her end in the rooms of Fatty Arbuckle. Gold-framed paintings hung on walls adorned with polished marble.

Vollmer was about to call to order the Twenty-Ninth Annual Convention of the International Association of Chiefs of Police (IACP), and the people in front of him were the best and brightest in global law enforcement. It was the culmination of a year of hard work—he was elected president of the IACP in 1921 and had toiled to bring the convention to the West Coast for the first time. There were delegates from 260 cities, including overseas visitors from Denmark, Australia, and the Hawaiian Islands. He really wanted it to go well.

Archbishop Edward Hanna opened proceedings with a prayer, and there were speeches from Chief Dan O'Brien and from the mayor of San Francisco, "Sunny Jim" Rolph Jr., before Vollmer took to the stage and declared the meeting open.

Discussions over the four-day event ranged from the best way to shield a car from shotgun fire, to the psychopathic personalities of criminals and how they were influenced by the environment. "The only subject we haven't included is that of the airplane thief," Vollmer told newspapers before the conference. "We don't have to deal with him just yet, although we probably will in a few years when airplanes become as popular as the automobile."

The meeting was also a chance for Vollmer to evangelize about the new policing methods he was bringing to Berkeley. He urged the assembled chiefs to create a national database of identification files, to study criminal psychology, and—of course—to start using the lie detector.

On the afternoon of the first day of the conference, John Larson set up the apparatus in front of a tightly packed crowd of men in linen suits and straw boaters, for a demonstration on the roof of the hotel.

This time, Vollmer and Larson watched on, and O'Brien played the suspect for a lie detector test conducted by William Pinkerton, the head of the famous private detective agency. (William, a portly seventy-seven-year-old, was the son of the agency's founder, Allen Pinkerton, who rose to fame after he helped foil an 1861 plot to assassinate Abraham Lincoln on the eve of his inauguration.)

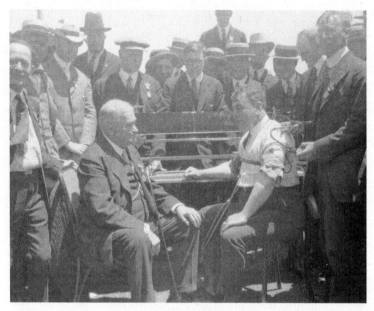

William Pinkerton quizzes Chief Dan O'Brien on the lie detector as John Larson (standing, center) and August Vollmer (standing, right) look on.

Meanwhile, at the Hall of Justice a few blocks away, O'Brien's colleagues were trying to do what the lie detector had failed to—make some progress in the Henry Wilkens case. They interrogated Arthur Castor, who had arrived back in San Francisco in chains after his arrest in Eureka, and was now residing in Cell number 1 in the federal wing of the county jail, which occupied the top floors of the Hall. Rows of stacked cages were arranged around a central courtyard, with a narrow walkway running around each level, an aviary for the jailbirds of the city.

Arthur had been charged with check fraud and was awaiting trial, but despite repeated rounds of questioning and the threat of a lie detector test, he maintained his innocence regarding Anna Wilkens's murder. He stuck to his original alibi and told Matheson that he knew nothing about the Hudson touring car that had been rented in Walter's name, which matched the one seen on the night of the killing.

Matheson pinned his hopes on finding Walter. "We'll have him here in two or three days," he told reporters on June 17.

The next day, police arrested four men suspected of stealing $25,000 worth of jewelry and furs from Arthur Herbst and his wife, Martha, in a carjacking a week before Anna's murder, in the same part of the city. The men had been driving a Hudson when the police apprehended them, and so they became the latest in a long line of suspects to be presented to Henry Wilkens in a police lineup.

Henry and the kids had left San Francisco for Redwood City the morning after his lie detector test, to escape the glare of press suspicion. He told police they could get hold of him via his friend William McNevin—and they did, calling him back to the city on numerous occasions to peer into the faces of whoever Matheson's men had picked up this time.

But Henry didn't recognize the four men presented to him on June 18, or any of the dozens of others he saw in various police lineups during the month. Each time he was shown a new array of suspects to look at, Henry's eyes slid past Arthur Castor, who had been keeping his mouth firmly shut.

The police department still didn't know about Henry's secret meeting with Robert Castor—District Attorney Matthew Brady had decided to keep that information close to his chest for now.

So, parade after parade ended with Henry shaking his head, and Matheson and his men going back to the drawing board. But while they struggled, Brady was putting a plan into action.

IMPS AND DEMONS

In the last week of June, a boy in his late teens was brought into the police lineup, taking his place among the hardened criminals plucked from the cells. Henry walked down the line with a practiced air now, and the officers in the room prepared themselves for the usual shake of the head. But this time, Henry paused. He knew that each suspect he eliminated only tightened the net around himself. He looked carefully at the newcomer. "That looks like the fellow," he said, finally. "I believe it is."

The stunned youth was placed in a cell two doors down from Arthur Castor. When the lights of the county jail went out that night, Arthur could hear the boy's sobs echoing through the darkened building. "Oh my God, I didn't do it," he cried. "They're going to railroad me."

For Arthur, it seemed like the perfect situation. He was still facing the bad check charge, but this new kid—whoever he was—would divert any suspicion for Anna's murder away from him. But Arthur was never quite as ruthless as his brother. He kept thinking about what the kid had said to him as they were being led back to their cells. "I guess I'll hang," he'd wailed. "As God is my judge, I didn't have anything to do with it."

Arthur's conscience wouldn't let him sleep. All night, he paced his cell, long face creased into a frown. When he did finally drift off, it was to dream of being tormented by "imps and demons." Eventually, he gave up on sleep and sat on the hard bed until the thin dawn light filtered in through the iron bars on the windows.

That morning, his mother, Minnie, came to see him. "They've got an innocent kid in there," he said, his blue eyes welling with tears. He sank to his knees on the floor of the cell and told her everything.

Walter had picked him up at about five thirty AM on the day of the murder in a rented Hudson touring car. Arthur said his brother hadn't told him what he wanted to do—just that he needed someone to help with a little job and that there was "$500 in it," which he promised to split fifty–fifty.

They got to Felton at about noon, where Walter turned off the highway and onto a dirt track, eventually parking the car under a big tree by the side of the road, which was bordered by a wooden and barbed wire fence to separate it from a railway line. Walter got out of the car, crawled through a hole in the fence and then up onto a railroad embankment overlooking Felton Auto Park, where Henry and his family were camping.

Arthur watched his brother walk back and forth along the track until he lost sight of him behind the trees. Walter returned a couple of minutes later and said he had signaled Henry Wilkens. A few moments later, Henry popped out from another hole in the fence about seventy-five yards behind where the car was parked, carrying a bucket. Arthur stayed in the car, watching in the mirrors as Walter and Henry had a brief conversation. When Walter came back, he was holding a roll of bills. "He wants us to stick around until four o'clock," he said.

The brothers drove back into the town of Felton itself, where Arthur bought half a dozen oranges and two packs of pastries called Panama Creams. They drove back to the hole in the fence, ate the food, and then sat around for a while, waiting. At one point, Arthur got out of the car and wiped the Hudson down until it shone. Then they sat around some more.

"At one time during the long wait, I could hear voices and singing coming from the auto park on the other side of the railroad bank, Arthur remembered. "And so I got out of the car myself and climbed through the fence, and crawled up the bank and looked over. Right nearby I saw Wilkens, and there were some children near him, and he was singing. I crawled back again and came to the car."

At about four PM, they heard the sound of engines starting up. Walter crawled through the hole in the fence to investigate, and returned with a strange look in his eyes. "Well, they're starting—let's go," he said. "We'll have to make this short and sweet."

"I didn't realize what he meant," Arthur said later. "Or I'd have killed him then and there."

Arthur started the Hudson and drove up to near the entrance to the Auto Park, then waited until Walter pointed out the yellow Premier with the Wilkens family inside. He told Arthur to follow. When the convoy stopped for ice cream in Saratoga, the brothers did the same. Arthur bought two cones at an ice cream stand, crossing paths with Henry and his friends as they visited the neighboring stand. Walter took over the driving when they returned to the road, and as it got dark, Arthur noticed Henry's stop signal flashing over and over again.

As they climbed the hill into the city, Walter told Arthur to take the wheel and ordered his brother to force Henry to the side of the road.

"What's the idea?" Arthur asked.

"You'll see pretty soon," Walter replied. "Don't get excited. If you hear a shot, go like the devil when I get back in the car."

Peering back through the darkness, Arthur heard shouting and a gunshot, and then Walter appeared from the mist like a ghost and jumped back into the car, swearing at his stunned brother to drive, drive, drive. Walter was clutching an empty wallet. He thrust it angrily in Arthur's direction. "The dirty skunk double-crossed me," he screamed.

"For God's sake, Walter, who fired that shot?" Arthur shouted back.

"Forget it," replied his brother, "and ride like hell away from here."

* * *

Minnie Castor was used to the antics of her wayward sons—her glassy blue eyes were world-weary—and she said little as she listened to Arthur's story. But she knew what was right and what her late husband, the police officer, would have wanted from this sorry mess. "No matter what happens to you, tell the truth," she told her son, advising him to come clean. "Don't let an innocent boy go to prison."

But the next day came and went, and Arthur still hadn't confessed to the police. That night, when the lights went out, he could hear the boy wailing again, his cries cutting through Arthur like a bullet. "I couldn't stand it when I heard that boy cry in the cell and knew he was innocent," he said.

The next night, Sunday, June 25, policewoman Katherine O'Connor pulled Arthur in for another round of questioning on the Wilkens case.

O'Connor was in her late forties and had been working at the Hall of Justice as a social worker when the city decided to hire its first policewomen in 1913. At first, she was confined to working with women—minding teenage delinquents or consoling the widows of murder victims—but she quickly proved herself to her skeptical colleagues and was soon assisting on everything from gang-related shootings to mysterious disappearances. She played a key role in uncovering the clandestine abortion clinic at the "Mystery Castle" near Salada Beach, where William Hightower had buried the body of Father Heslin. Now she was working with the DA's office.

Her perceptive hazel eyes had seen it all—and she could tell by the worry lines on Arthur's face, the redness in his eyes, and the fact that he'd brought an attorney with him that he was finally ready to talk. "I didn't want to see Wilkens hang the murder on an innocent man," he said.

By four AM, O'Connor had extracted a ten-page written statement, which Arthur signed at the bottom of each sheet. He told her everything and then repeated his story to district attorney Matthew Brady and assistant DA Isidore Golden.

When he was finished and had been taken back to his cell, the two men exchanged wry smiles. The lie detector had failed to crack the case, but Arthur Castor had been undone by a much simpler trick: it turned out that the sobbing boy in the nearby cell was never really a suspect. He had been planted there by the DA's office to guilt Arthur into confessing.

THE THIRD DEGREE

At Siegler Springs, a holiday resort about a hundred miles north of San Francisco, Henry Wilkens was finally starting to relax. He'd spent a few calming days with his children and his sister-in-law, Helen Lange, enjoying the beauty of the mountainous setting and the crystal-clear waters that bubbled up from underground.

For the first time since Anna's death, the tightness in his chest had begun to dissipate, and he felt like there was a light at the end of the tunnel. He had no idea what was happening at the Hall of Justice or of the chaos that was about to engulf him.

On the morning of June 27, the day after Arthur's confession, Henry was standing outside the family's tent when he saw four men approaching. His car was parked nearby—he'd gotten it back from the police and done his best to get the bloodstains out of the fabric of the seats.

He spotted the group from a distance—their suits and ties were out of place in the natural surroundings. As they got closer, a chill ran through him when he recognized the white hair and sturdy gait of Matthew Brady, the district attorney.

Brady was picking his way over the soft ground toward Henry, accompanied by *The Examiner* reporter Oscar Fernbach and two imposing men who very urgently wanted to speak to him. One of them grabbed Henry roughly by the arm. "Come here," he said. "We want you."

It was a "grueling interrogation." The men dragged him away from his children "without hat or coat," Henry claimed. They took him first to the nearby city of Lakeport and then all the way to San Francisco.

But instead of going to the Hall of Justice for a formal interview, the group ended up in a room at the St. Francis Hotel, where just over a week earlier August Vollmer had been preaching the gospel of humane policing, with the lie detector at its heart.

But the chiefs of police were gone now. Henry said he was "grilled for hours" while Brady and his assistants drank whiskey. It's not entirely clear what happened to Henry during the hours he spent in Brady's company, but at 5:20 the next morning an ambulance was called to his flat on Vallejo Street. He was "taken suddenly ill" with severe stomach pains and rushed to the Central Emergency Hospital, where he was diagnosed with "acute appendicitis." (He was accompanied by a police officer and booked in under a fake name.)

Later, Henry accused Brady and his men of subjecting him to the third degree. The term—used to describe a brutal questioning by law enforcement—is often attributed to Thomas Byrnes, a New York detective in the 1880s whose brutal manner earned him the nickname "Third Degree Byrnes," derived from the steps he supposedly ascended through with stubborn suspects: the first degree is persuasion, the second is intimidation, the third is pain. But it really takes its name from a Masonic initiation ritual and the intense interrogation candidates had to undergo to reach the third degree of master mason.

By the 1920s, police had become adept at an array of third-degree methods—from psychological tricks, like the one Brady pulled on Arthur Castor, to techniques that crossed the line into torture.

In his book, John Larson lists some common tactics of the time: starvation, sleep deprivation, shining a bright light directly into a suspect's face. There was the "sweat box," where captors set up a roaring stove in the neighboring cell, steadily increasing the temperature and throwing in "vegetable matter, old bones, pieces of rubber shoes" to make a terrible, stinking heat; and the cold-water hose, blasted at a suspect in between questions. But the simplest method remained the most effective, and one of the wisdoms passed down from veterans to rookies was the skill of inflicting physical pain without leaving a mark. "In this technique the stomach is the favorite site for the administration of the blows," Larson noted.

But Henry still denied any involvement in his wife's murder, and the newspapers were unimpressed by Brady's tactics. "District Attorney Brady seems to be taking considerable risk," wrote *The Santa Cruz Evening News*. "His fiasco in the Arbuckle prosecution should cause him to prepare a strong case before he decides to charge a man with murder."

Henry's attorney called his client's treatment "brutal and inhuman" and likened the district attorney's behavior to kidnapping. John Larson was appalled. Not only had his lie detector apparently failed to determine the truth in this case, but its failure had also led to a collapse back into the more brutal forms of interrogation he was so keen to eradicate.

*　*　*

While the district attorney's office was making progress, by fair means or foul, police efforts to find Anna's killer continued to stumble. Brady had decided not to tell them the full details of Arthur's confession, so they were still scrambling around, pursuing new leads.

On July 3, Henry—bent double from the pain in his stomach—made a partial identification of a twenty-year-old called Clayton Hall during a police lineup. Hall was from a prominent family in Santa Rosa and had been arrested on an unrelated charge of grand larceny, accused of stealing another passenger's luggage during a steamship journey from Honolulu.

But during questioning, Hall admitted to being the driver of the car that had forced the Wilkens family to the side of the road, and he named two accomplices, Frank Mason and Fred McGregor, who Hall said had fired the fatal shot. Hall gave a detailed account of the slaying to Duncan Matheson, explaining how he'd met his accomplices at Coffee Dan's restaurant and went from there to the Panama Hotel, where they picked up two guns, and then on to Nineteenth Street, where the murder took place. He even specified the location of a candy store on Market Street where he'd spent one of the stolen $100 bills.

Henry told police that Hall was the same height and build as the man who had shot his wife, and that his bushy eyebrows and his voice matched too. "I cannot positively identify Hall, but he closely resembles the fellow who acted as leader in the robbery and who killed Mrs. Wilkens," Henry said. "The resemblance coincides with the description which I gave to the police immediately after the robbery and murder."

He had been in the hospital ever since the interrogation by Brady and his men—moving from Central Emergency to Mission Emergency and then finally to Franklin Hospital in Haight-Ashbury, where he was reportedly in quite a serious condition. Nonetheless, Henry had been adamant that he wanted to go to the Hall of Justice that day to view the latest police lineup and to appear in front of the grand jury, which had convened to discuss Hall's confession. (In the United States, grand juries are used to determine whether there is enough evidence to pursue a prosecution, and on what charges.)

He needed surgery, and his doctor warned him he was jeopardizing his life, but Henry didn't care—he refused to go under the knife until he had put his side of the story across. "I am going before the grand jury if it is the last thing I ever do. I want to help clear up this awful situation and, if I can, clear myself of any suspicion that certain authorities seem to have."

But that night, Clayton Hall refused to reiterate his confession in front of the grand jury. A chastened Matheson was forced to admit that there was little evidence to suggest that Hall had anything at all to do with Anna's murder. In fact, Matheson now believed Hall was mentally unstable—and that the two accomplices he'd named, whom police had spent a week searching for, were entirely fictional. A few months later, Hall was charged with insanity.

Meanwhile, Henry—side still throbbing with pain—sat in an antechamber outside the grand jury room for an hour and a half, waiting to testify, but the call never came. After Matheson finished his embarrassing tale of police incompetence, the grand jury took a "sudden adjournment" on the advice of Matthew Brady, who was perhaps worried about what they might make of Henry's pain-wracked appearance when he entered, or keen to keep news of Arthur's confession close to his chest while he continued to build his case.

* * *

After he recovered from his injuries, Henry returned to Siegler Springs to be with his children and his sister-in-law. Soon afterward, the family relocated to Redwood City, about twenty-seven miles south of San Francisco, where Henry found work in a repair shop and tried to rebuild his shattered life. Before leaving San Francisco, however, he found time to hire an attorney: forty-nine-year-old Frank Murphy, a short, fat man with a prominent double chin and a liver-spotted forehead, below a crop of limp, flat hair that was parted in the center and which—when he really got into it—gave him the appearance of a water buffalo on the rampage.

Murphy was born in Elmira, New York, and had come to San Francisco in 1901, where he quickly became one of the most prominent attorneys in the city—he was hot-tempered, but skilled at directing that fury in the service of his clients. He had, in the past, been charged and acquitted of jury tampering and had previously represented the chief of police and the mayor in a case against the Board of Education. Henry would need every bit of that experience.

On the morning of Friday, July 14, district attorneys Matthew Brady and Isidore Golden, a childhood friend of Brady who had been one of the key voices in the Arbuckle trial, held a meeting with detective Duncan Matheson and a host of senior men from the police department to discuss the case against Henry Wilkens.

A bitter rivalry had developed between the police and the DA's office over the case—Brady thought the police had botched the investigation; Matheson was furious at Brady for withholding information. But now, they put their differences aside.

In Brady's office, the men ran through all the evidence they'd collected in the six weeks since Anna's murder: Arthur Castor's confession, the witness testimony from Jacob Gorfinkel, the numerous statements from Henry that had been proven to be lies, his secret meeting with Robert Castor.

Afterward, they secured two arrest warrants. The first was for Henry, who was in the process of moving his family into a new house at 20 Hudson Street in Redwood City when the police arrived. His belongings were still piled up in the street outside as they drove him away. The second warrant was for Walter Castor, who had parted ways with Annie Downs and was thought to be lying low somewhere in northern California.

"It was the unanimous conclusion of all those present that if the confession of Arthur Castor and the facts and circumstances developed as a result of the investigations referred to were in accord with the truth, there is a very powerful case against the accused," read a typewritten statement from the DA's office that ran in *The Chronicle* the next day. "A vast mass of corroborating, detailed circumstances has been uncovered that would indicate the substantial truth of the confession."

But Henry stuck to his story. From his cell at the Hall of Justice, he denounced his arrest as a "frame-up" and said the Castor brothers and their attorney were plotting against him to collect the reward money.

Frank Murphy leaped to his client's defense on the front page of *The Chronicle*. "The arrest of Henry Wilkens is the most high-handed and outrageous abuse of official power ever recorded in the State of California," he wrote. "The story of his abduction by District Attorney Matthew Brady from the county of Lake to this city, and of the indignities and torture inflicted upon him in endeavoring to extort from him a confession of a crime of which he is innocent, is well known: and the participation of the District Attorney of this city and county in that abduction is a thing that ought to bring the blush of shame to the cheek of every citizen in our State."

He accused Brady of arresting Henry to distract attention from the "scandal and infamy" that the case had already brought upon him. "Wilkens is innocent of this crime, and his innocence will be proven in court," Murphy said. "And those responsible for his brutal persecution will be made to pay, and pay dearly."

* * *

Henry's days passed slowly. In the gloom of his cell, where the light struggled to penetrate, he could hear the raucous singing of the other prisoners, rising from the rows of stacked cages.

He pined for his kids. "Have you seen my children?" he asked reporter Ernestine Black when she visited him there on July 18. His voice was "husky with sobs," she wrote, and "tears rolled down his cheeks." "I am assured that they are being well taken care of, but I have no idea where they are."

He bounced between floors at the Hall of Justice, from the jails to the courtroom of Judge Sylvain Lazarus, who was presiding over Henry's arraignment, a preliminary hearing that would determine what crime he would be charged with and whether he would be granted bail.

Throughout the second half of July, Henry sat hunched in a high-backed chair in the courtroom as eleven witnesses methodically chipped away at the picture he'd tried to paint of a loving family torn apart by a random act of violence.

Anna's family and friends told the court how he'd beaten her until her fair skin was left mottled with bruises. Jacob Gorfinkel cast doubt on Henry's recollection of the night of the murder. And a languid Arthur Castor—leaning back into a wooden chair, wearing a crumpled suit with collar upturned and tie askew—repeated his story with all its damning details: the meeting at Felton a few hours before the murder, the roll of bills Henry had handed to Walter, the flashing taillight Henry had used to signal the bandits before his wife was shot. It was, wrote *The Examiner*, "one of the most remarkable" confessions ever made.

Occasionally Henry whispered something to his attorney, Frank Murphy, or spoke in low tones to the reporters who were covering the case inside the packed courtroom, but generally he sat in silence, sometimes breaking into quiet tears. When Arthur stated his version of events, the blood seemed to drain from Henry's face, and it looked like he might faint. After that, he kept his head bowed—occasionally closing his eyes and placing his head in his hands. "If he is an actor, if his grief is not genuine but simulated, he is a star," wrote Black.

At the end of the hearing, Henry Wilkens was denied bail. Things were looking good for the DA's office. Brady and Golden now had a month to prepare a murder trial against Henry. But trials were expensive. They wanted a confession. "Wilkens in my opinion will never confess," Golden told reporters, however. "He is another Hightower."

Both sides were convinced that their chances rested on locating the man who Arthur had pinpointed as the shooter and who would either implicate Henry Wilkens or exonerate him. They needed to find Walter Castor.

A WILD SORT OF COUNTRY

In July 1922, one of the biggest strikes in American history brought construction on the railroads to a grinding halt. More than four hundred thousand workers took part, in protest at a 12 percent pay cut—and the railway companies brought in strike breakers to do the work.

In what became a bitter dispute, the men crossing the picket lines faced physical threats and ostracism from the community. In Pennsylvania, a crowd of women and children pelted them with rotten eggs and sour milk, and in some places the rail firms had to build temporary accommodation at their sites so strike breakers wouldn't have to leave. Tens of thousands of private guards were hired to protect them as they worked.

It was an unenviable job—but the perfect one for Walter Castor, who was running out of money. After fleeing Eureka following his brother Arthur's arrest, he'd bounced around the picturesque mountain towns of northern California, looking for work, and had found it during the strike—at a Pacific Railroad site in Gerber, under the fake name Frank Collins.

The remote setting and lax employment checks offered a good place for him to lie low while the police continued what was becoming a nationwide manhunt. Already, Walter's photograph, fingerprints and a detailed physical description (including his hat size, 6¾) had been circulated up and down the West Coast. By mid-July, with a warrant out for his arrest, they were being sent farther afield, to major towns and cities all across America.

But Walter was never good at lying low. His impulsive ways were always close to the surface, and he quickly came to the attention of local police in Gerber after trying to coerce a Filipino laborer into shooting one of the strikers. Walter disappeared from the work camp on July 13 and arrived back in San Francisco two days later, hoping to reunite with Annie Downs and to scrape together enough cash for a dash to the Mexican border.

He headed for 828 McAllister Street in the bustling Filmore district, and the second-floor apartment of his uncle Henry Castor, a seventy-one-year-old who was slowly dying of colon cancer. Uncle Henry lived with his wife, Frances, and Marguerite Bramlett, a nurse who had been hired to help tend to him during his final days. She was in her thirties and had just moved north from Los Angeles.

When Walter arrived at the house, he introduced himself to Bramlett under his railway alias, Frank Collins. For a few days she didn't suspect anything. Then, on Thursday, July 20, there was a knock at the door. Bramlett was in another room, so Frances answered. It was a bill collector—one of a band of oft-maligned officials who went door to door, collecting money due for utilities or at local merchants and forcibly chasing up debts.

By then, Anna Wilkens's murder case had been the talk of the town for weeks, and the Castors' potential role in it must have been well known, because when Frances handed over a $100 bill in payment, Bramlett heard the collector joke: "This is not one of the Wilkens bills, is it?"

That's when it dawned on her who "Frank Collins" really was. "I walked into his room and asked him why he had mixed himself up in the case," she told reporters later. "It was the money!" he cried. "I didn't shoot the woman, though." He said Henry had pulled the trigger.

Walter was not in a good mental state. He stayed in the house all day, bouncing between nervousness and hysteria, and haunted by dreams of Anna's dead body lying on the ground. He kept a gun strapped around his waist, and he told Bramlett that he'd rather kill himself than be captured by the police. "I feared that the police would eventually come to the house and that Walter would start shooting on sight and probably kill someone," she said. Sometimes, when he left his revolver and cartridge belt on the table in the kitchen, she thought about grabbing them.

Soon, Walter's lover, Annie Downs, also arrived at the house on McAllister Street. They'd parted ways after fleeing Eureka in the wake of Arthur's arrest, but now they made plans to go into hiding together.

The police had unpicked the complex relationship between Downs and the Castor brothers, and she was trying to keep a low profile in case she led them to Walter's hiding place. The couple spent their days peering out of the window, looking for the undercover officers who they suspected were now stationed outside. When Downs went grocery shopping, she borrowed Bramlett's long coat and hat to use as a disguise.

"We all knew that the house was being carefully watched," Bramlett said. "Many times, Walter would look out the window and spot some plainclothes man whom he knew. He feared the police, and every time the doorbell rang he reached for his revolver."

When Walter wasn't crashing around the house in an anxious daze, he worked on a letter—a full account of what had really happened in the days before and after Anna's death, which he told his family he was planning to mail to Detective Matheson once he'd made his escape to Mexico.

* * *

It had been a frustrating few weeks for the police department. After Arthur's arrest in Eureka, Matheson told reporters his officers were just days away from bringing Walter back in for questioning, but as time passed, the rumors had become scarcer. There was a sighting here, a suspicious presence there, but little concrete evidence. By the time police had managed to chase down the leads, which came from all over California, Walter was invariably gone—if he'd ever been there at all.

On Sunday, July 23, Walter finally cracked and left the safety of his hideout. He was gone for four or five hours and came home steaming, stumbling drunk. "How he ever missed being caught then, I can't see, because he was in no condition to know what was happening," Bramlett said later.

Any lingering hangover Walter might have been suffering from— and he got such terrible headaches, even sober—was made much worse the following afternoon, when Detectives Thomas Murphy and Richard Tatham arrived at the house looking for him. They'd received a tip-off—a phone call to Matheson's office from an unknown female caller who confirmed where Walter was staying.

Walter hid in a back room as Frances opened the door. While the officers were in the hall, he grabbed his gun, cartridge belt, and coat, and ran into the laundry room, which had a hatch leading up to the roof. As the detectives searched the apartment, Walter crouched in silence on the roof, watching the trapdoor and clutching the revolver close to his thumping chest.

* * *

This near miss prompted Walter and Annie to find a new hideout, and they paid $12 for a room at 1920 Green Street, where they posed as Mr. and Mrs. Frank Burns. Walter told the landlady that he was "Shrimp" Burns, a daredevil motorcycle racer (the real Shrimp Burns had been killed in a crash the previous summer, in August 1921).

On the night of Wednesday, August 2, Robert Castor turned up at the room on Green Street after his shift, determined to win Annie Downs back from his brother. But things soon descended into a violent row, ending in a "primitive" and bloody fistfight between the two brothers. "Robert Castor told his wife that if she was prepared to reform and behave herself, she could return to him," reported *The Chronicle*. "She flouted him. He went away."

Downs left too, and Walter spent the rest of the night smoking and drinking himself into a frenzy and making plans. When police searched the room a week later, they found hundreds of cigarette stubs in an ashtray, an empty bottle of moonshine whiskey with a bottle of carbonated water for mixing, the peel of a dozen oranges, and enough used coffee grounds to have "made coffee for a family for a week."

The morning after the fight, Thursday, August 3, the police received another phone call from their mysterious female source, with another tip-off. This time, she said, Walter was hiding at Annie Downs's aunt's house—a "shack" at 2A Charlton Court, a narrow side alley off Union Street, which was overlooked by Walter and Annie's rented room.

Detective Tim Bailly and Patrolman George Stallard set off to investigate, in one of the SFPD's "heavy" cars—probably a dark wagon with black blinds over the rear windows and "POLICE PATROL" painted on the side and front in neat capitals.

Stallard was driving. He had just turned forty and was tall and slender, with sharp brown eyes, light brown hair, and more than a decade of police experience. Bailly sat next to him on the car's front seat. He was sixty-six—with thinning hair offset by an enormous bushy moustache—and was one of the oldest and most popular men on the force.

Bailly had spent years running the night shift and still had the bags under his small dark eyes to prove it. In an era marked by brutality and graft, he was one of the good ones. He had "a perfect reputation," according to *The Chronicle*, and never had a complaint filed against him. "He was tactful in handling cases and several times was given honorable mention for his courtesy in persons asking his service."

They drove to a corner on Pine Street to pick up Jere Dinan, another SFPD veteran, who was meant to be on the morning shift but hadn't turned up. Dinan—a stout, hard-looking man with pale eyes and a wispy moustache—was San Francisco's chief of police during the earthquake, appointed on a promise to make the force more efficient and less corrupt (he was one of the first people August Vollmer learned from when he took over in Berkeley). But he lasted less than two years before being forced to resign on charges of perjury.

In 1915, Dinan was demoted from detective and put back on street duty in a case of apparent retribution by an officer he'd wronged during his tenure as chief. But by 1922, he was back in the unofficial uniform of the detective—dark suit and tie, waistcoat, and the ubiquitous homburg hat.

The trio set off downhill, descending into streets still cloaked in morning fog. They arrived just after eight. Stallard stopped the car on Union Street while Bailly and Dinan walked up to the house to investigate—one to the front, one to the back. "We pounded on the door—hard—so anybody could have heard us," Dinan said. "Nobody answered."

So, they smashed it down and started a slow and careful search of the four rooms. They knew Walter was dangerous—he'd threatened to kill one of their colleagues for putting him in jail the first time around.

Everywhere they checked was empty, but then their attention turned to a little closet in the corner of one of the bedrooms. There was a faint rustling from inside. Dinan and Bailly crept toward the closet with their weapons drawn, then yanked it open, expecting perhaps to see Walter staring back at them with a gun of his own. Instead, they found Annie Downs, bundled up in a corner, trying to hide under some clothes.

She told them Walter had been there, but that they were too late—he'd left at midnight, she said, and she didn't know where he had gone. She didn't tell them about the fight—or the apartment across the street, where Walter had spent the night drinking, smoking, and eating oranges.

Dinan, Bailly, and Stallard went back to the station to report the news, but were ordered straight back to the house on Charlton Court. "We want that Downs woman," said their commanding officer. "Better go back and get her."

They returned with reinforcements, in the shape of Ernest Gable, a forty-five-year-old who had served in the city's mounted division and in its nascent motorcycle squad; and Barney Riehl, the department's bomb expert, whose brown eyes carried the wary frown of a man who spent his life dealing with explosives.

This time, Downs was ready to talk. She told them Walter was hiding at his mother's house at 1425 Kansas Street on the western side of Potrero Hill, a working-class, immigrant area that sloped down to the butcheries and shipyards of Mission Bay.

The officers took Downs with them and headed toward Kansas Street. But on the way, they decided to make one last check at the McAllister Street address to see if Walter might have gone back to his uncle's place. It was something Dinan would regret for the rest of his life. "Maybe if we hadn't made that stop, we might have got to the house before he got inside, and then we would have had a better chance," he said.

* * *

By the time George Stallard parked the car just short of the house at Twenty-Sixth and Kansas, the morning mists had vanished, revealing a clear, bright day. The detectives discussed their plan of attack. "We knew [Walter] would be armed and would be a dangerous man in a corner," Dinan said.

At first, they thought about sending Downs up ahead to try and "trick Walter into thinking it was just an ordinary visit." But Kansas Street was all steep hills and gravel banks—"a wild sort of country"— and the gaps between the houses hadn't been filled in by San Francisco's voracious real estate market, so it would have been all too easy for Downs to slip away.

Dinan and Bailly, the two senior officers, decided to take Downs with them to the front door, and sent Gable and Riehl to the back to shut off any potential escape routes.

The Castor home had a tired, old-fashioned air—it was the last in a row of "huddled little houses" with narrow steps leading up to the porch, to compensate for the sloping terrain. The paint was peeling off the wooden paneling. It looked, wrote one unimpressed reporter, "drab, dull, and not at all like the lonely refuge chosen by fictional crooks."

Dinan, Bailly, and Downs walked up the steps and rang the bell. Nothing happened. They pressed it again, and this time they heard it ringing through the house, followed by a slow shuffling of feet.

Finally, the door opened and Minnie Castor appeared. Walter and Arthur's mother was short and frail, with a wrinkled face and clear, pale blue eyes. Her sparse gray hair was flecked with yellow—she had been painting the kitchen floor when the doorbell rang.

"We're police officers," Dinan told her. "I know you've been bothered a lot, but we've got a straight tip that Walter is here."

"No, he isn't here," Minnie said. "I don't see why everybody is bothering me all the time about him."

Downs chipped in. "Why, he told me he was coming here," she insisted. "He was with me last night."

The officers pushed past Minnie, who offered little resistance, and into a short, dark hallway that smelled of paint. The house had four rooms—two at the front, two at the rear. A door at the end of the entrance hall led into the kitchen. It was slightly open, and they could see a large stove and a small dining table with the remains of someone's breakfast—a half-eaten melon—still sitting on it.

On the right and left of the hallway were two more doors that opened into the bedrooms. Dinan and Downs went into the right-hand room, which was largely empty save for a bed with a metal frame. Bailly went left, into what appeared to be Minnie Castor's bedroom.

It was a neat little room with a rug on the floor and a dark wooden dresser with a photo of her late husband, Charles Castor. He'd served alongside Bailly and under Dinan during the latter's tenure as chief of police, before being shot dead by a fugitive on the run from the law. Bailly glanced at the photo of his fallen colleague, which showed a stout man with a thick moustache in a round police helmet.

At the back of the bedroom, another door led into a living area. Through the opening, Bailly could see a piano pressed against the wall, below a portrait of a young woman holding a bouquet. But what he couldn't see from where he was standing was the other doorway, on the right-hand side, the one leading from the living area back into the kitchen. That's where Walter Castor was hiding when he shot Detective Bailly in the chest.

WHOLESALE SLAUGHTER

Walter Castor had trained the gun, in his good right hand, on the doorway from the front bedroom into the living room, and he pulled the trigger as soon as he saw Tim Bailly step through it. Jere Dinan heard the shot and rushed back into the hallway from the other bedroom. Bailly came staggering toward him with his features twisted into "kind of a smile."

He was clutching his chest and blood was already seeping through his shirt onto his hands. "I'm shot, Jere," he said. He lurched past the bed, leaving a crimson trail on the white sheets, and then collapsed between bed and window, his blood soaking into the rug and spreading across the floor.

The fugitive darted back into the kitchen, leaving scattered furniture in his wake. He cursed and fired a bullet at Dinan, which whizzed along the hallway and buried itself in the wall behind the detective. Dinan glimpsed a figure in a dark jacket and white shirt, and then Walter slammed the kitchen door shut before the stunned officer could react.

Dinan grabbed his gun and tried to follow. But Walter had either locked the door or barricaded it shut. There was an explosion of splinters as a second bullet came roaring at Dinan through the closed door. He returned fire in a wild daze. "I remember firing two shots at him, but after it was all over, I found four empty shells in my gun, so I must have fired four times," he said.

Walter ran to the back of the house, to try and escape through the kitchen window. But Barney Riehl and Ernest Gable were waiting for him—they'd walked up the steps to the back door of the house and found it locked, and had taken up positions in the back garden, which was ringed by a low wooden fence. Riehl remembered two or three distant gunshots. "Then suddenly there were two shots seemingly closer to us," he recalled.

The kitchen windows had grimy screens, which meant Walter could see the officers, but they couldn't see him. He may actually have recognized the men who'd arrested him twice in the past: Riehl, seven years prior on the manslaughter charge that put him in prison; and Gable, a few months back for the burglary charge that he was still on probation for. He aimed his gun through the screen and fired twice.

Outside, Gable glimpsed the faint outline of a hand in the window, and then he couldn't see anything at all. Walter had shot him in the face. The bullet hit Gable just above the right eye, driving a piece of skull into his brain. Riehl noticed his partner suddenly stiffen and drop to his knees, holding a hand to his forehead. Blood poured out between his fingers.

Riehl dodged around the corner of the house with his gun drawn and his heart racing. At the same moment, Dinan came hurtling down the front stairs, calling for help. "Get an ambulance," he yelled. "Bailly's hurt!" But it was chaos outside too. Then he heard an angry shout from inside the house.

After failing to escape through the kitchen, Walter had come back to the front of the house and spotted Annie Downs, the woman who had betrayed his hiding place to the police, hiding from the gunfire in the spare bedroom. She tried to run, but there was nowhere to go. Walter shot his lover in the back of the head and then stepped back into the hallway and turned the gun on himself.

Dinan opened the front door just in time to see Walter's body hit the floor. He was slumped at a crooked angle in the narrow hallway, with his neck propped up against the wall and his legs stretching back into the room where Downs lay dead too.

He'd shot himself just under the right ear. There were powder burns on that side of his face from the gunshot. Blood and brains dripped from the back of his head, down the skirting board and onto the floor. He had another gun and fifty rounds of ammunition on a cartridge belt around his waist.

Dinan's hands were shaking. He bent down to check the body and retrieve the gun, a .38 caliber revolver—the same type as the one that had killed Anna Wilkens. He went to the bedroom, where Bailly's body lay still on the rug, and picked his way through the scattered furniture at the back of the house to check on Gable. He slid open the kitchen window, to find a shaken Riehl pointing a gun at him. "Don't shoot!" Dinan shouted. "We've got him, Barney."

It had been less than three minutes since Minnie Castor had opened her front door, and three people were dead. She'd run from room to room during the shooting, screaming at Walter to put the gun down. She was still screaming when reinforcements arrived: twenty firemen who'd been at a colleague's funeral nearby, riot squads from the Mission and Potrero station, and Chief O'Brien in one of the department's newest vehicles, with a machine gun mounted on the front.

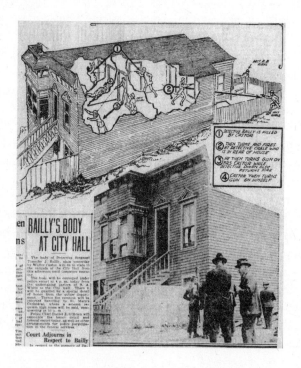

Dinan stood on the back porch in his hat and jacket, leaning on the railing and staring blankly into the distance while his colleagues dealt with the aftermath. They laid Annie Downs on the bed in the room where she'd died, and covered the body with a sheet. They searched Walter's pockets and found $28.45 and Marguerite Bramlett's address and telephone number. An ambulance arrived to take Gable to Mission Emergency Hospital, where doctors raced to save his sight.

*   *   *

The next day, the city reeled from the killings. Bailly's body rested "in the stilled and shrouded rotunda" of City Hall, surrounded by floral tributes and with two police officers keeping watch at all times in a guard of honor. Surgeons removed a bone fragment from Gable's brain with the aid of an X-ray machine—a delicate and risky operation in which they removed his right eyeball from the socket, picked the shrapnel out of his head and then pushed the eye back into place. (Gable recovered almost all his sight and was back on the beat before the end of the year.)

A crowd of hundreds gathered outside the Castor house on Kansas Street, whispering to each other about what the morning's newspapers were calling "wholesale slaughter" that read "like the story of a dime novel thriller." Police tried to push them back, but some evaded the cordon and rested on the fence behind the tiny backyard, peering in.

Inside, behind drawn curtains, nineteen-year-old Elmer and fifteen-year-old Harold Castor were trying to erase the marks of what had happened, with trembling hands. They scrubbed at the rugs and the floor, and filled the bullet holes in the walls and casements with putty.

Their mother was catatonic. Minnie Castor lay in the darkened bedroom of the house where Bailly had met his doom, and refused to leave—hair tangled and still streaked with paint, face white and swollen with tears. Her sons tiptoed in and out, but their anxious questions "met only a glassy stare."

Minnie didn't seem to know who she was or what had happened. "Where am I?" she asked over and over again, raving wildly while three policemen held her in a chair. "Did I fall down?"

At the Ingleside Jail, where he'd been moved after getting death threats for "squealing" on his brother, a shaken Arthur Castor gave interviews with his wife, Mary, by his side, squeezing his hand for support. "Walter is better off dead," he said. "But I'm terrible sorry about those two officers. I know them both, and they were fine fellows too."

"It proves what I said—that Walter was absolutely crazy," he went on. "I told the officers time after time that if they ever tried to take Walter, he'd shoot. He's that way—everybody knows he's crazy. I was afraid of him myself at times."

Walter's death was a blow for the prospects of Henry Wilkens, who still stuck to his story of a vast conspiracy against him. "Oh God! This is awful!" he cried, when he got the news, voice rising to a fearful pitch. "Now they will railroad me. But they can't hang an innocent man. They can't do it. They never can do it."

"I only wish they had taken Walter Castor alive," he said, wringing his hands in his cell in the Hall of Justice, "so that he could have told the truth and have proved that this is all a frame-up against me."

He blamed Arthur. "I believe that Walter was simply hounded to death by the officers, acting on the story framed up on him by his own brother," he said. "He wasn't crazy—he was simply hounded into shooting these officers and committing suicide by the thought that he didn't have a chance against this frame-up."

Henry seemed to have sunk back into the deep depression that marked the days leading up to his lie detector test, and worried wardens at the Hall of Justice placed him on suicide watch, to the fury of syndicated newspaper columnist "C. K."

"Why this desire to prevent him ending his existence?" C. K. wrote. "Would it not be the easiest solution? If his life is guarded and saved, his trial will cost the taxpayers a considerable sum. Even if found guilty of a most heinous crime, it is a ten-to-one bet he never will be hanged."

But by nine PM on the day after the gunfight, as the prison curfew bell clanged and the inmates started to settle in for the night, Henry's mood had changed. Ernestine Black from *The Call* found him buoyant. He scoffed at the interviews Marguerite Bramlett was giving to the newspapers, saying Walter had told her that Henry paid $5,000 to have

Anna killed. "Five thousand! Why, where would I dig up that amount of money?"

"With his lips he says he is sorry that Walter Castor is dead," Black wrote. "But he holds his head high, his eyes are bright, he talks with animation overlaid with confidence."

* * *

At nine thirty on the morning of August 5, Tim Bailly's funeral procession left City Hall for St. Mary's Cathedral—a full battalion of policemen in uniform, led by Chief O'Brien and Mayor Rolph, moved solemnly north along Van Ness Avenue as the municipal band played Chopin's funeral march. Spectators lined the sidewalks, with their heads bowed and their hats in their hands.

Behind them came the pallbearers, among them detective Leo Bunner, who had swapped shifts with Bailly on the morning of the shooting. There were four cars loaded with flowers—white roses and purple asters—and a line of 250 more, carrying friends and family to the cathedral, where they sang a solemn mass. Afterward, Bailly's body was carried from the church and taken to Holy Cross Catholic Cemetery in Colma, where he was buried under the six-pointed star of the San Francisco Police Department.

(Walter Castor's body was returned to the family home and placed in the back room. A simple wreath hung on the front door.)

After the service, police sought to avenge their fallen colleague with a burst of decisive action. The massacre on Kansas Street had left Chief Daniel O'Brien and the district attorney's office convinced that Walter and Henry had conspired to kill Anna Wilkens. The biggest weakness in their case against Henry Wilkens was the lack of anything approaching a motive—he did not seem to have gained financially from his wife's death, for instance.

They quizzed him at the Hall of Justice and interrogated Robert Castor, who had arrived at the house two hours after the deaths of his wife and brother and was immediately arrested.

Now Robert told police that Walter had returned to San Francisco to try and meet up with Henry, and that together the two men were plotting to pin the crime on Arthur—but that by the time Walter arrived back in the city, Henry had been arrested, so he was forced to quickly change his plans. ("I don't believe this statement," said Arthur when reporters put this to him. "Walter never would throw this on me.")

In Berkeley, John Larson read about the bloodshed at the little house on Kansas Street with a growing sense of horror. By now, he was convinced that Henry was guilty, which meant that his lie detector had failed to uncover the truth. His invention hadn't worked, and now three more people were dead, and a police officer was in the hospital, fighting for his life. But Larson did his best to push those thoughts to the back of his mind—he had more pressing things to attend to.

On August 9, a short story appeared on page three of *The Examiner*, noting Larson's marriage to Margaret Taylor, the first person he'd ever conducted a formal lie detector test on during the College Hall investigation. After the wedding, the couple were "kidnapped" by a party of college cops, who handcuffed them together and drove them out into the countryside as an exuberant prank.

Two columns over, one of the happiest moments of Larson's life was juxtaposed with one of his biggest failures. District Attorney Matthew Brady was cutting short a trip to Yosemite with his ailing mother, to rush back to San Francisco and begin preparations for Henry's trial. It would be one of the most heated legal battles in the history of the city—and it opened with a stunning revelation.

CHICKEN DINNERS

O n Monday, August 14, 1922, Frank Murphy stood in the marble-floored waiting room of the Third and Townsend Depot, San Francisco's main train station, scanning the faces of arriving passengers for the woman he knew would make or break his case.

The evening sunlight streamed through the station's high windows and gleamed off polished floors, where homebound commuters waited for their trains on wooden benches.

The attorney was not a particularly patient man, and it was unlike him to be running an errand like this. But he knew how important his influence on this particular witness could be for his client, Henry Wilkens, whose case was going in front of the grand jury that evening to finally decide if there were reasonable grounds to charge him for murder and take him to trial.

At seven fifteen PM, the Southern Pacific service from Redwood City pulled into the station with a rush of steam and a screech of iron, and a young woman in a dark, wide-brimmed hat stepped off it and surveyed her surroundings as other passengers jostled past her. Murphy spotted her and raised a meaty hand in greeting—he recognized Helen Lange, sister of the murdered Anna Wilkens, from his meetings with Henry to discuss the case.

Lange was tall and thin, with fairer, more delicate features than her late sister, and her flaxen hair seemed streaked with gold in the evening light. Her blue eyes were sharp and alert, her nose finely pointed. There was a black mourning band around one arm. Heads turned as she strode toward him.

Murphy had promised to escort Lange safely from the train station to the Hall of Justice and back. But first he wanted to talk to her alone. He knew Lange had the potential to be a key character witness for the defense. She'd seen Anna and Henry's marriage and could impress upon the grand jury that Henry was a devoted husband—a passionate, sometimes angry man, yes, but not someone who could ever harm his wife in cold blood.

But she also had a secret—one that could derail the whole case. In the weeks since Anna's death, rumors had begun to swirl about Henry's relationship with his pretty young sister-in-law.

* * *

Helen Lange arrived in San Francisco on February 20, 1922, a few months before her sister's death. She had spent the previous two years training to be a children's nurse at a hospital in Germany, but she decided to come to America to support Anna, who paid for part of the journey. Like her sister, Lange was kept under strict supervision by her parents. She was not allowed to fraternize with other young people. She "never went to a party, had never been kissed."

Having her sister with her helped Anna immeasurably. She'd been pining for home—missing her family and perhaps struggling with the rising tide of anti-German sentiment that followed the war. Lange was someone Anna could confide in when her husband wouldn't listen, and she was great with the couple's two young kids. As a mark of her gratitude, Anna gave Lange a gift—a thin gold ring, set with a tiny, sparkling diamond.

But things soon turned sour. Henry had been growing more distant from his wife over the previous year, and he seemed to take an unhealthy interest in his sister-in-law. Anna noticed that her sister and her husband's absences from the flat on Vallejo Street seemed to align—when Henry was away for work, Lange was out seeing friends. When Henry went out to run errands, he took Lange with him. Anna let her jealousy overcome her.

"Sometimes Wilkens would take his bookkeeper home after work, and then my sister—ill and nervous—would tell all around the neighborhood that he was taking other women out in his car," Lange said. "Sometimes she would actually accuse me of trying to get her husband away from her. I don't believe she knew what she was doing when she said that, because later on she would say she was sorry and that she knew I was a friend to both of them."

She even blamed Anna for Henry's violence. "You know how neighborhoods talk? People gossiped about what my sister said, and it came back to Wilkens. He has a very quick temper, and when he drank, as he sometimes did, he used to fly into rages. My sister drank too—it hurts me to say these things about both of them, but I must tell the truth."

Anna was right to be suspicious. In April, she fell ill, and during the two weeks she was in the hospital, Henry made his move. "Henry Wilkens attacked me in his home last April, two months after I had arrived from Germany," Lange said. "Soon after that I formed an attachment for him, and our relations continued up to the time he was taken into custody at Siegler Springs."

When Anna returned home from the hospital, Lange found a job as a hotel maid in Redwood City and spent less and less time at the family apartment. But her relationship with Henry only intensified. The couple shared kisses "morning and night," Lange admitted. Afterward, Henry tried to characterize these as wholly innocent. "It is true that Helen and I sometimes kissed each other, but always in the presence of my wife and never but in a perfectly natural spirit," he said.

They started seeing each other secretly. In the evenings, Henry took Lange out for long drives, treating her to "chicken dinners" at Uncle Tom's Cabin, a roadside restaurant in San Bruno. He was working later—staying at his garage so he could talk to Helen on the phone without Anna overhearing. But someone else was listening in.

In early May, the woman Lange was working for in Redwood City telephoned Anna Wilkens to tell her that her sister and her husband were having an affair. In fact, unbeknownst to Anna, Henry and Lange were actually together at that very moment—on a weekend away in San Jose, where they'd checked into the St. James Hotel together, posing as married couple Mr. and Mrs. Albrecht.

When they got home, a furious Anna was waiting for them. She threw Lange out of the house and demanded that her sister return the gold ring she'd given her. Lange spent the night at the Federal Hotel in the city, where Henry joined her later that night. They might have stayed longer, but the next day Henry got a phone call from the sisters' uncle, demanding to know where Helen was and threatening to call the police if Henry didn't produce her within the hour.

On May 10, a sheepish Henry returned to the flat on Vallejo Street. A tearful Anna greeted him at the door. "I've done something awful," she said. She'd hired an attorney and filed for divorce.

*   *   *

Murphy sat Lange down in his office. Later he insisted that he just wanted to calm her nerves and had no intention of trying to tell her what to say in front of the grand jury.

They talked about her relationship with Henry, and she blushed as she admitted to having dinners alone with her brother-in-law on a couple of occasions. She asked Murphy whether she should tell the grand jury about this. He told her to tell them everything (he said).

But he was worried there might be more. He'd read the rumors in the papers. A week earlier, Henry—who was making plans to study law from his cell—had merely laughed when reporters told him police were investigating an affair as one possible motive, and Lange painted her sister as a depressed, jealous woman. "If Henry Wilkens had been in love with me and had wanted to get rid of his wife so that he might marry me, I certainly must have suspected it," she said. "We were just friends, that is all, and I will never believe he did the awful thing of which he is accused."

"I put the direct question to her whether she was in love with Henry Wilkens," Murphy said. "She answered 'no,' that she was a loyal friend to him." It wasn't the first time he'd pressed the couple on their relationship, but now he asked again whether Lange had ever "been intimate" with Henry.

"I am a good girl, Mr. Murphy," she said in a line that could have been lifted straight from a detective noir novel. "I want you to believe I am a good girl."

At the Hall of Justice later that evening, Lange showed no sign of nerves as she waited patiently outside the grand jury room for her turn to give evidence. She chatted amiably with a couple of interpreters and spoke to a reporter in German as Murphy paced the corridor, smoking a cigar. His fears were justified. Helen Lange's first appearance was only the start of his troubles.

She spoke good English, with only a light accent, and the panel were impressed with her poise. "She appeared to be a sophisticated, entirely self-possessed young woman, pretty and with a reasonable command of the English language for a girl who has been in the country since February," said Otto Jungblutt, the chairman of the grand jury.

But over two hours of questioning, Assistant DA Isidore Golden pried out something approaching the truth. It was a far less innocent picture than what she'd told the newspapers.

Lange admitted to the kisses but said she'd stayed in the hotel on her own. She described how Henry and his wife would argue, and told the room about Anna's jealousy and her drinking. This proved too much for one member of the grand jury. "Why don't you remove that black mourning band that you wear on your sleeve?" snapped Elizabeth Hayes. "Don't you know that you have insulted the memory of your sister by the admissions which you have made here."

Grand jury proceedings were meant to be confidential, to avoid prejudicing potential jurors or ruining the reputations of people who turned out to be innocent. But Lange's evidence was front-page news the next day. It wasn't the killer blow Golden had been looking for, but her testimony offered a plausible enough motive for the state to take into the trial.

Murphy was furious about the leaks. He said the DA's office was dripping "poison propaganda" about Henry into the minds of the populace, and dared them to publish the full transcript of her testimony. "It will show how she was bulldozed and bullyragged—called a liar repeatedly by the deputy district attorney—and treated in the most cowardly and shameful manner."

He also claimed the DA's office had known the whereabouts of Walter Castor for ten days before the mass shooting on Kansas Street but hadn't told the police because they'd been conducting secret negotiations to offer him immunity in exchange for testifying against Henry. Because of this, Murphy argued, Brady and his men were "directly responsible" for the deaths of Tim Bailly and Annie Downs. (Murphy never presented any evidence for these assertions, and this argument did not resurface.)

The police kept digging. Lange spent most of the next week being questioned by detectives Kate O'Connor and Henry McGrath. On Thursday, August 17, they showed her the register from the hotel in San Jose, where she'd told the grand jury she had stayed alone in early May under the fake name "Ms. Albrecht."

But the guestbook entry didn't say that. It read "Mr. and Mrs. Albrecht," and detectives were already convening handwriting experts who could match the penmanship to Henry's own. Confronted with her deception in black and white, Lange finally faltered, and the facts came tumbling out.

A special session of the grand jury was hurriedly assembled— ostensibly to decide whether Lange and Murphy had committed perjury by lying at the first hearing, but really as a means for the DA's office to get more information into the public record (to drip more poison, as Murphy might have put it).

Officials made a big show of secrecy. The grand jurors didn't know why they'd been summoned, and Golden made them raise their right hands and swear not to repeat anything that they heard. (Henry's friend William McNevin happened to be on the grand jury and had to recuse himself when he found out what case they were hearing.)

The reporters buzzing around the Hall were barred from speaking to Lange before she gave evidence. But despite the security, the hearing quickly became a teaser for the salacious material that would spill out at trial.

Lange's sobs could be heard echoing through the halls outside the grand jury room as she admitted that her relationship with Henry had continued even after Anna's death—carefully hidden from the detectives and well-wishers who came calling on the apparently grief-stricken family.

On the first or second night after the murder, Lange recalled—with Anna's body still at the morgue—she'd taken her sister's place in Henry's bed, lying awake in the dark as he "dreamed and moaned and tossed and talked of shooting, shooting, shooting."

After she finished her story and agreed to testify for the state in exchange for immunity from prosecution, Lange told the grand jury that she'd been "coached" by Murphy to lie to them before. The attorney was barred from giving evidence in his own defense, so when the grand jury voted to indict him for perjury, he complained to reporters instead. "This is simply an attempt to hamper my efficiency as an attorney and to deprive Wilkens of my services in his defense," he said.

It was a very different Helen Lange who left the Hall of Justice late that night. The jaunty smile had evaporated, and she was red-eyed and "almost on the verge of a collapse" as she was led slowly out of the grand jury room by Kate O'Connor, who would be maintaining a close eye on the state's star witness. Brady finally had his motive, and the trial was less than six weeks away.

AN AID TO THE STORK

On the morning of Monday, September 25, 1922, Henry Wilkens shaved, neatly combed his hair, and changed out of his striped prison clothes into the dark blue suit he'd bought for his wife's funeral.

His normally tanned skin had taken on a "prison pallor," but otherwise he seemed to be in excellent health despite his long stay in the Hall of Justice. He'd even gained some weight.

At the arraignment, just over a month earlier, he'd looked a broken man—entering the courtroom with his head downturned and breaking into "husky" sobs. But a visit from his children on September 6—the first time he'd seen them since his arrest—seemed to revitalize him. He hugged and kissed them, and "his eyes filled with tears."

The weeks since Helen Lange's revelations about their affair had passed in a flurry of motions and hearings. The grand jury voted to delay attorney Frank Murphy's perjury trial until after the Wilkens case had been settled. Murphy made a number of failed attempts to try and get Henry's case dismissed—leaning on obscure technicalities and mounting a desperate attempt to charge the remaining Castor brothers with conspiracy to frame his client.

The police department and the district attorney's office were holding regular conferences to discuss their strategy, but tension between the two arms of the law had been building all summer. On the afternoon of September 1, all the detectives working on the case had been summoned to a heated "showdown," where they were questioned about their work so far, in front of Chief O'Brien and Commissioner Roche as well as Matthew Brady and his assistants from the DA's office.

Assistant DA Isidore Golden accused the detective squad of failing to cooperate with the DA in gathering evidence. He said the detectives assigned to the Wilkens case had been "disinterested" in it, except when gossiping to outsiders.

Matheson fiercely denied this. His men had continued their search for physical evidence throughout the summer. They'd seized the yellow Premier from where it was still parked, outside the house in Redwood City, where Henry had been arrested, and took Arthur Castor back over the route he and his brother followed as they trailed the car from Felton to the city.

Anna's rings were key items of interest. Henry said they had been snatched by the bandits, but Arthur denied seeing them. If police could prove that Henry still had them or that he'd thrown them away, they'd have a key piece of physical evidence to contradict his story. They hired plumbers to search the sewers of the two hospitals Anna had been taken to, where Henry was seen pulling at her hands as she lay dying on the operating table.

* * *

At ten minutes before nine, Henry was handcuffed and led downstairs in chains to Department Twelve of the Superior Court for the first day of his trial for murder. It promised to be "one of the most sensational" in San Francisco history, and the corridors outside the courtroom were packed with spectators, held back by a special detail of five policemen.

Henry shared a few words with reporters on his way into the courtroom, a large square space with carved, dark wooden paneling on the walls, stretching up to a high ceiling. He was "ready to go" he said. "I will be acquitted. I am confident it will be shown I am the victim of a frame-up."

The room was already crowded with 126 prospective jurors, whose names had been drawn from a hat. The morning sun flooded in through windows that admitted no breeze—by the afternoon, the air would be stifling.

At ten AM, Bailiff Fred Schulkens rapped the gavel to call the court to order, and Judge Louis Ward stepped up to a raised dais at the front of the room and sat in a high-backed leather chair behind a wide wooden desk. Ward was forty-five and had only been a judge for a few years after a successful career as an attorney. His brown hair was streaked with gray and combed back from an owlish face. When he frowned, which he did often, his dark eyebrows formed a sharp "V" above hazel eyes, hidden by small round glasses.

In 1920, Ward presided over the trial of gangster "Spud" Murphy, who he sentenced to fifty years in prison, but the Wilkens case was undoubtedly the highest profile one of his career so far. He was a stern hand, quick with the gavel, but showed compassion when the occasion demanded it—twice before, he'd called early adjournments to allow attorneys to rush home in time for the births of their children. *The Call* dubbed him an "aid to the stork."

On tables spread out before the bench, the players in the impending drama took their seats for the first time. The prosecution team of Matthew Brady, Isidore Golden, and Leo Friedman were to Ward's left as he looked out over the courtroom, with Murphy and Wilkens to his right at the defense table.

A handful of spectators squeezed onto the oversubscribed benches at the back of the room. But those expecting fireworks were disappointed because the first three days of the trial were consumed by jury selection.

One by one, jurors approached the bench with reasons why they couldn't serve—work commitments, the railroad strike, the war in Turkey—and, one by one, Ward told them to sit back down. Even Henry cracked a smile at some of the excuses on offer.

Already, it was obvious this wouldn't be a clean trial. That night prospective jurors received calls from unknown numbers advising them to "get on the jury" or asking whether they had German heritage (like Henry and Anna Wilkens).

But by six fifteen PM on September 27, a jury of twelve had finally been selected. Their photo appeared in *The Call*: nine men in suits and ties, mostly middle-aged and balding, and three younger-looking women, wearing smart dark dresses and hats. They were all White, and their professions ran the gamut of 1920s industry: ranchers;

sales reps; and manufacturers of paper boxes, elevators, and adding machines.

A little after ten AM on Thursday, September 28, Isidore Golden stood up in front of the jury and began his opening statement for the prosecution. He spent ninety minutes outlining his side's case against Henry Wilkens, which had been building in force ever since Anna's murder. The state would, Golden promised, produce witnesses who would prove Henry had known Walter Castor for years, that he'd met with the Castor brothers both before and after the shooting, and that Helen Lange was a "good and virtuous girl," who had been "debauched by her own brother-in-law in her own sister's home."

It didn't matter, Golden told the jury, whether it was Walter or Henry who had actually fired the fatal shot—because it was Henry who had plotted the murder, Henry who had conspired with Walter on how to pull it off, Henry who had paid him the cash to do it. It was Henry who had lied—about the make of the car he'd seen speeding away from the scene, about the number of passengers in it, and about Anna's rings being stripped from her fingers during the robbery.

In fact, Golden said—and a smile played across his lips as he dropped this bombshell—Helen Lange had found the rings, the rings Henry said had been stolen by the bandits. The state would introduce them as evidence that he was a liar and a murderer.

"The outcome for this defendant means life or death for him," Golden said in closing. "It means imprisonment or liberty. We shall prove that this defendant entered into a combination or confederation or understanding, known legally as a conspiracy, with Walter and Arthur Castor, by which Mrs. Wilkens was done to death."

Over the next few days, the state worked its way through a list of thirty witnesses, starting with the doctors who had treated Anna's gunshot wound at the hospital. Frank Murphy used his cross-examinations to try and muddy the waters—tying witnesses up with questions of dates and times, and breaking Golden's flow with well-timed objections.

On Friday, Golden began painting a picture of Henry and Anna's troubled relationship when he called Eleanor Lewis and Gertrude

Stirness, who'd witnessed their fight at Calistoga on Easter Sunday, when Henry had threatened to kill himself and his daughter. Anna's aunt and uncle talked about the bruises they'd seen on her arms the last time she visited them. Two mechanics from the Garford Truck Company confirmed that Henry and Walter worked there together in 1918.

But as the first week of the trial ended at noon on Friday, September 29, the state had yet to land a really decisive blow. Things were just warming up, though, and when they returned to the courtroom on Tuesday, it would be time for the prosecution's two star witnesses to take the stand.

THE RISING TIDE

The first week of October marked the start of the World Series between the New York Giants and the New York Yankees—a contest that gripped America. In Minneapolis, a window washer fell from a third-story ledge onto the sidewalk, and his first question when he came to was "What's the score?"

But while crowds formed at bulletin boards around the country with the latest from the baseball, in San Francisco the Henry Wilkens trial was the hottest ticket in town—with seats harder to come by than a place at the Polo Grounds to see Babe Ruth.

Henry had watched the first week of his own trial with the dispassionate air of a man waiting for the streetcar. But on the morning of Tuesday, October 3, when Kate O'Connor led Helen Lange into a courtroom that was "jammed to suffocation," he seemed to "perk up."

Lange was wearing a black, wide-brimmed sailor hat and a modest dark blue dress with a white collar, under a gray tweed storm coat to keep off the rain that had been falling for days. Henry gave her a "long, impenetrable look" as she took her seat in the witness chair and swore to tell the truth, the whole truth, and nothing but the truth. "His eyes seemed to bore right through her."

But Lange did not return his stare. Throughout her testimony, she avoided looking at Henry, and on the rare occasions her eyes flicked in his direction, he quickly dropped his own gaze to the floor. Lange seemed calm and answered Golden's preliminary questions in her lightly accented English.

The only thing betraying her inner turmoil was a small muscle in her throat that "throbbed as though a wild bird were imprisoned there."

Jurors and spectators leaned forward, hanging on Lange's every word as the prosecutor slowly teased out every detail of her affair with Henry Wilkens.

"While Mrs. Wilkens was in the hospital, I want to ask you whether or not you had intimate relations with the defendant?" he asked at the end of one barrage of questions.

"Yes," Lange admitted.

"More than once during the two weeks?"

"Yes."

Halfway through Lange's testimony, Golden held up the registration book from the hotel where she and Henry had stayed together under fake names. The entry for the fictional Mr. and Mrs. Albrecht, in Henry's handwriting, had been marked with a penciled "X." Golden passed it around the jury box, and when he was satisfied that they'd all understood its importance, he moved on to scrutinize Helen's behavior in the aftermath of her sister's death—over the frequent objections of a powerless Frank Murphy.

"Now Miss Lange, were you a good girl before you came to America?" Golden asked.

Murphy almost spat his objection, rising to his feet with a surprising turn of speed for a man his size.

"Objected to upon the ground that it is incompetent, irrelevant, and immaterial," he shouted.

"Sustained," said Judge Ward.

But Murphy couldn't stop Lange from recounting the moment, a few days after the murder, when she'd opened a bureau drawer in the Vallejo Street apartment and found a small tin box that rattled when she shook it. There was jewelry inside: three rings, two set with a single diamond, the other with both a green and a white stone; and a diamond lavaliere necklace like the one Anna had worn on her wedding day.

Lange instantly recognized Anna's rings. But she'd read in the newspapers that they had been stolen in the robbery. She confronted Henry about it, and he told her that he'd been mistaken but that it was too late to change his story now. "I was lying about the rings," he told her. "I thought the robbers took the rings from your sister, but after, I found the rings in the house, and I was lying about that, and I will keep on lying about that because if I tell the truth now, then the people will think I am always lying."

Henry initially told Lange she could keep the jewelry, but when she visited him in prison in August, he was concerned about the police finding it. "Mr. Wilkens told me to take the ring away—nobody knows about it, the ring, and I should put it away," Lange told Golden, explaining how Henry had asked her to throw it into the bay.

Two of the rings and the necklace were introduced into evidence, but there was a third ring that was never mentioned in the court transcript—one small secret Lange managed to keep back. When she had looked in the tin box she found in the bureau, she'd seen the small, gold ring that her sister had given her as a gift when she'd first arrived in America, and then angrily demanded back when she found out about the affair.

Well, there was nothing Anna could do to stop her now. As she told the courtroom about her affair with her murdered sister's husband, a tiny diamond sparkled on Lange's slender finger. It was a symbol of sibling love, transformed into an emblem of betrayal, and she was wearing it on her right hand.

* * *

Helen Lange still didn't believe Henry had plotted to murder her sister, but she knew her testimony had been damning. After Murphy cross-examined her—a perfunctory fifteen minutes—she maintained her composure until she had to walk past Henry to take her seat in the front row of the audience, passing close enough to touch her lover. He did not look up as she walked past, nor turn around when she sat down directly behind him. She stared at his back for a few moments and then put her head in her hands and wept.

Arthur Castor was led into the courtroom after lunch for his turn on the stand. Deputies removed his handcuffs, and he sat coolly in the wooden witness chair in a light suit, waistcoat, and tie, with his blond hair combed back and his feet crossed loosely at the ankles. Unusually, Lange had insisted on staying in the courtroom to hear Arthur's testimony. As he was sworn in, she bent forward and listened intently, hoping for something in his story to put her mind at ease.

Arthur calmly, quietly, devastatingly talked Golden through his version of May 30—how Walter had picked him up early that morning with the promise of $250 for a "little job" and how he'd trailed the yellow Premier north toward the city and forced it to the curb on Nineteenth Street. "I heard a shot and a woman screaming, and Walter came running up and ordered me to drive off," he said.

He said he'd met Henry twice before the murder—once the previous week, when the mechanic repaired a car for the brothers, and then two days later, when Arthur and Walter went to Henry's shop on

Pacific Avenue and sold him a tire. Arthur had been scathing about his brother after the shooting on Kansas Street, but when he talked about Walter's suicide now, tears welled in the corners of his eyes.

Golden also teased out more details about the police lineup, where Henry had pretended not to recognize the Castor brothers. "He didn't say anything, but he sort of frowned at me," Arthur recalled, while Henry played with a pencil and stared down at a blank sheet of paper in front of him. Lange's testimony had taken its toll on the accused. "His color is bad, he slumps in his chair and is evidently engulfed in depression," wrote Ernestine Black.

* * *

So far, "occasional sparks had flown" between Murphy and Golden, according to *The Chronicle*, "but nothing had exploded." That changed a couple of hours into the next morning's session.

Murphy had Arthur Castor on the stand on cross-exam and was pressing him on some unsavory details of his personal history and on the confession he'd made to police in the presence of his attorney, William Herron.

For weeks, Murphy had been telling reporters and anyone else who would listen that it was Herron and Arthur who had cooked up the plot to frame Henry. Herron—a young, thin man with the look of a vampire—was sitting at the back of the courtroom, behind the massed ranks of lawyers from the district attorney's office, and he bristled when his name was mentioned.

He objected loudly to Murphy's line of questioning, and Murphy fired back in his brusque manner—questioning Herron's right to intercede in a case in which he had no involvement. At this, Herron's slick black hair rose "like a cockatoo's crest," and he countered: "You have been making a lot of charges, and I'm going to give you a chance to prove them."

Eventually he calmed down and agreed to drop his objection. "I am willing to let down the bars," he said. But Murphy couldn't resist one last jab. "You will probably be thrown behind some other kind of bars one of these days."

That sparked chaos. "You shall not insult me!" Herron shrieked, stepping toward Murphy with clenched fists.

"I'll show you up," Murphy yelled back. "You don't dare take the witness stand."

The courtroom buzzed. The bailiff was on his feet, smashing his gavel and poised to break up a physical altercation. From the prosecution bench, Golden made feeble attempts to interject—"Just a moment"—but no one heard him. The court reporter tried in vain to keep up with the verbal duel. Arthur Castor leaned back in the witness chair and enjoyed the show.

Judge Ward let this play out for a minute or two and then started talking in a low, ominous voice. He told Murphy and Herron that their behavior was contemptuous, and ordered them both to be locked up for twenty-four hours. Herron folded his arms and said he was ready to surrender. Murphy folded his and refused to go without the proper paperwork.

Bailiffs shooed out the crowd, and the two attorneys were escorted upstairs, where, at the receiving desk of the county jail, they stood grinning at each other like two troublemakers outside the principal's office. Downstairs in the nearly deserted courtroom, the look of bewilderment on Henry's face was slowly replaced with a smile.

* * *

Word of the entertainment on offer in Courtroom Twelve spread fast. On Friday, October 6, the day after the heated argument between Frank Murphy and William Herron, a ninety-minute queue of keen spectators snaked through the halls outside the courtroom, anticipating more fireworks. "An enterprising peddler of sandwiches and camp stools might have made a small fortune," observed *The Examiner*'s Oscar Fernbach. But they were left disappointed. "Honey fairly oozed from the tones of the attorneys."

The state continued its slow dismantling of Henry's story. On Monday, Robert Castor replaced Arthur on the stand and described his meeting with Henry on the corner of Pacific and Broderick after his lie detector test. Henry was in a buoyant mood that night, Robert said, and had triumphantly declared that police couldn't touch him as long as he didn't identify Arthur and Walter.

Jacob Gorfinkel, the attorney who'd helped Henry get Anna to the hospital, was the last to take the stand after a long day, but the jury listened attentively as he swore that he'd seen Henry pulling at the glove on his wife's left hand as she lay dying at the hospital. It left the jury with the impression that Henry was trying to remove Anna's rings before the police saw them, in an attempt to corroborate his own story.

As a lawyer himself, Gorfinkel made an impressive witness, and Henry looked grim as he watched the jury absorbing this new evidence. Murphy tried to poke holes in Gorfinkel's story—but only succeeded in drawing out more damaging evidence, including the revelation that Henry had known as far back as the night of the shooting that the car that had pursued them was not a Dodge. He'd been lying to police from the start.

Two days later, Henry's accountant, Kathleen Landel, described how, a few weeks before Anna's death, he'd started asking her not to enter certain transactions into the records because he didn't want his wife to know how much money he had. A divorce suit was incoming, he told her, and he didn't want to pay Anna maintenance. "The way he grinned as he told me about it gave me the impression that he thought he 'put something over' on her," Landel said.

Henry had shown little outward emotion while watching the parade of witnesses over the previous few weeks, but Golden had one more trick up his sleeve. On the afternoon of Friday the 13th, the state recalled Helen Lange. At the renewed sight of his lover, Henry "lost all control of himself." She was fighting powerful emotions too, and tears rolled down her face as she told the jury how the "unholy relations" with Henry had continued after Anna's death.

When she left the witness stand, Lange was led into Judge Ward's chambers, where grief and shame washed over her like the rising tide. "Why did I have to tell it?" she cried. "Why did I have to tell it?"

In the courtroom, the prosecution rested its case. The jurors glared at Henry, who sunk into his chair, wiped his closed eyes dry, and placed a hand over his trembling mouth to quiet his sobs.

THE TWILIGHT ZONE

All summer, John Larson wondered whether he might be asked to give evidence in the Henry Wilkens trial. But the call never came.

It made sense when he thought about it. Although Larson had told the press he thought Wilkens was innocent, privately his doubts had grown to the point where his testimony would probably have weakened the defense's case rather than strengthened it. And Henry had already admitted to deceptions that the lie detector had failed to catch—about the length of his preexisting relationship with Walter Castor, for instance.

So, instead of being in the courtroom on Friday, October 6—as Arthur Castor's testimony dragged into a third day—Larson was on an "auto drive" in Berkeley, standing by the side of San Pablo Avenue, stopping drivers for minor infractions: driving without a license, without taillights, without plates.

Larson and his colleagues made more than fifty arrests that evening, although few of the culprits shared the fate of Henry Villa—the former Berkeley cop who'd clashed with Larson and who was sentenced to twenty days in the county jail for speeding on the same day.

Any pleasure Larson might have taken from Villa's demise was undercut by his concerns about the lie detector. The machine's speedy ascent through the American justice system had been halted too. After the Henry Wilkens debacle, Larson heard rumors that the SFPD had decided never to use the polygraph again. And in July 1922, a landmark case set a precedent that would see it banned from most courtrooms for decades.

It centered on the murder of Robert Wade Brown, a prominent doctor in Washington, DC. Brown was the president of the National

Life Insurance Company and the "richest Black man in Washington." On Saturday, November 27, 1920, he was hosting friends after a college football game when a young man knocked on the door. The doctor went to speak to him, and a few moments later his guests heard gunfire from the front hall. Brown had been shot at point-blank range. There was a gun on the floor next to the body, but the culprit had vanished.

Brown's murder stunned the country's Black community, but for months police made no progress in catching the killer. It wasn't until August 1921 that they finally charged James Alphonso Frye, a twenty-five-year-old First World War veteran.

Frye had been arrested a few months prior on an unrelated robbery charge. During the investigation, Frye's sometime boss, a dentist named John Francis, told police that Frye had admitted to killing Brown.

A week later, Frye formally confessed to police. He said he'd accidentally shot the doctor during a struggle after he went to the house to get gonorrhea medicine, and Brown refused to give him any because he couldn't pay. "I tried to run to the door, and he grabbed me again and knocked me down, and I told him to put his hands up, and he kept on hitting me—hitting me on the head—and in the struggle, I think that my gun was fired," Frye said.

But by the time of the murder trial, Frye had retracted his statement. He said a police detective had tricked him into confessing by promising to drop the robbery charge and split the $1,000 reward with him if he did. Frye said his former boss, John Francis, was the real culprit and that he'd only made the false confession because he knew he had an airtight alibi.

However, when the witness to that alibi refused to come forward, Frye was left scrambling to clear his name. His case attracted the attention of William Moulton Marston, whose work on blood pressure had inspired John Larson's lie detector, and who had just started teaching a course on legal psychology at American University in Washington.

Marston's class—held two evenings a week, from March to June—was unique. It drew on his experiences at Harvard under Hugo

Munsterberg and relied heavily on experiments and live demonstrations. With the Frye case, Marston spotted the opportunity for another "class project" and a chance to promote his work on lie detection, which had proceeded on a parallel path to John Larson's.

In his last few years at Harvard, Marston had started to dabble in criminal cases. He always had one eye on fame, and he wanted to set a precedent for the admission of lie detector tests as evidence in court. He'd been writing to Larson for updates on the Wilkens investigation, which he thought might prove a useful test case.

On June 10, 1922—the day after John Larson's lie detector test on Henry Wilkens—Marston visited Frye in his cell to conduct his version of the deception test. Marston, a handsome man with dark hair and a strong chin, attached a blood pressure cuff to Frye's arm and jotted down notes as they spoke. "He asked me several questions, none pertaining to the case, then suddenly he launched upon several questions going into every detail of the case," Frye recalled. After the test, Marston declared that Frye was telling the truth—that he was innocent.

But to qualify as an expert witness, Marston would have to convince the trial judge William McCoy to let him testify. On July 19, 1922, he took his lie detector to the courthouse, where he tested the equipment on Frye in a corridor outside the courtroom. Frye's new defense team—both students of Marston—presented McCoy with a stack of scientific papers about blood pressure deception tests, including some of Larson's work and Marston's own dissertation.

But McCoy spent less than five minutes looking over these before making his decision. He would not let Marston take the stand. "If we are going to have a systolic test, you will have to test every witness who testifies in the case," he said. "If there is any science about it, we might as well apply the science to every witness." He dismissed the scientific papers as "pamphlets," and said he would read them properly after getting back from holiday. "I see enough in them to know that so far the science has not sufficiently developed detection of deception by blood pressure to make it a useable instrument in a court of law."

It was, in his view, not the place of science to make determinations of truth or falsehood, or of experts to weigh a man's sworn statements.

That, the judge said, "is what the jury is for. . . . When it [the lie detector] is developed to the perfection of the telephone and the telegraph and wireless and a few other things, we will consider it," he said. "I shall be dead by that time, probably, and it will bother some other judge, not me."

On July 20, 1922—the same day Frank Murphy was grilling Arthur Castor in a preliminary hearing on the other side of the country, Frye was found guilty of second-degree murder and sentenced to fifteen years in prison. In December 1923, the DC Circuit Court of Appeals affirmed McCoy's judgment and set a precedent for the admission of new forms of science into evidence.

The Frye standard tried to draw a line in the "twilight zone" between experimental technology and solid evidence. It states that a new technology must have gained general acceptance in the field in which it belongs in order to be accepted as evidence in court. It remains the law in some jurisdictions—including California and Illinois—but in most others it's been replaced by the more prescriptive Daubert standard, which sets out a number of additional requirements, including peer review and testability.

Together, these two standards would mostly bar lie detector evidence from American courtrooms for the next century. Eventually, the machine would twist its way into every other corner of the justice system, but for now the fate of Henry Wilkens would be settled by the jury—and his attorney, Frank Murphy.

THE CASE FOR THE DEFENSE

Frank Murphy stood in front of the jury just before noon on Monday, October 16, and began his opening statement for the defense. His ruddy face already had a sheen of sweat, and his belly strained against the buttons of his waistcoat. Henry's fate hung in the balance.

"I am glad," Murphy began, "that the time has come for Henry Wilkens to speak for himself and submit evidence to dispel the suspicion that has resulted from the cruel and unrelenting prosecution to which he has been subjected."

It had been a bruising few weeks for his client, but over the next ten days, Murphy would try to muddy the waters as much as possible, to sow the seeds of reasonable doubt in the minds of the jurors. He planned to do it with character witnesses who would show that Henry was a loving and devoted husband; he argued that the couple's fights were just like those of any other marriage and that although, yes, Henry had knocked Anna's tooth out, they had both been drinking—and in any case, the tooth had already been loose.

He also planned to do it by providing evidence that Henry was the helpless target of a scheme concocted by the Castor brothers and Arthur's attorney, William Herron, and that his client had been tricked into that suspicious-looking meeting with Robert Castor at Pacific and Broderick on June 9.

But mainly he planned to do it by attacking the integrity of Arthur Castor—a wily schemer, from a family of crooks and murderers, who was implicating Henry in exchange for his own freedom and whose troubles with authority had already begun to come out during his cross-examination. If Murphy could tarnish Arthur's reputation in the eyes of the jury, Henry might just have a chance.

Murphy spent most of the morning outlining his case and then—with a theatrical flourish that he must have enjoyed immensely—he called District Attorney Matthew Brady to the stand as his first witness. The courtroom buzzed with excitement as Brady stood up from behind the prosecution desk and approached the witness chair.

In a short but heated exchange, Murphy accused Brady of using "third-degree" tactics on Henry when they'd seized him from Siegler Springs. There was no evidence to back this up—just Henry's word against Brady's—but it was an inspired opening gambit because it planted the seeds of conspiracy in the jury's minds early on and ensured the controversial Brady's name would be dragged through the mud too.

Overall, though, the opening days of the trial didn't go quite as Murphy hoped. He called four witnesses from the camping party to testify that Henry had been with them for the whole trip and couldn't possibly have snuck away to meet Walter on either the Sunday or the Tuesday, as the Castors had described. But three of the four witnesses crumbled on cross-examination—admitting that Henry hadn't been in their sight for the entire time and that he could easily have found fifteen minutes to sneak away.

He dredged up former cellmates of Arthur's—interior decorator Louis Burkhart and fraudster Earl Coburn—who spun remarkably similar stories about how Arthur had been offered immunity by Brady in exchange for testifying against Henry, and how the whole thing was an inside job prompted by a tip-off from one of Henry's employees that he'd be carrying a lot of cash on the way back from the camping trip.

Both witnesses were shredded on cross-examination by Isidore Golden. It soon came out that Burkhart had previously been charged with lying in court and that in fact he had a habit of inserting himself into trials as a witness in cases that he had little to do with.

The jury seemed unimpressed with the parade of inmates Murphy was bringing out in Henry's defense—a check forger and an apparently professional perjurer were not the star character witnesses he'd promised in his opening statement.

*   *   *

On Monday, October 23, the expectant crowd finally got what they'd
been waiting for when Henry Wilkens took the stand. He was wearing his blue suit and had fixed a black mourning band around his left
sleeve. He looked well rested—he was clean-shaven, and his eyes were
clear and bright. He spoke slowly, mumbling a little at times in his
strong German accent.

Over three emotional days of direct and cross-examination, Henry
described his homelife and gave his account of the physical altercations
he'd had with Anna, which the prosecution had spent so much time
on: how he'd grabbed her so hard by the shoulders that it left bruises
and how ashamed he'd felt afterward. "Both Mrs. Wilkens and myself
were so intoxicated at the time that we did not know what happened,"
he said.

He described the moment Anna found out about his affair with her
sister and how he'd come clean, how Anna had forgiven him and how
they'd agreed to put it in the past. Henry even wrote a check for $50 to
cover the fees that Anna's divorce lawyer was demanding to drop the
suit.

"Was there any reason you wanted your wife to die?" Murphy
asked.

"I should say not," Henry answered.

Henry's voice weakened as he described the events of May 30. He
denied leaving the campground to meet anyone. As he talked through
the shooting and the frantic race to the hospital, tears rolled down his
cheeks, and he dabbed at his eyes with a handkerchief.

Murphy patiently built up his case—layering small contradictions
in Arthur's story on top of each other in the hope that they would prove
greater than the sum of their parts. He tried to show, for example, that
the Wilkens family had initially planned to return to San Francisco on
Sunday and had only extended their camping trip until Tuesday at the
last minute, so Henry couldn't have arranged the killing in advance.

With Murphy's help, Henry tried to explain his strange behavior after the murder. On June 9, he said, he'd been lured to a meeting at Pacific and Broderick by a telephone call from an unidentified man who then attempted to blackmail him. He said he'd only realized it was Robert Castor when he saw him in court.

And he tried to blame Arthur's attorney, William Herron, for conspiring against him. He said Herron had contacted him out of the blue, claiming that for $5,000 he could stop him from getting "mixed up" in the case and keep him out of jail. Herron already seemed to know about the affair. "You've got two children," he said. "You can't afford to have this woman's name come up."

Henry baulked at this offer, he said, but admitted to paying Herron $100 then and there to see what he could find out from policewoman Kate O'Connor and contacts at the DA. They'd had a couple more meetings after Henry came back from Siegler Springs, but then the next time he saw the man was in court, where he was representing Arthur Castor—whose testimony threatened to send Henry to the gallows. Murphy argued that Herron's meetings with Henry had simply been a ruse to mine him for information that could be used to frame him.

* * *

But it wasn't the content of Henry's testimony over these few days that stuck in the jury's mind, as much as the tone. With Murphy, the defendant was composed and cordial. But when he was being quizzed by Leo Friedman—a slender thirty-two-year-old who had taken the baton from Golden for cross-examination—Henry's attitude changed completely. "He looked and breathed open defiance," wrote Fernbach. "He seemed no longer able to give a single calm or unhesitating reply, save when it was fraught with abuse for the prosecution."

Friedman started his cross-examination by asking Henry why he hadn't taken Anna to a nearby house for help after the shooting and why he hadn't fired his pistol at the bandit who had just shot his wife—why, in fact, he hadn't even taken the safety catch off the gun.

Henry spluttered and hurled his responses. His voice rose in pitch and tone, and it took a supreme effort to force it down toward normal. "Why don't you ask me civil and decent questions?" he shouted at the prosecutor.

From there, Friedman moved on to the beating at Calistoga—demanding to know if it was true that Henry had grabbed his wife by the throat and left bruises on her arms. "Yes," Henry growled. "And there would be bruises on your arms, too, if I took hold of you."

Murphy looked crestfallen. With one outburst, Henry had undone all of the attorney's careful work, and as the jury went home that evening, it was with the image of an angry, snarling Henry at the front of their minds. "If the prosecutor's plan was to show the jury that the defendant possessed a temper, he succeeded," wrote *The Chronicle*.

The next day, October 24, Friedman took Henry over the day of the shooting for a second time, over Murphy's objections. Henry broke into tears, as he had done each time he was asked to remember the car chase, and pointed a shaking finger at his tormentor. "If your wife had been killed, Mr. Friedman, would you want to be asked these questions over and over? I—"

The rest of the sentence dissolved into sobs, and as Henry collapsed into his chair and covered his face with his hands, there were tears in the jury box too. Judge Ward called a short recess, and the jurors were escorted into his chambers to regain their composure.

But Friedman was merciless. When the trial resumed, he continued his forensic questioning, patiently drawing out the inconsistencies in Henry's stories.

He struck a note of incredulity that was echoed on the faces of the jury, particularly regarding Henry's meetings with Herron and the mysterious phone call he said had lured him into meeting Robert Castor on June 9.

"Did you ask this man what he wanted to see you about?" Friedman asked.

"No."

"Did you ask him in connection with what he wanted to see you?"

"I didn't ask him any particulars at all."

"Weren't you curious to know what he wanted to see you about, at all?"

"Well, curious—otherwise I would never have went out there, if I wasn't curious to find out."

"But you didn't ask him?"

"I didn't ask him."

"No. Now you don't run out of your shop every time somebody phones to you and says they want to see you on an important matter?"

"That is my business."

"Do you run out of the shop every time somebody phones to you and says they want to see you on an important matter?"

"If somebody wants to see me, no matter on what kind of a business, I am there for that purpose to go and find out."

"You go there to fix machines?"

"Absolutely."

"And when people call you up to fix machines, they tell you it is a wreck or something?"

"They usually do, yes."

"You generally take your shop car when there is a wreck?"

"Absolutely, if there was a wreck."

"If there was a wreck. But you didn't take the shop car this night?"

"No."

"You didn't think it was anything connected with your business?"

"I didn't know."

"Did you have any idea what this man wanted to see or speak to you about?"

"No, I did not. I had no idea whatever."

"So, you went out to see this man at eight o'clock at night, who called you up and merely told you his name was Roberts, a man you didn't know, and when you went out to meet him on the streetcar several blocks from your house, you went out without any idea in your head what he wanted to see you about?"

"I did."

"Have you ever done any such thing before?"

"No. And I was never in such a frame of mind before, Mr. Friedman."

* * *

Finally, on the afternoon of October 24, tangled up in inconsistencies, Henry made a desperate attempt to wrestle control of the narrative back from Friedman. He turned directly to the jury and gave an extraordinary speech in which he tried, falteringly, to explain why he'd kept the details he'd been describing over the last few days hidden for so long.

"Ladies and gentleman, I have been married ten years," he began. "I am proud to say that I have never laid a hand on any woman living. My wife was the only one I ever loved, and I always will stick to this."

"Miss Helen Lange came in the end of February, out from Germany. It was her sister. She tried to do her very best—she was happy and contented at home—and I will say it is a disgrace for me to say that I just simply—the temptation was there, and I went out with Helen Lange, her sister. I know I done wrong."

Henry's voice cracked with emotion as he described how he'd confessed his affair to Anna. In the jury box, Mrs. Anna Murray broke into silent tears.

"All right, Henry," Anna Wilkens had said. "Forget all about it, and we will go on another honeymoon trip. But please stay away from Helen."

And he had—he swore that he'd reconciled with his wife and broken it off with Lange, who he said had tried to stop him getting back together with Anna. After their sojourn in the hotel, Henry said he didn't see Lange again until a day or two after the murder.

"And she was like a mother to the children; I didn't have a living soul—no aunts, no uncles, on my side; no sister or brothers over here," he said. "The children liked her; it was an impossibility to throw her out of the house."

So, they settled back into a relationship of convenience and grief, but Henry knew how it would look to outsiders. "I was ashamed of what I had done. I wanted to keep it away from my children. So, when they asked me, in the district attorney's office, about going to Pacific and Broderick, I said I had not gone because I knew if I did, they would find out about Helen Lange and the thing I was ashamed of."

It was a powerful speech, and it seemed to resonate with the jury. Henry had "managed to make his statement that his wife was his only real love ring with truth or something akin to it," wrote Ernestine Black.

But Friedman wasn't finished with him. The next morning, he picked up where he had left off, hammering Henry—who looked like he hadn't slept—again and again on the same few points. Why hadn't Henry returned fire? "It was because I could not work the gun with my right hand," he shouted. "For God's sake, don't ask me those questions again, Mr. Friedman."

The prosecutor combed back through the statements Henry had made to the DA's office in June, about the whereabouts of Anna's jewelry—statements that didn't match the story he was telling now. The defendant was cracking under the pressure. "I lied!" he yelled at the end of one round of rapid-fire questions. "I lied to protect Helen Lange and because I knew it would mean much in your eyes."

A TRUE MARINER

Fierce winds lashed the ferries making their way across the bay and whipped the signal flags of the Merchant Building to stiff attention. Rain hammered the windows of Courtroom Twelve—a percussive backdrop to a stormy trial. But on Thursday, October 26, the best entertainment was on the street outside.

It started innocuously enough. Leo Friedman was cross-examining one of Frank Murphy's defense witnesses when he happened to mention that Murphy had been indicted for perjury by the grand jury just before the start of the Henry Wilkens trial, for allegedly coaching Helen Lange.

Murphy was furious. He accused Friedman and district attorney Matthew Brady of using "dastardly, cowardly" tactics to drive him off the case so Brady could secure his political future. Judge Ward had to step in. "You've had one experience in this court, Mr. Murphy," he warned.

"I can't help expressing myself. I am a human being and a man."

"You will restrain yourself, Mr. Murphy. You are going to restrain yourself if it is necessary to take a recess. If you do not, there are other methods."

But Murphy would not restrain himself, and later, Brady rose to his taunts. After one acerbic aside, Brady was on his feet, moving toward Murphy with clenched fists.

"You will keep quiet, Mr. Brady," Ward said. "If there are any difficulties between you and Mr. Murphy, they can be settled outside of this courtroom."

He probably wasn't expecting to be taken seriously. But during the lunchtime recess, while the jury were in the basement observing

Henry's yellow "death car," Brady and Murphy were on the street outside the Hall of Justice, two gray-haired men advancing on each other
with arms raised as a crowd gathered around them. They were separated by police before a punch could be thrown.

The courtroom battle had been long, and bruising too. In *The
Examiner*, Oscar Fernbach joked that at least "28.3 percent" of the four
thousand pages of transcript the trial had generated so far must consist
of bickering between opposing counsel.

There were a few final swings before the closing arguments. The
state called a cashier from Henry's bank, who said he'd taken money
out of a trust Anna had set up for the children and put it into his
personal account. Murphy promised surprise witnesses and delivered a
bizarre conspiracy theory involving private investigators pressing their
ears to the door of a hotel room where William Herron was allegedly
discussing the Wilkens case.

The prosecution denounced that as a "futile attempt to befog the
main issues of the case," and they were right. It highlighted how desperate Murphy was to make his conspiracy story stick, despite any corroborating evidence, and it gave Leo Friedman the ideal place to begin
his final assault.

* * *

Each side would get an unlimited amount of time to sum up their case,
followed by a brief final statement before it was handed over to the
jury to deliberate. Over the next two days, in a twelve-hour speech
that lasted the remainder of Tuesday and all day Wednesday, Friedman
patiently, methodically, and eloquently dismantled the defense's case.

He started by accusing Murphy of trying to, at every turn, "inject
into the record matters that had nothing whatever to do with the guilt
or innocence of Henry Wilkens." He trashed the "ridiculous and unbe-
lievable" evidence from Louis Burkhart, the interior decorator who was
briefly Arthur Castor's cellmate.

Murphy looked grave, and Henry squirmed in his seat as Friedman
described him as a wife beater and bruiser who had violated moral
and ethical law by striking up a relationship with his sister-in-law. He

talked about how, whenever Anna complained to friends about the way he treated her, Henry would use the excuse that his wife was "crazy or drunk."

"There were three concerned in the death of Anna Wilkens," Friedman said, echoing Henry's original statement to the police. "But they were not all in the Hudson car. Two of them were in that car, and the third sat next to Anna Wilkens in the Premier."

Friedman asked the jury why Henry—a skillful driver in a much faster car—hadn't been able to escape the Castors in the rented Hudson that night and why, if it was truly a random holdup, the brothers had bothered renting a car and driving all the way to Felton when there were surely greater riches in the city itself.

He asked them why Henry, who pulled out his gun when he thought his wife was being robbed, was not ready to take revenge on the man who shot her. "The highwayman shot Wilkens's wife. Then he turned and ran," Friedman said. "And did Wilkens, the man who was boiling up with rage, shoot him in the back as he ran? He did not. What did he do? Ladies and gentlemen, he put the pistol back in its pocket.

"That is the story of the holdup," Friedman continued. "He didn't stop at a house. He didn't rush for assistance. He was a member of an unholy trinity bent on the destruction of this woman, and he wanted to delay her getting to a physician long enough to accomplish his purpose. That is the story. A lie from start to finish."

And finally, with his voice ringing clearly around a courtroom that he'd held transfixed in a tense silence, the young prosecutor asked the jury to find Henry guilty and to sentence him to death.

* * *

Frank Murphy stood up the next morning facing one of the biggest challenges of his career. Friedman's speech had been electric—as spectators filed out of the courtroom, they were heard describing it as one of the best seen in the Hall of Justice in years.

"Ladies and gentlemen of the jury," Murphy began in response, "one of the greatest responsibilities I have ever assumed in my life has been defending Henry Wilkens against all sorts of opposition and all kinds of obstacles that have been placed in my way. If my footsteps have faltered, if I have at times been disappointed, I have been buoyed up by the knowledge that Henry Wilkens was innocent, and I stood between him and a band of hungry wolves who sought to destroy him.

"When I thought of the two little children rendered motherless by the murderous hand of Walter Castor, I felt that I would be shirking my professional responsibility if I did not see to it that they were not rendered worse than motherless by the perjury of Arthur Castor," he said.

Over the next five hours, Murphy walked a tightrope between sympathy and sarcasm—pulling on the jury's heartstrings while excoriating the testimony of Arthur Castor and throwing doubt on the motives of the prosecution's other witnesses.

"We have listened to this veritable Niagara of words from the lips of Mr. Friedman," he said. "We have been submerged in a sea of language, and the storm has thrown us off our course. And as a true mariner, it will be my purpose, through this hurricane of words, to again establish a true course which would lead you to a correct verdict."

He dismissed the swathes of evidence about Henry's relationship with Helen Lange and his treatment of Anna. "Henry Wilkens is on trial for murder, not for infidelity nor for adultery nor for battery on his wife," he said. "It seems to me that these incidents have been thrown in here, not so much to prove motive, but to prejudice the jury."

And then he came to the crux of his case. You could put aside the wrangling over names and dates and secret meetings—this was the one thing that Henry's fate rested on more than anything else. "The fact that the prosecution cannot get away from in this case here is that it begins and ends with Arthur Castor," Murphy said. "He is the foundation of this case, the cornerstone—if you do not believe him, there is nothing left to this case. There is nothing on which the prosecution can ask you to convict."

Finally, on Friday, November 3, after 119 witnesses and six weeks of arguments and tears and tension, the case was handed over to the jury. There had been a brief final statement from Murphy for the defense and a much longer one from the returning prosecutor, Isidore Golden, its length seemingly determined by how long he could talk before his throat started hurting.

Murphy pointed out the imbalance between prosecution and defense—the "heavy burden" of going up against three or four members of the DA's office, plus a cadre of police officers ready to run down new leads and interview potential witnesses as their names came up in court.

He said he was representing not just Henry Wilkens but his children too—and he asked the jury to consider the consequences to Henry Jr. and Helen of branding their father the murderer of their mother. "Henry Wilkens is not asking for sympathy," Murphy said while looking for it. "He is not asking for mercy. He is asking for justice."

Golden had the last word. "The cry of 'frame-up' is the ancient and worn-out defense of every criminal," he said after an impassioned defense of the district attorney's office—not "human wolves," but guardians against those who have "transgressed the law of God and man."

Only then did he turn his attention to Henry—demanding a verdict of first-degree murder and the death penalty. "His every word has been a lie," he said. "His grief has been faked, his illness feigned. He has 'pulled the sob stuff' in order to try to influence you jurors. He is the greatest actor I have ever seen in this Hall of Justice. He fooled the chief of police, he fooled the captain of detectives, he fooled everybody until we found out the truth."

* * *

At 5:40 PM, Judge Ward dismissed the alternate jurors and then spent half an hour giving the remaining twelve strict instructions on the points of law around the case, plus the three verdicts they could choose from: first-degree murder, second-degree murder, and not guilty.

The jurors filed out of the courtroom, which remained packed with spectators, hopeful of a quick verdict. But as the evening wore on, the crowd thinned. By eight fifteen, when the jury returned from dinner, only a third of the seats were occupied. A group of women chatted, knit, and shot "expectant glances" at the door to the jury room. By midnight, there was still no verdict, and the jury was sequestered for the night, under police guard, at the Washington Hotel.

Rumors seeped out anyway. The jurors had taken seven votes, some said, and the running tally stood at ten to two in favor of conviction. On the other hand, dismissed alternate juror Herman Schroeder had told *The Examiner* he would have voted not guilty. "I would not believe the testimony of convicts and jailbirds," he said.

At nine thirty the next morning, Henry Wilkens was brought from his cell and placed in his usual seat in the courtroom, with Frank Murphy at this side. At eleven forty-five, Ward sent for the jury. They still hadn't reached a verdict, but they had taken several votes, and foreman Howard Tibbetts was hopeful. They asked for lunch to be sent to the jury room.

At around four PM, after almost twelve hours of deliberation, the jury returned to the courtroom again. "Have you reached a verdict?" Ward asked.

"We have not," said Tibbetts. "The vote stands six to six and has been unchanged for ten ballots. There is no hope of coming to a decision."

The jury was hopelessly deadlocked. The first ballot had been seven to five for acquittal, but all ten after that had been tied—paper-box manufacturer H. A. A. Muhs was the only one to change his mind. All three women voted to acquit.

At four forty-five PM on Saturday, November 4, Judge Ward reluctantly discharged the jury. There would be an expensive retrial, and the whole circus would start again in a few months.

Henry sat back in his chair as the verdict was announced. He had many more months to endure in prison, but took heart from the fact that six jurors—seven if you included the alternate—thought him not guilty. "I am innocent," he said. "The next trial will prove it."

Brady declined to comment, but Isidore Golden told *The Chronicle* that his colleagues at the DA's office were more convinced than ever that Henry was guilty.

For the jurors, who were seized upon by reporters like ravenous seagulls swooping in the bay, neither side had come across well. Most had made up their minds long before closing arguments began, said juror Kathlyn McKee. Horace Rice, who had also voted not guilty, leaned on "reasonable doubt" to explain his decision. Tibbetts said the six who had voted guilty considered Henry's testimony a "tissue of lies."

The twelve divided jurors did agree on one thing: they didn't trust either Arthur Castor or Henry Wilkens. "It was a hard case to decide," said Tibbetts. "There was so much untruth, and there were so many lies on both sides."

BRIDGE OF SIGHS

It was a long winter. Soon after the trial, Frank Murphy suffered a collapse "brought on by his strenuous efforts on behalf of Henry Wilkens." He spent a few days recovering his strength at a health resort, and then one night in jail.

The contempt charges he and William Herron picked up early in the trial had been bumped back in a succession of Saturday hearings, but in November both men finally surrendered to serve their twenty-four hours behind bars.

Murphy made something of an event out of it. On the morning of November 17, when reporters found him at his office gathering together cigars and reading material to take into his cell at the Hall of Justice, he'd promised new sensations in the retrial. "Within the next few days, I shall make public some revelations about the Wilkens case which will amaze the citizens of San Francisco," he said.

During Murphy's brief incarceration, friends sent him—presumably as a joke—a giant wreath in the shape of a horseshoe that was almost as tall and wide as he was, and had a banner reading "GOOD LUCK, FRANK" in large capital letters. Murphy wasn't allowed to take it to his cell, so the floral display was set up on the "bridge of sighs" leading to the federal wing, from where it scented the halls of the prison.

The rest of 1922 passed in a battle of affidavits and delays. The retrial was initially scheduled for November 27 but was pushed back by illness, scheduling conflicts, and the holidays, so it wasn't until February 1923 that the group of weary lawyers gathered in front of Judge Ward to begin again.

The retrial followed largely the same pattern as the first. Arthur and Robert Castor took the stand again, followed by Helen Lange. There were tears and tantrums—again, Henry got emotional when his sister-in-law took the stand, and found it hard to control his temper under cross-examination. But overall, it was a much more subdued affair.

The frenzied press interest had died down—the news cycle had moved on, and the papers were no longer sending their star columnists into the courtroom to drink in every word.

Most of the witnesses were the same, and even Henry's account of the shooting had been smoothed by repeated retellings and shorn of its inconsistencies—although he still cried when he told it.

On Wednesday, March 7, over the vigorous objections of Frank Murphy, information about the divorce suit Anna had filed was introduced into evidence for the first time.

Two days later, Leo Friedman began the prosecution's final arguments. He spoke for a day and three-quarters, finishing on Monday afternoon by asking the jury to find Henry guilty of first-degree murder without recommendation—a verdict that would mean death by hanging.

Murphy stood up on Tuesday, March 13, to plead again for his client's life. He attacked the "tottering and perjured story of Arthur Castor" and drew laughter from spectators as he ridiculed the state's case.

He tried to twist the prosecution's evidence in Henry's favor—arguing, for instance, that if Henry really had taken Anna's rings on the night of the murder, he probably wouldn't have hidden the evidence in an unlocked drawer in his own home. Henry's temper was also a sign of his innocence, Murphy said, because "those quick to anger are slow at plotting."

The jury was handed the case at five minutes past four on Thursday, March 15, 1923. By eleven fifteen PM, they had taken ten ballots and were reportedly split nine to three, although in which direction, no one knew. "Absolutely no chance for a verdict tonight," the foreman told Ward. "May we send for our nightclothes?"

There was still no verdict by two PM the next day. Alternate juror John Gray told *The Examiner* he would have voted to convict. Henry sat nervously in his cell. He looked pale and unwell.

That afternoon, when the jurors asked Judge Ward for some clarification on the law concerning reasonable doubt, he called their attention to the cost of two trials and told them they must "exhaust every effort to reach a verdict."

But they seemed hopelessly deadlocked, and so when they knocked on the door of the jury room at about six thirty PM with the news that they had actually come to a decision, it was so unexpected that the courtroom was almost empty. None of the key players from the DA's office were even there.

As the jurors filed back into their seats, a few of them glanced over at Henry. He kept his eyes fixed on the jury box.

"Have you reached a verdict?" asked Ward.

"We have," said foreman Bruce Gibson.

He handed a slip of paper to the judge, who read it with an inscrutable expression and then handed it back. Gibson read aloud.

"We, the jury in the above entitled case, find the defendant, Henry Wilkens, not guilty as charged."

A smile crept across Henry's face. After ten months of suspicion and twelve weeks of sitting in court across two trials, he was a free man.

The unanimous verdict had been something of a shock, even to the members of the jury. The first seven ballots they took were all seven to five in favor of acquittal. After Judge Ward spoke to them about the cost of a third trial and urged them to reach a verdict, they took another ballot, and two jurors had switched sides. Two more switched by the ninth ballot, and by the tenth, all twelve agreed to find Henry not guilty.

Ward addressed the jury. "Ladies and gentlemen," he said, "you have reached a verdict, and though I will say that it does not meet my judgment in the matter, still I do not criticize any member who voted not guilty. I only say that if I had been in the room, I would have voted differently."

As the men and women who had settled his client's fate left the courtroom, Murphy thanked each of them profusely. "Congratulations, gentleman," said bank teller William Novakovich who walked over to shake the defendant's hand.

"I have been vindicated," an elated Henry told reporters. "I can now go home to my little kiddies, a free man without disgrace."

At that moment, the kids were at the home of Henry and Marie Crossfield, family friends who'd been looking after them since Henry Wilkens's arrest in July. They'd been in the courtroom earlier that day but had gone home, believing they were unlikely to hear a verdict that evening. So, they were stunned when a liberated Henry walked into their house on Twenty-Fourth Street with Frank Murphy alongside him.

Henry Jr. and Helen rushed to meet their father, jumping into his open arms. "Daddy! Oh, Daddy, is it you, really and truly, Daddy, is it you?"

Henry seemed dazed. Tears streamed down his cheeks, and he held his children close to his chest and sunk slowly to the floor. He sat there in that tight embrace for twenty minutes of contented silence until Marie Crossfield tenderly loosened his arms, and he moved to a chair. Then he scooped the kids up again for another round of hugs and kisses.

"Are you going to stay home with us now, Daddy?" Helen asked.

"Yes, dear," Henry replied, voice trembling. "I'm going to stay with you all the time."

A photographer captured the happy scene. Henry, who looked like he'd aged a decade in ten months, shook hands with a beaming Murphy while his son—dressed in a short-sleeved white shirt, tugged insistently at his sleeve. Murphy perched on the edge of a table, where little Helen—in a white dress, with her bright hair cut short—knelt by his side and planted a grateful kiss on his cheek.

"My acquittal I owe solely to my faithful friend and counsel, Mr. Murphy, whom my children and I will never forget," Henry had told reporters at the Hall of Justice. "I am going right home to my kiddies now, and Mr. Murphy is going with me."

But a week later, Murphy was dead.

TRUTH SERUM

Something had gone horribly wrong. Within days of the second trial ending, the jurors' stories began to leak out, and it became clear that the amazing late swing to a unanimous verdict of acquittal was not because of a change of heart, but due to a serious miscommunication between the judge and the jury.

When Judge Ward told the jurors that they must try their utmost to reach a verdict, they thought that he was ordering them to vote for acquittal. "The reason for having suddenly reached a verdict after an agreement had appeared impossible was that the jury felt that Judge Ward's last instructions were preponderantly in favor of the defendant," said one juror. "I guess that we were mistaken, however, in view of Judge Ward's later remarks that he would have voted guilty."

When they learned that they had misinterpreted the judge's instructions, the five jurors who changed their votes were distraught. Ward was perplexed by this turn of events. "I fail to see how the jury could have read in my instructions any ground for the acquittal of Henry Wilkens," he said. In any case, it was too late—a draw and then a defeat was a damaging result for District Attorney Matthew Brady, who had no recourse for an appeal.

Henry wasn't entirely in the clear, however. An organization called the Women's Vigilance Committee was pressing for him and Helen Lange to be kicked out of the United States as "undesirable citizens."

It was a sentiment shared by some of the jurors. "The least punishment he and Miss Lange should get is to be deported," said Lillian Gray, who wished she could change her vote. "I was hysterical and thought myself convinced of his innocence, but a few minutes later

I regretted my action and realized that I should have hung out for a guilty verdict," she said. "I was weak; I am ashamed of myself; there is no excuse for me."

Katherine Ringen—an alternate juror who had joined the panel halfway through the trial—believed the verdict might have been different if Ward's instructions had been interpreted properly. "As it is, Wilkens will have to watch his step now, even if he is free," she said. "His intimacy with Helen Lange probably bore some weight with the jury. I believe it would be a good idea to deport them, at least from California."

These calls quickly faded away, which was fortunate for Henry, because six days after the trial he found himself without an attorney when Frank Murphy dropped dead.

His doctors blamed an "acute dilation of the heart" brought on by incessant work on back-to-back murder trials for hastening his death. There was a hint of scandal—Murphy wasn't at home with his wife, Nonie, and his thirteen-year-old daughter when he died, but at the house of Rose Helm, a beautiful twenty-nine-year-old former nurse.

When the contents of Murphy's recently signed will were revealed, it emerged that he had left his wife just $1 and bequeathed the bulk of his $70,000 estate to Helm, including Henry's yellow Premier, which had been signed over to him as part payment for legal fees.

Henry spent the next few months battling with Murphy's estate to try and get his car back. At the same time, he was trying to rebuild his shattered life and make a fresh start somewhere outside San Francisco—and he found the unlikeliest of allies.

* * *

Throughout 1922 and 1923, John Larson conducted hundreds more lie detector tests as he honed his skills as an investigator and continued his efforts to scientifically validate the device. But he couldn't stop thinking about the Wilkens case.

He viewed it as a spectacular public failure for the lie detector. He was furious at the newspapers for sensationalizing the machine, and vowed never to talk to them about an ongoing case again. Although the results of his test tallied with the eventual findings of the jury, he felt in his heart that Henry was guilty—and Keeler and Vollmer agreed when they looked at the chart. Larson feared that his test, although it hadn't been introduced as evidence, had somehow influenced the trial.

So, all through the summer after the lie detector test, he kept in "close touch" with Henry. "Allow me to congratulate you on the termination of your trial, as well as to offer commiserations for the death of your friend," Larson wrote to Wilkens on March 27, 1923, less than two weeks after the acquittal. "I would be glad to see you at any time that you can get over onto this side. If you do find time to get over, ring me up and make an appointment."

In his book, Larson describes this as the natural next step in his investigation—but it's a staggering admission. He had designed the lie detector to be an objective, scientific instrument, but at the first obstacle he reached, Larson abandoned his impartiality by getting too close to the subject. By doing so, he set a pattern that has been repeated countless times since, across several different types of so-called lie detector.

After Henry was released, he left San Francisco, and Larson helped him find a job in Oakland, where he lived under an assumed name, to shield his children from the notoriety of the case.

Larson struck up a closer friendship, hoping to get to the truth. He "spent considerable time driving Wilkens about while he was looking for a house, using this opportunity to study his personality," he wrote.

You can almost picture the two men cruising around Berkeley together at the start of that long summer of 1923, outwardly friendly and cordial, but each secretly suspecting the other's motives—every word and pause carefully chosen, every facial expression and casual remark analyzed and reanalyzed. Henry Wilkens, a cold-blooded killer or a grief-stricken victim, depending on who you believed, and John Larson, a scientist and detective so desperate to be proven right that he had abandoned his scientific principles.

Eventually, Larson managed to talk Henry into taking another lie detector test—in private this time—but again he was disappointed. "The second record showed no essential differences from the first,"

Larson wrote. He didn't try to extract a confession, and he kept his own views on the case to himself. "More than once Wilkens volunteered statements to the effect that the test was much better than the writer realized," Larson insisted. But he still wasn't satisfied—and he made one last, desperate attempt to get to the truth.

* * *

A few years earlier, an obstetrician from rural Texas, called Robert House, had begun using the drug scopolamine as a form of "truth serum." The substance was normally given to women to ease the pain and dull the memory of childbirth, but House noticed that on receiving it, some of his patients fell into a suggestible state, somewhere between wakefulness and sleep, in which they could still answer questions despite being apparently unconscious.

On one occasion, at a home birth in 1916, he asked a patient's husband for scales to weigh the baby, and the woman, "still deep in twilight sleep," gave their precise location. "They are in the kitchen on a nail behind the picture," she said.

By 1922, House was convinced that scopolamine could be used to "make anyone tell the truth on any question"—he thought the drug might make it easier to coax suspects into revealing truths their conscious minds would rather stayed locked away. "The drug numbs the conscious will," House told reporters. "With this dormant, the subconscious mind will respond to facts. Questions propounded to a patient under such a condition invariably bring truthful answers. In more than five hundred cases, there is yet to be recorded a failure." It was remarkably similar to the rhetoric John Larson spun about the lie detector.

In June 1923, House visited San Francisco to give a talk on his findings at the American Medical Association and to test the drug on prisoners at San Quentin State Prison. In early June, Larson—who knew House was in the area and looking for "test material"—wrote to the doctor, asking whether he would use the truth serum on Henry Wilkens.

Remarkably, Henry also agreed—*The Los Angeles Times* suggested this was because he was "unsatisfied with the popular opinion of the verdict" and wanted to clear his name in the court of public opinion so he could go back to something approaching a normal life. "I am going to take every step to establish my honesty in the community," he said.

On the night of June 25—almost a year to the day since Arthur Castor's confession had changed the course of the murder investigation—Henry lay on a bed at Temple Hospital in Berkeley. Larson and August Vollmer watched as House, a severe, bald man with dark circles around his eyes, began the test by injecting the drug into Henry's left arm with a hypodermic needle. Another injection followed ten minutes later, and then a third.

The aim was to keep Henry just hovering in the suggestible state at the edge of unconsciousness that House called the "receptive stage." An hour after the first dose, he could no longer recognize familiar objects—a watch, a bottle, a knife. Two hours in, he was able to talk fluently and clearly.

Vollmer and Larson fired more than two hundred questions at a semi-somnolent Henry, but he stuck to the facts he'd told at the trial. There was one "interesting statement," Larson noted, as Henry was falling under the spell of the anesthetic. "I'm going to fool them," he had said. "I'll answer them in German."

House told Larson that he'd initially been inclined to judge Henry guilty because of that statement, but at the end of the test—after four hours of questioning that carried on until two AM—he was satisfied that Henry had given the truth.

Vollmer was impressed and christened the drug the "fourth degree"—a cleaner, better way of getting to the truth than even the lie detector. But Larson wasn't convinced. "That did not prove anything to me," he wrote. Henry had repeated statements that were proven false during the trial, and Larson knew from his interactions with him over the previous few months that he'd lied on several other questions, including denying that he'd had sex with his housekeeper. "If he could keep back one fact, he could also lie about the murder," Larson told Vollmer in April 1927. "The more I look at the record, the more confused I become, as I do not know whether the disturbances are due to his fear of detection, [or] his antipathy at the way he was being handled by the police, having been accused by the papers, etc."

Ultimately, Larson admitted to Vollmer that, with more experience, he would not have judged Henry as innocent, based on the record he gave in that first lie detector test. It was only the polygraph's second murder case, and both men agreed that it would have been unfair for an inexperienced operator to give a definite guilty verdict when the interpretation was so doubtful. But Larson doubled down, arguing that he would have gotten to the correct verdict if only he'd been able to test the Castor brothers, Brady, Murphy, and all the witnesses on both sides.

In October 1923, Larson left the Berkeley Police Department and moved to Chicago to take an academic job at the Institute for Juvenile Research. But four years later, he was still mulling over the Wilkens case. He wrote to Vollmer to try and arrange for Leonarde Keeler to run Henry on his improved machine, to see if that might provide a clearer record. "I have figured up a preamble which should tip him over if he were guilty as Keeler and Bill [Wiltberger] figure from his record, and I am inclined to agree with them if W[ilkens] is a normal individual. If we did and kept publicity out, there could be no ill-feelings on the part of S.F. officials."

* * *

With his name cleared by polygraph, truth serum, and jury, Henry slowly faded into anonymity—the newspapers recording only his efforts to get his beloved yellow car back, a $10 fine for speeding in 1924 and a strange incident in 1925, when he was accused of being a corrupting influence on his housekeeper's son, who stole a pistol from Henry and shot a police officer with it. The boy told of liquor-fueled parties in Henry's basement flat.

Eventually, Henry rebuilt his life as a mechanic. In October 1928, he dropped in to see Vollmer in his office while on holiday in California. He was driving a brand-new Packard 8 and was "sitting on top of the world," the chief told Larson regarding his "old friend."

Henry had set up successful businesses in Vancouver and Seattle, where he was living with his new wife. "She appears to be a very solid sort of woman, and they are quite happy," Vollmer reported. "His wife told me that he had a nervous breakdown about a year or so ago but is entirely recovered and now seems to be doing quite well."

If only Larson could have moved on so easily. "When I get out there, I want to renew my acquaintance with Wilkens and clean up certain matters," he replied. He never really stopped hoping for a resolution to the case. "There is still the possibility that someday this case will be cleared up," he wrote in his book in 1932. "Either by the confession of Wilkens, if guilty, since he is now immune to punishment, or, if innocent, by the confession of Castor that his story was a frame-up."

Henry Wilkens died of a heart attack at Stanford Hospital in 1953. He never did confess, and his case established a pattern of hype, premature use, and failure that's been repeated every time a new form of so-called lie detection has been invented.

The Wilkens case was the lie detector's first public failure. It made John Larson seriously doubt the wisdom of the machine he had created. Unfortunately, his protégé Leonarde Keeler's own ambitions knew no bounds—and he was about to take the polygraph out of the courtroom and spread it across America and then the world.

FIRE AND VENOM

Berkeley was burning. The grasslands to the east of town had been baked dry by the heat of a California summer, and on the morning of September 17, 1923, residents noticed a strange amber hue to the air and the smell of torched eucalyptus floating on the wind.

At around two PM that afternoon, the fire that was growing in the canyon swept over the hills in a half-mile wall of destruction. Charles Keeler's stylish wooden home had spawned many imitators in North Berkeley's richer neighborhoods, but the architectural wonderland was also a tinderbox. As the inferno grew stronger, the cedar shingles on the roofs of the houses "literally exploded," spreading the flames further.

Leonarde Keeler was one of the first on the scene, with his friend and hiking companion Ralph Brandt. The pair went from house to house, racing the flames to make sure the occupants made it out. They rescued a woman who refused to leave her new car and an old man who didn't want to abandon his burning house and "resisted so violently that the boys were obliged to knock him unconscious before they could carry him out."

Eventually, reinforcements arrived from San Francisco—troops of firefighters on ferries across the bay—but they found only chaos and dry hydrants. By the time the blaze was extinguished, with the help of a humid ocean breeze, more than six hundred buildings were destroyed and four thousand people were homeless. It was a miracle no one died.

Keeler liberated a truck from a burning garage and ferried refugees and their belongings to safety on the university campus. For days afterward, the nineteen-year-old helped his father in the relief effort, carrying messages and supplies to police officers in the burned-out neighborhoods.

As the town recovered, dust and smoke particles hung in the air for weeks, turning the pristine facade of City Hall a dull gray and wreaking havoc with Keeler's sinuses, which had been prone to flare-ups ever since the childhood infection that had almost killed him.

Keeler had just started college in his hometown, with the aim of becoming a doctor, but predictably, he was not a model pupil. He was sharp and intelligent but spent more time in the basement of City Hall with the lie detector, or tinkering with his machines and his menagerie in his cabin in the woods, than he ever did at class. He missed the popularity he'd enjoyed at University High—"he resented wearing a freshman beanie, hazing by upper class students, and the pressures to conform," recalled his sister Eloise.

And he was lonely. His high school sweetheart had married someone else, and his two closest friends—Ralph Brandt and Elwood "Doc" Woolsey, who he'd known since his Boy Scout days—had transferred to the "Southern Branch" of the university, better known today as UCLA.

They weren't the only ones who had moved to Los Angeles. In the spring of 1923, as the Henry Wilkens case was drawing to its dramatic conclusion, August Vollmer was approached by a secret delegation from the southern city, asking him to take over as chief of police. They were impressed by the work he'd done in Berkeley, they said, and wanted his help ridding Los Angeles of "vice and crooks."

Vollmer was initially reluctant. He felt guilty about abandoning Berkeley and leaving his girlfriend Pat Fell, an old flame he'd bumped into again while in San Francisco preparing for the policing conference the previous summer. Eventually, though, he agreed to go on loan for a year on a much higher salary, with the option of returning to Berkeley if things didn't work out.

He arrived in Los Angeles on August 1, 1923, ready to enact sweeping changes but facing a huge challenge. He was stepping up from a town of forty thousand to a metropolis of eight hundred thousand, and from a force with twenty-four officers to one with more than two thousand.

In his first few months, he reorganized the department, created a 250-strong squad of "crime crushers," and raised $1.6 million to hire more officers and build more jails. But Vollmer also met resistance from the city's power structures—corrupt politicians and lazy police officers colluding with criminals for financial gain; gangs and unions and the Klan all working against him.

He thought the lie detector might offer one potential route through the mire, and so he was delighted when Keeler agreed to transfer south in the winter of 1923, after being advised by his doctor that a warmer climate might help his breathing. In October, Keeler moved, with his friends Woolsey and Brandt, into a one-room shack on an empty lot in Hollywood, its shelves groaning with snakeskins and books and camping equipment.

Keeler found LA fascinating and appalling. It was not a city, he thought, but "an overgrown, weed-like village, that has spread all over the landscape." It was a "crook's paradise" and a lesson in human psychology, from the sprawling suburbs where the nouveau riche built their homes, to the con artists he encountered at the auction houses. "You can get more knowledge of the inside workings of people's brains in one of those sales in five minutes than you could from a year's study of some dry professor's book," he told his father. He doubted even the chief's ability to clean things up. "Unless the city officials can do away with the cause, I can't see how Vollmer can do away with the effect," he wrote. "It's like trying to cure a stomachache with a hot water bottle when the real cause is appendicitis."

During his last months in Berkeley, Keeler had been considering ways to improve the lie detector. With Woolsey and Brandt's help, he drew up plans for a more compact and precise version of the machine that would be easier to transport and that used ink pens and ordinary white paper.

When they were done, Keeler took the plans to Vollmer, who looked them over from behind the mahogany desk in his new office at the LAPD. "Go ahead and build it, Nard," the chief said. "I'll give you a chance to try it out."

For weeks, the three young men—who dubbed themselves the "Three Musketeers"—toiled on the instrument, with the aid of a professional mechanic the chief recommended. "But while we all helped, Nard did by far the greater part of the work," Woolsey said. "It was definitely his invention."

It was a trying time. The boys couldn't afford rent, food, and the cost of parts for the machine. They siphoned electricity from their neighbors to test it. Keeler was tearing through what was left of his inheritance from his mother, and Woolsey and Brandt flipped a coin to decide who would have to go out and get a part-time job (Brandt lost). Eventually, Keeler's father, Charles, had to send a check.

Finally, in January 1924, the new lie detector was ready. Ticker tape wound crazily through a tangle of wires, with a naked bulb at one end. But despite its looks, it was an improvement on Larson's original model. It could give an absolute reading of blood pressure instead of a relative one, allowing an examiner to quantify precisely how much of a change a particular question triggered.

Keeler would improve it further in the years that followed—creating a sleek enclosure and adding a mechanism that automatically marked the chart when each answer was given, and a system to counteract fidgeting and thwart those who tried to trick the test by tensing their muscles on the control questions.

For now, he nervously presented his work to Vollmer, who was secretly rather unimpressed. "That first machine of Nard's looked like a crazy conglomeration of wires, tubes, and old tomato cans," Vollmer said. "But I kept my promise."

That same night, Vollmer led Keeler to an interrogation room at Central Police Station in LA, to test his new machine on a murder suspect. "We feel sure he's guilty," Vollmer said. "But so far we have no proof."

It was January 24, 1924, and the suspect was Bert Vernon, a landlord accused of shooting one of his tenants in a row over eviction. It was the first lie detector test conducted in the city, and a crowd of interested reporters and officers gathered as Keeler fastened his new equipment to Vernon.

He ran several rounds of questions, each time pointing out the places on the chart where he thought the record showed deception. Finally, Vernon nodded slowly. "You're right," he said. "I lied."

The crowd "surged into the room." Reporters peppered Keeler and Vollmer with questions, and cameras flashed. The chief paid Keeler $25 for his efforts and told him that "from here on out he could have all the cases he could handle."

It was a triumphant moment for the "Three Musketeers," who celebrated with a "huge roast beef dinner," according to Eloise's probably exaggerated account. "As they left the restaurant," she wrote, "newsboys were shouting, 'Extra! Extra! All about the lie detector. Murder suspect confesses! Read all about it!'"

There was no spare room in the police department, so Vollmer set Keeler up with a makeshift office in one of the jail cells—to enter or leave, he had to summon a guard. From there, Keeler ran tests on "suspected murderers, burglars, rapists, bootleggers, and owners of gambling joints."

"Subject material was plentiful, and I was fortunate enough to have some of the keenest criminals of the south attempt to fool the machine and so gain their freedom," he wrote. "Santa Barbara, San Diego, and Bakersfield added their share of material."

* * *

At around nine PM on Saturday, March 8, 1924, Keeler arrived home from working on a case, put some water on the stove to heat, and then stepped outside to talk to Woolsey and Brandt, who had spent the day tinkering with the lie detector.

A few minutes later, Keeler noticed a pink glow at his feet and looked up to find the "entire interior" of the shack in flames—the fire started by the stove, or perhaps as a result of the "bootlegging" of electricity they'd done to test the device. All their possessions were destroyed, including the prototype lie detector. Keeler quickly began work on a new and improved version. But the sharks were starting to circle.

When he'd first arrived in LA, before moving in with his friends, Keeler had stayed with Hiram Edwards, a family friend and UCLA physics professor. Edwards was a helpful ally for the redesign of the lie detector—he helped Keeler build a better version of the "tambour," the crucial link between the tubes measuring breathing and the pens that recorded the results. But Edwards wanted to race ahead on commercialization—and Keeler didn't think the device was ready for that yet, and he didn't want anyone else muscling in on what he was increasingly starting to think of as "his" machine.

"It seems to me that this work is altogether too much in its infancy to start anything in a commercial way; and besides, my interest is more in the results obtained than in the actual mechanics," Keeler wrote to Larson, who was in full agreement.

"You did right to keep out of the commercial proposition of Edwards, for I think it would ruin you scientifically," he replied.

As Keeler rebuilt the machine after the fire, he turned to another family friend for help. Charles Sloan was the crime editor of the *LA Times* and a skilled machinist, and Keeler moved in with him so the pair could work in Sloan's workshop. Together, they built a new, more reliable version of the device, which ran on AC power—but Keeler's time with Sloan also opened his eyes to the lie detector's dark potential.

* * *

In April 1924, the two men drove 130 miles north, to the isolated hamlet of Los Olivos, to play their part in an elaborate scheme involving a neighborhood feud, an unsolved murder, and the Ku Klux Klan.

William Downs, the local postmaster, was accused of murdering his neighbor John McGuire, a disheveled blacksmith who'd been engaged in a decade-long battle with most of the settlement's hundred residents.

Things came to a head when the unpopular McGuire started spreading rumors that Downs had sexually assaulted his own children, and then pulled a gun on him in his shop. Downs called the police, and McGuire spent a month in the Santa Barbara Jail.

Three days after he returned home, in December 1923, McGuire was killed by a terrific explosion that destroyed his house and severed his legs. The circumstances were more than suspicious—not one of the locals rushed to McGuire's aid, even though the blast was so loud it could be heard thirty miles away in Santa Barbara. There was a freshly dug trench running from the Downs property to McGuire's that could have been used for a fuse, and before he died, McGuire—who had been dragged from the wreckage by telephone workers—accused Downs of orchestrating his demise.

But without the cooperation of locals, the investigation stalled for four months, until the district attorney's office decided to set a trap. Willard Kemp, the DA's new assistant, was also the head of the local chapter of the KKK. He told Downs the best way to avoid prosecution would be to get in tight with the local police by joining the Klan. To do that, Kemp told him, he would need to go through an initiation ceremony.

But it was just a ruse to get him on the lie detector. Keeler and Sloan donned Klan robes and joined twenty real members of the group in the initiation room for the fake ceremony. Downs was led in and strapped to the apparatus. "Mr. Downs, we have received certain objections to your candidacy, and for this reason this machine was brought from Los Angeles," Keeler said in the deep slow voice he adopted for lie detector tests. "In the solemn secrecy of this room, you may answer the questions put to you without fear or favor, for we must ask you, that the records of this organization may be kept clear of all unworthy names, questions pertaining to the death last December of John J. McGuire. Have you any objection to the test?"

Downs had been blindsided. He had no choice but to agree to the test—although he denied any knowledge of the murder. Keeler switched to a testing protocol known as the guilty knowledge test.

The examiner runs through various options, the theory being that the closer they get to the truth, the stronger the subject's physiological response will be. Larson honed it in Berkeley, practicing on the homeless by trying to determine their state of origin.

Keeler read Downs the names of twenty-five locals suspected to have played a part in the killing. He examined the charts and singled out five men for further interrogation. A posse was sent to round them up, and after thirty-six hours of uninterrupted questioning, Keeler had elicited strong reactions from two men: wealthy rancher William Crawford and machine shop owner Harvey Stonebarger. After another thirty-six hours of interrogation, Stonebarger fell to his knees in tears and told Keeler that Downs had planned the murder with his father, and he'd helped them lay the charge. It was, Sloan told Larson, "one case which the district attorney admits would never have been solved without the machine."

But at trial, the men were acquitted. On the stand, Stonebarger recanted his confession and accused the prosecution of resorting to "inhuman third-degree" techniques in their use of the lie detector. Keeler didn't think he'd done anything wrong, but Larson was horrified by his protégé's "clowning tactics."

In Larson's view, this was exactly the kind of outcome he'd created the lie detector to prevent. He likened it to torture. "It is better to lose the material than to have to resort to these methods," he wrote.

* * *

By the fall of 1924, August Vollmer had worn out his welcome in Los Angeles—and he was worn out himself, tired of the constant battles with his own officers, sick of the politics.

Billboards had appeared around the city, funded by the gloating underworld kingpins he'd tried to eradicate: "The first of September will be the last of August." His enemies even cooked up a sex scandal involving a woman named Charlotte Lex, who claimed Vollmer had broken a promise to marry her and sued him for $50,000. He moved back to Berkeley.

Keeler left LA not long afterward—not least because, without Vollmer, he'd lost a valuable source of income. The Three Musketeers all transferred from UCLA to Stanford, where Woolsey and Keeler developed an unusual business to help pay their tuition.

They kept thirty fully grown rattlesnakes in cages on the second floor of an abandoned water tower behind their cottage. Keeler fed them hamburger meat through a bicycle pump, and every other week he carefully "milked" them of their venom—prying open the mouth with a forked stick and using pincers to squeeze the viscous yellow poison into glass jars, which they sold to a company that used it to make antidote.

Keeler still had his sights set on becoming a doctor, but he continued to neglect his studies (his grades at UCLA were so poor that his father had to write to the dean to get him transferred to Stanford). He dodged class in favor of an impressive range of extracurricular activities, from taking flying lessons to trying to make a motion picture in the snowy Sierra Mountains.

He took women on long drives around the Bay Area in his brand-new Ford—often speeding, drinking, or both. "Be careful," he once warned his friend Agnes de Mille as she was climbing into his car after a trip to the movies. "There's a sack on the floor in the back full of live rattlesnakes."

However, Walter Miles—a professor in Stanford's psychology department—took an interest in Keeler and gave him space and equipment to work on the lie detector. He continued to refine the instrument and his interrogation techniques.

He tested sleep-deprived students and mental patients at Palo Alto Veterans Hospital and calibrated his machine against the model John Larson had left behind in Berkeley. He tested his friends while they were under the influence of amyl nitrite (procured from his uncle, a doctor). The only person he couldn't put on the machine was himself. The first time he tried it, he discovered a heart abnormality—a relic of his childhood illnesses that emerged when he was under stress.

It was Keeler who developed the backdrop of many interrogations even today—a quiet, undecorated room, a one-way mirror, an experimental procedure where the suspect is shown the chart and asked to explain the irregularities before being retested. "This ritual was designed to focus the subject's mind on the matter at hand, make her conscious of the stakes of deception, and put her in the position of having to explain herself," writes Ken Alder. "Under those conditions, Keeler discovered, an astounding number of people would tell him everything he wanted to know."

Slowly, Keeler became an expert at extracting confessions—not just because of the machine, but because of his skill or charm or sheer force of personality combined with the presence of the polygraph. But, as with the case in Los Olivos with the Ku Klux Klan, John Larson was not happy with the methods his former assistant was adopting.

There was, for instance, the "card test"—a trick that Keeler used at the start of interrogations. After hooking someone up to the lie detector, he presented them with eight playing cards and asked them to choose one and hold it in their mind. "Don't let me see it. Just look at it and put it back."

Then, as Keeler flipped each card over, he asked the subject to deny that any of them were the chosen one—the idea being that the polygraph machine would be able to correctly identify the real card.

The card test had two purposes: First, it gave Keeler an idea of what a known lie looked like on the chart for that specific subject. But more importantly, it demonstrated the supposed power of the machine—if it could correctly guess which card you were thinking of, what else could it do?

It's a technique still used by some polygraph operators today (known as a stim test), but Keeler made sure of success, using the sleight of hand he'd learned as an amateur magician to stack the deck. To the person strapped into the machine, it might have seemed like the polygraph was reading their mind, but really it was all about Keeler.

* * *

One person saw through his trickery. In the summer of 1926, Keeler ran a polygraph test on Kay Applegate, a headstrong young student from rural Washington with fair, wavy hair and rosy cheeks.

Applegate was bold and independent, with a "slow way of talking" and a taste for adrenaline. Late one night, she and a friend pulled off a college prank—they snuck into the psychology lab and attached a mannequin to one of the devices used for measuring muscle reflexes.

When college authorities threatened to unleash the lie detector to find the culprits, the girls snuck back into the lab, dressed the mannequin in purple underwear and attached it to the machine. "It created a sensation, and we are strongly suspected but so far have maintained our innocence quite beautifully," Applegate wrote to her parents.

Keeler had used his card test on dozens of people by then—he once boasted that only two out of sixty suspects had managed to beat it. So, Applegate certainly caught his attention when she fooled the test (by only pretending to look at the card when he showed it to her).

The pair soon struck up a close friendship. Keeler took Applegate out for long drives and showed her his snake farm and the photos he'd taken on his mountain expeditions. He thought Applegate was "startlingly brilliant," he told his father. "I only wish I had the keen mentality she possesses."

* * *

John Larson's disapproval of Keeler's tactics stemmed in part from his desire to see the lie detector gain acceptance from his scientific peers. He felt that cheap parlor tricks and sensational trials would weaken its position and damage his own reputation.

Despite their vastly different backgrounds and outlooks on life, the pair had become good friends during their travels around California with the lie detector. "You'll be as famous as Edison in invention and as great as Vollmer in crime," Keeler once told Larson.

From Chicago, where he moved in 1923, Larson sent encouraging letters to Keeler. "Keep up your good work and remember that it will be from workers like yourself who are patiently and tirelessly trying every known method, testing these experimentally, who will ultimately do the most constructive work in research," he wrote.

As Keeler used the machine in more cases, Larson preached caution and talked about the careful work still needed to validate it. But it was too late. The genie was out of the bottle. The polygraph may not have been admissible in court after the Frye ruling, but thanks to Leonarde Keeler, it would soon reach into almost every other aspect of the justice system—and beyond, into business and politics.

Over the next few years, Larson and Keeler drifted apart. Keeler took secret steps to take the polygraph to market—preparing a patent application and meeting with manufacturers to discuss mass production. But he found it difficult to cede control—he wanted approval on every unit sold to prevent bad investigators from ruining the lie detector's reputation. He also knew—even if he didn't say it publicly—that a large amount of the machine's efficacy derived from his own experience and skill.

Vollmer continued to prod the pair to cooperate, but Keeler's communications became sparser, to the extent that Larson had to write to Vollmer to get updates on how Keeler was progressing.

"This is the third time he has asked me to have you write to him, so I am leaving it up to you to do as you please in the matter," the chief told Keeler in May 1925. "My advice, however, is to keep in contact with Larson, because I am sure he will do much to help you, and you will undoubtedly be able to contribute something to his researches."

"Yes, I am certainly ashamed of myself for not having communicated with Larson before," Keeler replied. "I know mighty well that there is no one that can help me more than Larson in this work, and hereafter I intend to keep in constant touch with him."

But their collegiate relationship was dissolving. They had fundamentally different perspectives on the lie detector: for Larson, success meant scientific and legal recognition; for Keeler, it was commercial revenue and widespread usage.

In March 1927, Larson wrote to Keeler from Chicago, again chasing for updates on the lie detector and struggling to hide his frustration. "You might not be glad to receive this communication as it might look as though I were calling you on the carpet because I have been unable to hear from you for some weeks," he wrote. "That is, I want to find out who's who and what each is doing. You were going 100 percent in deception experimentation and construction of apparatus until you hit Stanford, and then something seemed to happen."

Keeler blamed others for leading him astray—he said the likes of Hiram Edwards, Charles Sloan, and Walter Miles were only helping with the device in order to stake a claim to the riches it would surely bring. He told Larson that Miles had tried to stop him from displaying the lie detector publicly.

"After all your kindness, help, and advice, you were the incentive which started me in this work, and you certainly deserve to know what I was doing," he wrote. "I have made it clear to Miles that whatever I am doing under him or in his department that I should be free to disclose any developments to you."

But eventually, the two men who'd once worked so closely together on the machine were driven apart by it. Larson spent the rest of his life trying to stop Keeler from spreading the polygraph across America, while Keeler sought fame and fortune, but found only misery and mistrust.

Chicago was waiting for them.

PART FOUR

PART FOUR

STOOL PIGEON

Max Dent moved through the darkening city like a ghost. It was just after seven thirty PM on Tuesday, October 8, 1935, and the thirty-four-year-old had stepped out to buy cigarettes.

He was short and slight, with dark curly hair and a boyish demeanor. "His thin, angular face was all bones and ears," wrote one reporter. As he climbed the stairs to street level and stepped into the murky night, he seemed wary. He walked in odd bursts of speed, broken by long pauses where he'd jerk his head around like a scared rodent.

Dent had just finished dinner with his parents, Annie and Joe, at the family's apartment, in the basement of a three-story greystone at 1859 South Lawndale Avenue, on Chicago's West Side. Their worried faces were still in his mind—his father, short and stout, with a shock of dark hair and his gold teeth glinting below a thick moustache; his mother, stocky and gray haired, her frown lines deepening when her son insisted on leaving the house.

They'd come to the United States from eastern Europe—Dent was born Mordke Trelisky, on October 12, 1901, in Kiev, and landed in America as a five-year-old on the SS *Merion*. It was a cattle-class ship, built for the scores of immigrants seeking stability in the New World—life savings sewn into their coats. They eventually settled in Chicago, where Joe set up his own smithing shop in the growing Jewish community in Lawndale.

Chicago was a cruel, noisy, stinking city—at the confluence of the railroads that crisscrossed the continent, it became a nexus for all that was rotten in America. It was a place of industry and hard labor—from the steelworks, which belched their fumes into the cold night air, to the

203

infamous stockyards, where millions of cattle and pigs arrived each year to be butchered. They used every part of the animal, if not for food and clothing, then for glue, machine grease, candles. The people were used up too—ground down through injury or illness until the vultures picked them clean.

By the mid-1930s, Chicago was in the grips of the Great Depression. The manufacturing industry had collapsed—shedding half its workforce between 1927 and 1933. Payrolls were down nearly 75 percent; home foreclosures had increased fivefold; and more than 160 banks had closed. Business competition turned ugly—a barber who undercut his rivals was prone to having his windows smashed.

Even the ultra-wealthy in their grand homes along Lakeshore Drive couldn't ignore the "desperate and ragged" who begged at junctions, queued at the breadlines, and slept on benches or under bridges until they froze to death. Men were driven to organized crime out of desperation.

In Lawndale, where the Dents lived, Jewish families who'd fled persecution in Eastern Europe packed into cramped apartments—each three-story greystone might be carved into four or five units, housing dozens of people.

The neighborhood was usually alive with outdoor activity—a "constant procession" of peddlers hawking food, milk, ice, or coal. There was the knife sharpener, the umbrella man, the pop man selling soda and seltzer water, news boys shouting extras, insurance collectors, and even ambitious Christian missionaries.

But tonight it had been raining, and the streets were quiet, the asphalt slick and shining under the electric lights. A chill mist had settled on the city, taking on a yellow hue where it curled around the iron lamp posts. But Dent had no overcoat—it was as if he didn't feel the biting gusts of wind or the cold drops settling on his face as he walked south, down Lawndale Avenue. He stayed in the shadows.

When he reached Ogden Avenue, a wide main street cutting diagonally through the neighborhood, he relaxed a little. He passed kosher butchers and small-scale factories and the ticket office for the Lawndale station for the elevated train, whose tracks ran overhead. Local businesses filled the air with the smell of cigars and laundry detergent. Dent ducked into a drugstore to buy his cigarettes.

A few minutes later, he turned back onto South Lawndale Avenue toward home. The crowds thinned out, and he adopted the same cautious gait, looking around in all directions, walking as fast as he could without drawing attention.

He was about halfway up the block when a dark shape emerged from an alleyway between two houses and stepped out in front of him. Dent froze, turned, tried to break into a shambling run. A hail of gunshots pierced the quiet night.

*   *   *

For a few moments, a blanket of silence descended on the street. Cars slid past and commuter trains rumbled by on the elevated tracks that ringed the city like an "iron crown." Then the neighborhood slowly came to life: Window frames slid up, doors creaked open, footsteps edged down wooden steps.

Dent was lying face down on the concrete outside 1918 South Lawndale Avenue. His body was curled like a question mark, head pointing southwest toward Cicero, where Al Capone's men still held sway, arms outstretched, still imploring his assailant not to shoot. His feet were splayed out toward home, and his head was resting in a pool of blood that mixed with the rain on the pavement and ran away in a tinted stream. He had been shot four times in the back.

Seven blocks away, at the crumbling Lawndale District Police Station, the phone on the sergeant's desk jangled. He picked up the receiver. "Twenty-fourth district," he said, and then listened for a minute. "We'll send somebody right over."

He dispatched officers William Fenn and Arthur Vanderpoel, who climbed into a dark police sedan and turned on the heaters, which had little effect on the chill. "Probably just a family squabble," Fenn said as they pulled out onto the main road. "They always pick the worst nights."

By the time the squad car arrived on the scene at 7:55 PM, there were two dozen or so men milling around on the street. Their suits and waistcoats were getting soaked through by the rain, but they still peered grimly at the body from under dripping hats.

Fenn and Vanderpoel stepped out of the car and into the cold night air, wearing dark raincoats over their uniforms. "Who saw this?" they demanded, but there was no answer from the residents of a city where talking to the police was rarely a good idea. They'd seen a few members of the crowd slip away as they strode toward the scene. The rain was still coming down hard.

Fenn was the more experienced of the two officers—a slender man in his late forties, whose brown hair was soon plastered to his forehead by the downpour. He pushed the onlookers back behind a wooden fence that separated the sidewalk from the road. Then he walked over to Dent, bent down close to him, and wrapped his fingers around the man's wrist to check his pulse. His skin felt cold.

The crowd held its breath as the officer crouched there by the body, and the only sound was "the slap of rain on concrete." Fenn stood up with a grim expression and turned to his partner. "Suppose you make the calls," he said. "I'll stand watch here and get started."

Vanderpoel nodded and went to look for a police box or a house with a phone so he could call into the station and get the coroner and the Homicide Squad to the scene. Fenn took off his raincoat and draped it over the body, but Dent's pale hands were stretched out over his head and stuck out of the top. He stooped again to adjust the shroud.

"Now," he said when he was done, turning to the crowd, "who is he? Anybody know him?"

There was no answer. "So he's a stranger? Don't live round here?"

It might have been a gang murder, Fenn thought, or maybe the body had been dumped out of a moving car. He peered into the anxious faces around him, searching for answers. Then a small voice rang out, and a thirteen-year-old boy with blond hair and inquisitive blue eyes stepped forward. "I think it's Max Dent," he said.

The boy's name was Clarence Stachowiak, a neighbor of the Dent family. He hadn't seen the shooting, but he had seen Annie Dent—Max's mother—walking down the street a few minutes before he heard the gunshots. "Maybe five or six," he said. "They weren't real sharp or loud."

Fenn scanned the crowd again. "Where's Mrs. Dent?" he asked.

"She ran over here, then she ran home or somewhere after the shooting," someone replied.

"Here she comes now," said someone else, and the crowd turned to the north and watched the pale-faced, gray-haired woman hurrying toward them on stubby legs. The group split to let her through, and she passed down the aisle between them to where Fenn still stood next to the body. She lifted a corner of the coat, peered beneath it, and then turned away, face twisting in pain. She screamed "That's my son! It's my Max, my Max! He's dead!"

Fenn placed a gentle hand on her shoulder, and she looked up at him with wide eyes. "Take it easy," he said. "You've got to help us."

She straightened.

"Did you see it happen?" Fenn asked.

She nodded. Her face was stiff and drawn in the glow of the streetlights. Water dripped from the end of her nose—Fenn couldn't tell if it was tears or rain.

"Tell me about it," said the officer, in the softest tone he could manage.

"I saw him, my son Max," she said slowly. "He was coming this way."

There was a cacophony of background noise—sirens screamed and loud voices shouted instructions as more police cars and an ambulance arrived. The coroner's physician and his assistant set to work on the body, throwing curious glances at Annie Dent before they began.

But she was oblivious to all around her as she told Fenn how she'd been so worried about something happening to her son that she'd followed him out of the house.

As she crossed over Nineteenth Street on her way south, she'd seen Max walking toward her, illuminated by the lights of the el train as he passed underneath the tracks. "Then he started to walk faster toward me," she said. "Then he started to run."

She told Fenn that two men had come out of the alley and approached her son. Or was it one? She couldn't be sure, and she was getting flustered. "I–I am all mixed up," she said.

"Sure, Fenn said patiently. "Take it easy."

In the brief silence that followed, Fenn could hear the murmuring of the crowd and the coroner talking to one of his interns. "Turn him over a little so I can see the other side."

Annie started up again. "Max ran across Lawndale, and the man was after him," she said. "I ran after them too. We ran right over to here. And the man started shooting. And Max fell down."

She'd heard five or six shots, and after her son had fallen down, she said, the man stopped and leaned over and put the gun against Max's head and pulled the trigger again. "The man that was shooting, he was a young man like Max, tall, kind of skinny, with a long dark coat on," she said. Fenn pressed her for more details, but she was in shock and rambling, clearly on the verge of collapse. Her neighbors led her home through the rain.

The other officers started a search. Fenn knew it would probably be futile—too much time had elapsed since the shooting, but it was worth a try. Police threw a cordon up around the neighboring blocks, questioned employees at the station and stopped trains from leaving. They set up blockades, positioned squad cars at strategic points, and then began moving in on foot, drawing the net ever tighter.

On Ogden Avenue, they peered closely at passing faces and scouted restaurants, taverns, and drugstores, armed with their description of the tall, thin man who Annie Dent had described.

At the scene, Fenn turned to the coroner's physician, who had his preliminary report ready. Max Dent had been shot in the neck, chest, and abdomen, and from the powder burns on his skin it seemed that the final shot was fired from close range through the back of the neck. "It was a professional job," said one of the officers. An execution.

Chicago was rotten with gang activity. Al Capone was at Alcatraz, serving his infamous sentence for tax evasion, but there were plenty of other mobsters who had stepped into the power vacuum. It was quite possible that Dent had become mixed up with one of them. But there was something else too.

The coroner's physician beckoned Fenn closer to the body. He flicked on a flashlight and turned it full on the dead man's face, which glowed pale and eerie under the beam. "Notice anything?" he asked.

Fenn peered at the body and shook his head. Holding the flashlight in one hand, the doctor used the thumb and forefinger of the other to lift one of Dent's eyelids, revealing a glassy stare. "Notice the pupil dilation?"

"A junkie," Fenn said, frowning.

"That's what I thought. The man was a user of narcotics. That mean anything to you?"

"Not now. But it might later on. It might mean a lot."

*   *   *

A mile to the north, a ticket seller at the el train station on Independence and Harrison was telling police about a nervous-looking man she'd seen boarding a train—a man who matched the description Annie Dent had given police. "I wouldn't recognize him just from your description by itself," she said from inside the metal cage of the booth. "But I remember him because he seemed so jittery. He kept looking over his shoulder all the time he was buying his ticket, like he expected somebody to come after him."

She had been worried she was about to get robbed. "He forgot his change, and I had to call him back to get it," she said. "And he wasn't dressed like the kind of man that leaves change lying around."

"Which way'd he go?" asked one of the officers.

"Eastbound."

"Where's your phone?"

*   *   *

Soon, police radios across the city were blaring with the more detailed description given by the ticket seller. Officers checked the trains and cross-referenced them with the schedules to find the service the man must have boarded. The conductor remembered the nervous, thin passenger who kept changing his seat and who fearfully eyed each oncoming rider. The man had asked him for the nearest stop to the Hotel Sherman, an opulent twelve-story venue on the corner of Randolph Street and a favored haunt of celebrities and politicians.

"And he got off there?"

"I didn't notice," the conductor said. "But he got off somewhere in the Loop."

The Loop was the swirling center of Chicago—a maelstrom of cars, trolley buses, and crowded sidewalks ringed by train tracks. The room clerk at the hotel hadn't seen anyone matching the description of the man they sought. But the house detective—a private security role that was already a noir novel trope—remembered seeing an odd character sitting briefly in a corner of the Sherman's grand lobby.

"He didn't stay long," the detective said. "Acted like he couldn't sit still. I was watching him; he didn't look like a guest to me—wasn't so well dressed. I thought maybe he was waiting for someone."

"You're pretty sure he isn't registered?"

"Positive."

"Where'd he go?"

"I don't know. He walked out and I forgot about him."

"He was alone?"

"That's right."

"Was there anything noticeable about him?"

The detective paused. "I wouldn't want to say for sure," he said. "But something about him reminded me of a narcotics addict."

The trail ended at the hotel. Officers quizzed the taxi drivers parked outside, and canvassed nearby bars and restaurants, but they were "poking around in the dark," and back at Lawndale station, witness statements were clouding things further.

One local said he'd seen a man running away from where Dent's body was found and jumping into a small two-door sedan. Another contradicted Annie Dent's story—describing the culprit as short and fat, not tall and thin. Estelle Cohen, a young woman in a thick fur coat, said there had been two men, and they'd driven off in a small dark car.

Meanwhile, officers had been digging into Dent's backstory. He was dressed better than you might expect of a junkie. He'd been a sailor, officers discovered, and then worked as a huckster, selling items door to door, and as a taxi mechanic, but he hadn't had a full-time job in almost ten years. Lately, he hadn't been doing much of anything, but his friends in the neighborhood said he never seemed short of cash.

Both the coroner and the hotel detective had mentioned drugs, so William Fenn set up a meeting with three agents from the Federal Bureau of Narcotics—Francis Burns Kennedy, Joseph Walsh, and Edwin Klein. And as it turned out, they were very familiar with Max Dent.

The murder victim was, the agents explained, one of their "stool pigeons"—an informant who fed them news about drug deals and helped them bring down dealers by making buys while they lay in wait (the term "stool pigeon" derives from a hunting practice where one bird was used as a decoy to attract others).

Fenn was stunned. He stared at the agents. "He was? Was he mixed up in any pending cases?"

"He could have been," said Kennedy. "He made several cases for me, and I think several for other agents."

Dent had been working as an informant for a couple of years, Kennedy said. He'd been scraping by when Kennedy first converted him into a state's witness. He could often be spotted waiting outside

Kennedy's office, and was well known by the city's own drug squad at Eleventh and State. "Seen him pretty often," Kennedy said. "He came to my office frequently during the last couple of years, sometimes as often as twice a day."

He often brought the drug squad people they'd not heard of before, mostly low-level dealers selling small amounts to friends and acquaintances. But he was prolific: on February 8, 1935, he informed against Gloster Waters and Horace Washington; on March 26 he informed against Edward Henderson; on April 5 he informed against William Turner and Mary Wilson; on June 5, he informed against Joseph Pitelka.

Overall, Dent had worked with at least three different detectives on the drug squad and had helped on maybe fifteen or twenty cases—which meant there were at least that many people with a motive for wanting him dead, each with enough friends on the outside to make it happen.

One account of the case likened the drug organizations to an octopus with endless tentacles. Picking off low-level dealers, as Dent helped government agents to do, simply angered the beast. And given the sometimes intimate relationship between police and organized crime in the city, Chicago was not a smart place to be a snitch.

As he mulled over this new information, Fenn realized the huge task facing him. Each case Dent had worked on would have to be carefully checked over—it could take weeks or months of work.

Police began by trying to match descriptions gathered from witnesses with the people Dent had sent to prison, but soon gave up: "tall and thin" and "short and fat" were too vague, as well as contradictory. Instead, they made a list of every defendant Dent had informed against, every witness in those cases, and their favorite haunts.

All but one had been settled, with the accused either being freed or sent to prison. There was only one case Dent had been an informant on that was still open, and it concerned a man named Joseph Rappaport.

PRISONER #32147

The morning after the killing was cold and gray, and a light rain was falling as police hunted for their new prime suspect. Joe Rappaport had spent the night wandering around Chicago in an anxious daze, hands in his pockets, head bent against the weather.

He was five foot six and slim—a well-dressed thirty-year-old with thick dark hair and a broad smile that reached right to the corners of his eyes. He was the first American-born child in a family of Russian Jews and lived with his mother, Etta; his sisters Martha and Rose; and his father, Israel, on the second floor of a two-story greystone at 3430 Douglas Boulevard.

Family life was difficult. Rappaport's father, Israel, had been a prominent local rabbi in Chicago until a decade earlier, when a severe bout of influenza left him virtually paralyzed. He was diagnosed with Parkinson's disease, and their once tall, imposing patriarch was now bedridden, speechless, and incontinent. The sisters spent much of their time caring for their gaunt, frail father, who looked much older than his fifty-seven years.

Rappaport had four years of education at Medill High but had to drop out before graduation and became the family's main breadwinner at a tender age. He spent four years as a bookkeeper, worked as a plumber and a clothing salesman, and drove a taxi for a while, handing over $30 to $35 a week to his mother, who gave him back a small allowance.

He spent his spare time playing basketball with friends at his old high school gym, and although he swerved the public dances, he met a woman—Hazel Romaine from New York, who worked in the theater industry. His mother and sisters did not approve of the marriage.

Rappaport also found other ways to supplement his income. In April 1929, he was convicted of drug dealing and sentenced to three years at Leavenworth Penitentiary in Kansas—a medium-security prison that housed bank robbers, gangsters, and spies, and was a tightly run ship under Warden Tom White (one of the main characters in David Grann's book *Killers of the Flower Moon*).

He was assigned prisoner number 32147 and cell A-319. He traded loving letters with his wife, who had returned to New York after his sentencing and was on the road a lot—she sent him telegrams from all over the country updating him on her movements. And he kept in close contact with his family too, marking birthdays and special occasions with telegrams sent from the prison. "May God remember you in his book of life and grant your prayers for yourself and those dear to you," he wrote to his mother on Rosh Hashanah one year.

The wardens put him on kitchen duty, and Rappaport mostly kept his head down until October 16, 1929, when he spotted Morris Bernstein, the man who had testified against him at his trial. It was Bernstein's first day at Leavenworth after a transfer from Detroit, and he was sitting in the lunchroom when Rappaport—who was working as a waiter—slashed him across the face with a knife as he walked down the aisle between the tables.

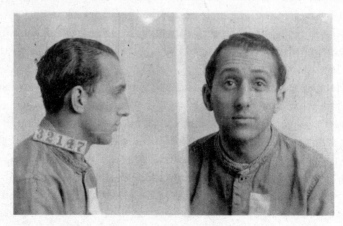

Joseph Rappaport.

Bernstein was left with a deep cut across his cheek that needed fifteen stitches, and the suspicion was that Rappaport had been aiming for the neck. He was put in isolation on a restricted diet and his letter-writing privileges were limited to one piece of correspondence a month for three months, sparking a flurry of concerned telegrams to Warden White from his family.

But the more serious consequence of the incident was that it cost him thirty days" "good time," and made him ineligible for parole at the first attempt—lengthening his stay in prison by six months. Rappaport's teenage sister Rose bombarded White with desperate letters, pleading with him to change his mind.

Her father's health was getting worse, she wrote, and her mother had suffered a nervous breakdown and been taken to Goodheart Sanatorium for the second time since Joe's arrest. "She believes her children are being burned alive and that her son Joseph is being tortured," wrote her doctor in a letter that Rose forwarded to White as evidence of their plight. They were in desperate financial straits—"without bread to eat" and borrowing money from friends and, at high interest rates, from loan sharks.

In a ten-week spell from late November 1930 to early February 1931, Rose wrote to White at least ten times. "My brother and only supporter is away from home. I have no one to look to for help," read one letter. "The thirteen months that Joseph has been away has seemed like thirteen years."

White wrote back, explaining the seriousness of what Rappaport had done and why he couldn't be given parole. "He looks like a clean-cut fellow, but he must learn how to control himself or else it is going to end up pretty bad with him sometime," he wrote.

But eventually Rose's persistence wore him down. When a report from Social Services confirmed that things really were as bad as she said they were, White dropped his objection to parole, allowing Rappaport to return home in August 1931. But now, four years on, he feared for his freedom again.

* * *

Rappaport had known Max Dent for a couple of years. At trial, Dent's mother, Annie, described how he would come to their house every few months and drop off a silk envelope for her son in exchange for a few dollars. Once, she peeked inside and found half a dozen little capsules containing white powder—heroin. But theirs wasn't solely a business arrangement—Rappaport considered Max a friend and had once stayed with the family for a few days.

That changed on February 4, 1935. Rappaport had just sold Dent sixty-two grains of heroin for $20 when agents Joseph Walsh and Francis Kennedy from the Narcotics Bureau appeared out of nowhere to arrest him.

Dent had been due to give evidence against Rappaport in the trial, which was just a few weeks away when he was gunned down. Assistant District Attorney Mary Bailey said she was "not surprised" by the killing, especially given Rappaport's previous attack on a witness who had testified against him.

On the morning of October 9, the day after Dent's murder, police visited the Rappaport family's eight-room apartment. It was filled with good-quality furnishings that showed considerable wear. This was a household that had fallen on hard times. They questioned Rappaport's siblings—his older sister, Martha, and his younger brother, Morris, who had only just been bailed after being granted a retrial on a manslaughter charge. But Joe Rappaport himself was nowhere to be found.

Police circulated his description over the radio network—an August Vollmer innovation that was now commonplace—and noted that it seemed to match that of the nervous man they'd tracked from Harrison station to the Sherman Hotel.

It wasn't until later that night, when the temperature fell and the rain drops turned to snow flurries, that they finally found him. At eight thirty PM, Rappaport walked into the Summerdale Police Station on the North Side. "I heard you fellows were looking for me," he said.

He was turned over to Captain Pat Kelliher at Lawndale Station for questioning. Rappaport told Kelliher that he'd left his house at about five PM on the evening of the shooting and walked a couple of blocks north to a restaurant at 3613 Roosevelt Road, where he watched a few rounds of pinochle, a popular card game in the Jewish American community.

After leaving the restaurant at 6:55 PM, Rappaport went to meet his girlfriend on the corner of Roosevelt and St. Louis (his marriage to Hazel had ended in divorce soon after he left prison). But she didn't show up, so he walked alone to the Lawndale Theatre, where he said he watched the musical romance movie *Naughty Marietta*; a newsreel with stories about Mussolini's invasion of Ethiopia; and footage of a boxing match between Joe Louis and Max Baer, which pitched a cult hero of the Black community against a former heavyweight champion.

Rappaport said that when he left the movie theater a few hours later, he caught a glimpse of a newspaper headline about Dent's murder, and he knew that it was only a matter of time before he was implicated in it because of the pending narcotics case. "His first impulse was to run." He jumped on an eastbound train at Independence and Harrison and headed for the Sherman Hotel. But he was so nervous that he couldn't sit still, so he left and wandered around the Loop—agitated and jittery because of the situation and, according to one account, because he was trying to stop using drugs. He was, it seemed, the nervous man whom the ticket seller and the conductor had told police about.

For the rest of the night, Rappaport bounced between el trains and hotel lobbies, trying to keep warm but too scared to go home in case the police were waiting for him. Scanning a newspaper the next morning, he read his own description in the paper and decided the best thing to do was to give himself up.

The police made Rappaport repeat this story again and again, trying to catch him out on minor details. But it seemed "just fuzzy enough to be probable," and Rappaport was unfazed when they warned him they would check every aspect of the tale. He agreed to submit to a lie detector exam and a paraffin test—where heated wax was pressed to the skin to draw out any gunshot residue that may have settled there. Then he said something that surprised them.

"Anyway, why should I want to kill Max Dent? He wasn't going to testify against me," he said.

"He wasn't?"

"No. He came up to me just a week or so ago and said he was sorry he'd framed me on that narcotics rap, that he'd been put on the spot by the agents and had to do it, but that he was going to make it up to me by skipping town and not testifying."

"You were pretty sore at him when he turned you in, weren't you?"

"Sure. Who wouldn't be? I thought he was my friend. But it was all patched up because he said he wasn't going to testify."

It was obvious that Rappaport was the man they'd been looking for from the train, but if his story about Dent planning not to testify was true, then he had no motive for the murder. It tallied with the testimony of Annie Dent, who told police that she'd visited the Rappaport home a week before the shooting to plead for her son's life. She'd promised Etta Rappaport that Max wouldn't testify and that he'd leave Chicago, although now that he was dead she had no doubt who was to blame.

When another friend of Max Dent's confirmed that he'd been planning to leave town instead of testifying, it seemed like Rappaport was in the clear.

But then Rappaport's alibi collapsed. While checking his story, police spoke to Jerry Frost, the booker for the Lawndale Theatre who said he hadn't had footage of the Louis versus Baer fight, so Rappaport couldn't have seen it there when he said he had.

And then, when they were going through Dent's personal effects, police found something even more damning. It was a note in Dent's handwriting, written on a scrap of paper from a memo pad:

> *If anything happens to me it would be caused from Joe Rapport*
> *[sic]. He has tried to put me out of the way several times on*
> *account of the case I have against him.*
> *Max Dent*

At first Rappaport tried to explain, to change his story. Eventually, he just stopped talking. "You don't have to talk," Fenn told him. "We know that you killed Dent. You were afraid he'd testify at your trial, and you wanted him out of the way."

The officer paused for a moment. His blue eyes met Rappaport's dark ones, blazing under the lights of the interview room. "But killing him didn't do you any good because all you did was pass up jail for the chair."

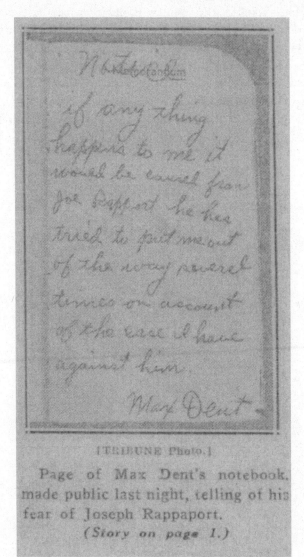

[TRIBUNE Photo.]

Page of Max Dent's notebook, made public last night, telling of his fear of Joseph Rappaport.

(*Story on page 1.*)

Despite the frenzy of police activity, Max Dent's murder made little impact on the front pages of the main newspapers. "Gangland elimination of a disconcerting witness is news only of passing interest in Chicago," observed one account. The city had long been the organized crime capital of the country. Prohibition may have ended, but the gangs and gangsters it birthed still had Chicago and its institutions in their grip. Territorial flare-ups between rival groups were common, and there were flourishing trades in drugs and people.

But where there were criminals, there were also criminologists, and a new breed of investigators had flocked to the city—including John Larson, August Vollmer, and Leonarde Keeler, who would soon get drawn into the Rappaport case in a hugely damaging way.

AN UNPOLISHED DIAMOND

August Vollmer had been dreaming of Chicago. For someone so calm and composed when awake, the chief was a surprisingly bad sleeper. He and his wife, Pat, had moved to separate rooms after he'd pushed her out of bed one night while grappling with a criminal in a nightmare.

In November 1927, he drifted into a dream of San Francisco Bay—the sweep of shore he knew so well, the moonlight rippling on the dark water. It was Vollmer's favorite place on earth, and all was cool and tranquil as he walked along the beach.

His waking hours had been occupied with dark thoughts of Al Capone and his mob, who had made nearly a hundred million dollars so far from their bootlegging and racketeering, and who were building a significant body count in their violent struggle for control of America's alcohol supply. John Larson was writing him regular missives from Chicago, painting a grim picture of a city in the grip of crime and corruption.

In the dream, a huge man appeared next to Vollmer, grinning a wide, sinister smile. He was wearing a black derby hat, and there was a sign on his chest, with a single word glowing in red: "Gangster."

Vollmer opened his mouth to speak, but the man disappeared "like a puppet suddenly jerked away." Another appeared in his place, with a different word emblazoned on his torso: "Thief."

More joined the parade, each marked out as a menace to society—the kind of men he'd worked so hard to keep off the streets of Berkeley and who were running riot in Chicago. Rapist. Robber. Con man. Kidnapper. Racketeer. Each man's face twisted into a sneer before he vanished.

Now Vollmer was standing on a cliff, looking at the waves crashing against the moonlit shore. When he turned around, there was a man walking toward him with a sign so bright it hurt Vollmer's eyes: "Killer."

He was a giant—dressed in black and advancing toward Vollmer with a gun in his hand. The chief leaped forward to try and wrestle it off him. The gun went off with a sound like a cannon. The man engulfed Vollmer in his huge arms, an iron grip stronger than anything he'd ever felt before. Soon he was on his back, and his assailant rained down painful, powerful blows with heavy fists. Vollmer raised his arms to try and protect his face. He felt a tide of anger rising up in him, and with a "burst of superhuman strength," he pushed the giant away, and both men jumped to their feet.

Now the momentum had shifted. He beat his fists against the phantom's face, and the man backed away until finally he toppled over the edge of the cliff and into the bay below. Vollmer heard a voice, faint but insistent, and getting louder. "August, wake up."

He was on his knees on the bedroom floor, where he'd been pounding the wall so hard with his fists that his hands ached.

"I'm glad I don't dream often," he joked with his colleagues. "I have enough of this crime business in the daytime."

* * *

Eighteen months later, on the cold wintry morning of February 14, 1929, a Chicago gangster called Bugs Moran was standing with his men inside a warehouse on Clark Street, awaiting the arrival of a truck full of hijacked whiskey. A big black car pulled up outside, and five men got out and entered. Two of them were dressed as police officers. They lined Moran's men up against a wall and murdered them in a barrage of machine-gun fire.

Moran, who'd managed to slip away before the bloodshed, blamed the killings on his rival Al Capone. Until then, the famous gangster had enjoyed a cult hero status in Chicago, where he was lauded for his philanthropy and applauded at sporting events. But the Saint Valentine's Day massacre shocked the public into demanding action and set in motion a chain of events that would reunite the three creators of the lie detector and pit their device against the city's criminal machine.

John Larson had already spent a few years in Chicago by then. He'd first arrived in the winter of 1923, just after the conclusion of the Henry Wilkens saga. He accepted a job at the Institute for Juvenile Research, where he hoped to use the polygraph to predict criminal behavior instead of just solving crimes after the fact.

In his first summer in the city, Larson was pitched into a very private case—trying to track down a group of pickpockets who'd stolen his wallet. He'd been squeezing onto an el train at La Salle Street station, carrying the lie detector in a bulky suitcase in one hand and a heavy textbook in the other, when two youths bumped past him.

Larson turned to apologize for blocking their way, and it was only as he saw them skittering off the train as the doors were closing that he realized they'd dipped into his pocket and taken his wallet, with $189 inside—almost a month's pay.

Chicago elicited "violent passions" in Larson, particularly when the desk officer at the detective bureau said there was really nothing he could do to help track down the culprits, a "dip mob" led by a character called "Immune Eddy," who recruited children from the slums and cut the cops into the proceeds in exchange for protection. Larson wrote to Vollmer, vowing to trawl the Loop looking for the pickpockets and to dish out his own punishment. "If they ever trip us again . . . I think that there won't be any necessity for complaint, for they will be taught a lesson through a few broken limbs."

When he wasn't itching for vigilante justice, Larson split his time between medical school and the Institute, where he was given a two-room lab and access to all the criminals he could possibly want: gangsters, bootleggers, murderers, and the depraved.

Crime was everywhere—Capone had a warehouse across the alley from Larson's basement office, and he was once roped into helping out on a raid of the premises by Elliot Ness, of the famed Untouchables, who rushed in without a gun but with his fingers formed into the shape of a pistol in his pocket.

This rich seam of material was Chicago's one "redeeming feature," Larson thought. He was simultaneously drawn to and repulsed by "its vast clinical wealth of disease—especially syphilis and crime and everything that is wrong with present-day civilization."

The city's institutions didn't exactly warm to Larson either. He was thrown out of the mayor's office during a presentation on the lie detector, when he explained how the device might be used to quiz city workers on corruption. The chief of police refused to even sit down for a demonstration.

He also clashed spectacularly with his boss, Herman Adler, the director of the Institute for Juvenile Research. They had run deception tests together in California and were working on a joint research paper, but by 1926 Larson had come to think of Adler as "a colossal joke."

Adler wanted Larson to quit his medical studies and work at the Institute full-time, and enraged him further when he fired his assistant during a round of budget cuts. Larson was frustrated by Adler's loyalty to the dirty world of Chicago politics: he was barred from telling the truth about goings-on at Joliet prison, where he was running regular tests on inmates as part of his research. "Any honorable work there was a farce," Larson wrote to Vollmer. "Either the convict was innocent and framed in by officials whom Adler said we could not and dare not expose, or he was guilty and was buying his way out through channels we must ignore."

When Walter Stevens, a mob fixer who had been arrested three hundred times but never charged, admitted complicity in multiple murders during a polygraph test but was still granted parole, Larson sensed that he was on the fringes of a vast conspiracy. He was not the sort of person who could leave that thread unpulled, and he got his hands on a carbon copy of a letter that implicated Walter Jenkins, the Director of Public Welfare—and Adler's boss.

Adler was furious, but Larson refused to drop the case. He became increasingly paranoid, seeing conspiracies and plots all around him, and sending angry letters to Vollmer, filled with slurs against Adler, including some that veered into anti-Semitism. "I wanted to choke him," he wrote.

From California, Vollmer urged Larson to be patient. "Try, if possible, not to engage in any row while you are there. This is selfish, to be sure, but it is necessary for you to be selfish for another year until you have that medical diploma in your hand—then shoot with everything you've got," he wrote. When it came to diplomacy, Larson was, in Vollmer's view, "a diamond that needs a little polishing."

In 1927, having received his medical degree, Larson finally decided to cut his losses at the Institute and take up a fellowship in psychiatry at Johns Hopkins Medical School in Baltimore. Leaving Chicago felt like a retreat—as if he'd let the criminals win. Adler already had a replacement in mind.

In April of that year, he'd met Leonarde Keeler, who was passing through Chicago with Walter Miles on a journey to the east coast to show his improved version of the lie detector to potential manufacturers.

It was a pivotal day in Keeler's life. He met Adler in the morning and secured the job that would take him to the city two years later, and then in the afternoon, he held a secret meeting with Larson to show him drawings of the new lie detector and get his advice on how to patent the invention. It was the first time they'd seen each other in person since the Berkeley fire in 1923.

The latest machine was a vast improvement on the original model: it had a ninety-foot roll of paper that could be turned at three different speeds, and dials and switches to control settings that used to be tweaked manually. The whole thing fit into a sleek wooden box measuring sixteen inches wide and nine inches tall, with storage space for the blood pressure cuffs and tubing. "The instrument is portable and always ready for immediate use," Keeler wrote in *The American Journal of Police Science*.

John Larson spent two intense years at Johns Hopkins working under Adolf Meyer, an influential psychiatrist who had limited patience for his new charge's dalliances with the lie detector.

By the end of 1929, he had a well-paid job in a psychiatric hospital in Iowa, but he was already falling out with his colleagues and itching to get back to Chicago, where Leonarde Keeler and August Vollmer had just embarked on a mission to clean up the city.

A PAINTED SPARROW

Leonarde Keeler left Stanford in the summer of 1929, without a degree but with hundreds of lie detector tests under his belt and a growing reputation for being the man to call when you had a particularly obdurate suspect to crack.

He landed in Chicago with the grand aim of ending corruption. He was twenty-five years old and as confident and headstrong as ever. "I am the first shot from the gun of destruction of political graft," Keeler told his father.

He took up Larson's old job at the Institute for Juvenile Research, living and working at the prison in Joliet. "I occupy a large room in the Warden's quarters," Keeler told his sister Eloise after Herman Adler showed him around on his first day. "Have a double bed and all the conveniences of a high-class resort." He had prisoners serving him: a renowned burglar as his valet, a thief as his waiter, a "nice kindly fellow who raped his daughter" to cut his hair. His research was focused on parole—an increasingly popular use of lie detectors today. Keeler planned to run thousands of tests on inmates and design a reliable means of determining which ones were likely to reoffend if released.

He missed California and the close friendship he'd been developing with Kay Applegate, but soon after he arrived in the "hot, humid, filthy, stinking" city, he got a letter from her. She'd quit a job at Boeing and was moving to Chicago too. The prospect excited and terrified him. "I don't know what this means," Keeler wrote to his sister. "It looks bad. I'm afraid I'll be responsible for her here—and that might lead to most anything."

Although they weren't yet a couple, Keeler found himself inexorably drawn to Applegate—her intelligence and bravery, her sense of adventure. After graduating in the summer of 1927, Applegate and a friend tried to get jobs on an ocean liner to Hawaii, and when they couldn't, they snuck on board anyway. They were quickly discovered but were allowed to complete the journey to Honolulu, where Applegate flipped pancakes in the window of a restaurant, worked in a pineapple cannery, and took flying lessons in a First World War biplane. "This caper amazed Nard," wrote Eloise. "He thought Kay the most fascinating girl he'd ever met—beautiful, intelligent, daring, unique."

Keeler had more success than Larson in drawing confessions from the prisoners at Joliet—he was more personable, better able to put himself on their level. Soon, he was using the machine to screen potential prison guards and working on live cases again—over the intense opposition of many Chicago police officers, who still considered the best form of lie detector to be "a clenched fist."

In 1929, Keeler got tangled up in the case of Decasto Earl Mayer, a thirty-five-year-old from Seattle accused of murdering a naval officer named James Bassett after stealing his car. Mayer and his mother were arrested while driving the stolen vehicle, and had Bassett's wristwatch and cufflinks among their effects.

Months after the killing, Mayer was still refusing to help prosecutor Ewing Colvin locate the body. Colvin wrote to Vollmer, who referred him to John Larson, who declined to get involved in such a high-profile case and passed him on to Leonarde Keeler. He would come to regret it.

Mayer had already been interrogated under the influence of scopolamine, the "truth serum" used on Henry Wilkens, and Keeler turned the screw further with what Larson disdained as a "fishing excursion."

Keeler spent a week firing questions at Mayer in an interrogation room set up in an old courthouse. "Is the body in a lake?" he asked. "Is it in a well?" Mayer initially treated the test as a joke, but Keeler painstakingly narrowed the search down to a cemetery near Mayer's old house. He was making him go through the graves one by one, when the suspect suddenly ripped off the equipment, "sprang like a cat," and smashed the machine. Keeler rushed at him, and two deputies dragged Mayer to his cell.

That night, Keeler resumed his interrogation of Mayer with a repaired lie detector. The prisoner looked gaunt and bleary, and his legs were strapped into special restraints known as "Oregon boots" that tightened when he tried to move. The next morning, in a private meeting with prosecutors, he offered to confess. Keeler was listening through the door and wired the news back to Chicago. "We actually obtained confession and soon will have body."

But when Mayer returned to the interview room, he recanted his confession and refused to look at the new maps Keeler had produced of the area where the body might be buried. Mayer kept his eyes firmly shut, and when deputies tried to pry them open, he rolled them up into his skull and convulsed as if having a seizure. They injected him with a sedative and pressed a chloroform-soaked rag over his face until he calmed down (Colvin claimed these were placebos).

The pictures of Mayer on the front pages of the newspapers the next day caused national outcry. The lie detector was meant to end the third degree, but this—the unwilling suspect, the psychological inter- rogation, the handcuffs, the Oregon boot—looked a lot like torture. A report into policing called it "one of the outstanding third-degree cases in the United States."

While investigators dug up graves in the cemetery in a futile search for Bassett's body, Mayer's lawyers obtained an injunction against him being questioned without an attorney present. The judge compared Mayer's treatment to the Spanish Inquisition and said it represented "a serious violation of his constitutional rights."

Keeler was mentally and physically exhausted by the case and the criticism—for weeks afterward he had a high fever and a persistent cough. John Larson was furious and embarrassed by Keeler's "antics." "If, as alleged, a subject has to be chained down, he should not be tested," he wrote.

"People included me personally in criticisms of the way the case was conducted—ways that were not in accordance with principles set by me," he complained to Keeler. "Principles set up for my own protec- tion and for anyone operating the test."

And it hadn't even worked—seven years later, Mayer's mother confessed to a cop disguised as a priest that Bassett's body had been split across several sites, none of which were anywhere near a cemetery. The lie detector evidence had been completely wrong.

* * *

Gus Vollmer's own arrival in Chicago felt like destiny. He'd been invited to join the University of Chicago as its first professor of policing administration. It was a big step for a man who had never even gone to high school, and Vollmer weighed it up for a long time before accepting.

His work commitments had been piling up, and in April 1929, the fifty-three-year-old had suffered a mild heart attack. But Chicago had been calling to him in his dreams. He decided that a change would be as good as a rest and took a seven-month sabbatical from the Berkeley Police Department.

The nation's leading voice on law-enforcement reform—"the father of modern policing"—was finally on the scene and ready to pit his methods against a city increasingly run by crime. Chicago was in the midst of a turbulent restructure—Capone's syndicate had consolidated organized crime and stuck its hooks into every institution, from the police to the prisons.

Vollmer and his wife, Pat, moved into an apartment on University Avenue. Leonarde Keeler and Kay Applegate were frequent visitors and grew to think of the Vollmers as foster parents—their family in the strange city far from home. They went to the theater together and met for regular dinners at Won Kow, a legendary Chinese restaurant on the South Side. Vollmer nagged Keeler to go to the doctor when his cough got bad, and when Keeler was considering proposing to Kay, it was Vollmer whom he confided in.

Although the chief was only in town to teach a class, he soon found himself immersed in the dirty world of police corruption and in a strange case involving a dead woman and her missing canary.

* * *

Anna Gustafson had high hopes for her new business venture. The café, called The Singing Bird, at 816 Cass Street, served home-baked delicacies made in her basement kitchen, and the forty-five-year-old hoped it would supplement the income she was already bringing in from paid lodgers.

The café's unique selling point was a canary called Nimble, a "rare and expensive" bird who had been trained to sing and do tricks. Gustafson had paid $100 for the bird, whose "merry singing" brightened even the dreariest Chicago day. She painted the tearoom's furniture a bright yellow to match Nimble's plumage.

But business was slow—it was 1929, and the country was stumbling toward the economic cliff edge of the Great Depression. Gustafson grew despondent. "The songs that Nimble warbled no longer cheered her."

On October 6, 1929, one of her lodgers—a young attorney called Philip Weinstein—found Gustafson lying dead on the kitchen floor. She'd turned on the gas jets to take her own life. Weinstein immediately alerted the police. As he walked through the rest of the house opening windows to clear the gas, he found Nimble still cheerfully singing in his cage in the tearoom upstairs. He placed the cage next to a window in his room and then left for the night, just as four police officers arrived to guard the scene until the case could be fully investigated. But when he returned the next night, the cage was empty. Nimble was gone.

Two days later, Gustafson's friend Lillian Weinberger turned up at the house to feed the bird. When the officer on duty told her Nimble was missing, she insisted on searching the house. She found the body of a yellow canary lying in a darkened corner of the tearoom. Weinberger crouched down and peered at the corpse. "But this bird is not Nimble," she said. "Her body was a different shade of yellow. Nimble was a more valuable bird than this one. This is just an ordinary canary."

The officers at the scene insisted that the bird was Nimble and told Weinberger it must have had a delayed reaction to the gas fumes. But the woman became doubly suspicious when she realized that items of her friend's clothing and silverware were missing too.

It looked like the latest in a spate of thefts—for years, things had been disappearing from the estates of the deceased while their homes were being guarded by the police. It was becoming an embarrassment, and an up-and-coming probate judge called Henry Horner decided to use this case to set an example.

Horner, a genial bald man in his early fifties, had developed a reputation for honesty and clamping down on graft and corruption, and he wanted to show the police that they could no longer break the law with impunity. So, for a few months—while the Wall Street Crash erased fortunes and plunged America into the Depression—Nimble's disappearance became one of the hottest stories in Chicago. It was nicknamed "The *Real* Canary Murder Case"—a nod to *The Canary Murder Case*, a 1929 movie about the murder of a showgirl known as "The Canary."

A month passed, and Gustafson's friends were still convinced that the dead bird had been switched. In early November, these "friends of Nimble"—as *The Tribune* described them—insisted on the body being exhumed from where it had been buried (by a janitor, outside the morgue) so that it could be examined by an ornithologist who could determine whether it was indeed a canary of the singing species (or even a canary at all—some suspected it might have just been a "painted sparrow").

Eventually, Judge Horner tracked down and questioned the four police officers who had been guarding the scene the night Nimble went missing. One of them, William Tobin, claimed the bird had flown out of the window while he was on duty, and then flown back in a few days later and immediately dropped dead.

Horner wasn't convinced, and after months of fruitless investigating, he decided that August Vollmer—the newly arrived professor of policing at the University of Chicago—might be able to help him navigate the case.

Vollmer happily recommended Leonarde Keeler and the lie detector—he hoped the case would "make an indelible impression" on Horner and smooth the machine's route into the courtroom.

On February 13, the three men gathered in Horner's chambers to run polygraph tests on the police officers closest to the disappearance. It worked. Four hours later, Horner had a confession. Tobin and another officer had conspired to steal the bird and then tried to clumsily cover their tracks. It was the first time in history a judge had used a lie detector to try and determine the facts.

In their next big case, the polygraph's creators attempted to go a step further. In April 1930, Larson agreed to set aside his qualms about the lie detector being used as evidence, and his growing doubts about Keeler's judgment, to assist his friend in a court case.

Two collection agents from Chicago were accused of robbing a bank in Black Creek, Wisconsin, but they pleaded innocent and passed Keeler's lie detector test. Keeler knew his lack of formal qualifications meant he'd struggle on cross-examination if allowed to testify, so "when plans were made, [he] shouted loudly for John L. with his experience and many degrees," he recalled.

On the penultimate night of the trial, the pair explained the machine and their findings to the judge—Larson talked through the science, and Keeler conducted a successful card test on the sneering chief prosecutor. "He kept his mouth shut after we quickly picked his card," he wrote.

But the judge was unmoved and refused to allow the lie detector evidence to go in front of a jury. Then, the next day, two men from Minneapolis confessed to the crime. The trial was stopped, and Keeler and Larson were vindicated.

Although they didn't get to testify, they were delighted that the lie detector had been proven right. They spent the weekend together in Chicago, dashing around the city to lunches and dinners, and trying to secure positions for themselves at a new independent lab that was opening to study scientific methods of crime detection.

* * *

After the canary murder case, Judge Horner struck up a friendship with Keeler—they'd meet and talk over whiskey at a men's club in the city. And he became a strong advocate of the lie detector.

In April 1930, for instance, he arranged to be tested on it in a demonstration for *The Tribune*. Keeler successfully performed his trademark card test on Horner in front of the police commissioner, the coroner, and a Colgate-Palmolive executive called Burt Massee.

Massee had been the foreman of the coroner's jury in the aftermath of the Saint Valentine's Day massacre and had personally financed the hiring of ballistics experts to give testimony during the inquest.

The grim evidence Massee heard as foreman convinced him that something drastic needed to be done to fight crime in the city. He put up the funding, and John Henry Wigmore, the dean of the Northwestern University Law School and an expert on the law of evidence, provided a site.

The Scientific Crime Detection Lab was the first private criminology lab in the United States. Wigmore was adamant that it be kept separate from the police department—the lab would cover its costs by charging a small fee for cases.

"No laboratory attached to a police department will ever have civic full trust and confidence," he wrote. "The powers of such a laboratory, as an engine of jealousy and spite and graft, to divert justice from truth and to injure the innocent, are enormous. Their possibilities of abuse are terrifying, because these scientific methods of proof are irresistible." He could have been describing the polygraph machine.

Northwestern's main campus was in Evanston, a northern suburb, but the Scientific Criminal Detection Laboratory made its home in the law faculty building on 469 East Ohio Street in downtown Chicago.

It was a huge space, filling an entire floor of the building, with offices at the front fitted with the latest scientific equipment and a firing range at the rear.

The atmosphere was strange but invigorating. There was an air of industry and quiet determination under the lab's high ceilings: men peered through microscopes at blood-stained fibers and soil samples, soundtracked by the occasional burst of machine-gun fire. There was a classroom for lectures and a darkroom for developing photographs.

Keeler managed to line up an arrangement where he and Larson could split their time between the medical faculty at Northwestern and the new Crime Detection Lab, but Larson tanked the interview. "The poor fish—he arrived in one of his hyper states of mind—without a damn for his appearance—talked around circles instead of the questions at hand, and had his feet so far off the ground that he made a poor impression," Keeler told Vollmer.

"I did my best to promote John—but that one meeting ruined everything," he continued. "I think if they really could know John, they would alter their opinion—but I can't budge them now." It was an embarrassing situation, Keeler said, particularly when he was offered a full-time job at the Crime Detection Lab and Larson wasn't.

Still, Keeler jumped at the chance to join and also convinced lab director, Calvin Goddard, to hire Kay Applegate as his secretary. She and Keeler had been dating for a while by then, and in August 1930 they were married—Judge Horner performed the ceremony and threw "an elaborate wedding dinner" at the Lake Shore Country Club in Glencoe, where the newlyweds danced on the polished marble veranda as the sun set over the lake.

The Keelers moved into a two-bedroom apartment on the West Side. Kay took fencing lessons and learned to sew her own clothes. In the evenings she'd cook for her husband and his colleagues, who came over after work to drink and smoke cigars, and listen to the police reports coming over the scanner. They spent their holidays in the wilderness—hunting and fishing on a two-week "pre-moon" in the Canadian woods for instance.

But Kay Keeler was soon bored out of her mind by this domesticated life. "She wanted to break the bonds her sex imposed on her, to compete on equal terms in what was still a man's world," wrote Eloise. She started taking an interest in the pioneering forensics she saw going on around her. Meanwhile, her husband's work with the polygraph had become the main focus of the crime lab's activities.

Burt Massee's fortune had been hit by the Depression, and lie detector tests became a crucial way of bringing in revenue—the proceeds split fifty–fifty between Keeler and the lab. Without him, lab director Goddard admitted in a memo, the venture would likely have gone out of business.

Meanwhile, Vollmer was still keen to get the whole gang back together again, so when Herman Adler resigned from the Institute for Juvenile Research in June 1930, he recommended John Larson.

He moved back to Chicago in October 1930, and for six months everything went well. A photo from the time shows Keeler, Vollmer, and Larson grinning widely—arms around each other's shoulders in a show of genuine warmth and camaraderie. The trio spent many happy evenings together discussing the lie detector and making plans.

They were finally all together in the crime capital of the United States, poised to strike out corruption and deceit. Their next case plunged the three men and their machine into the dark heart of Chicago's criminal underbelly.

THE REPORTER

On the afternoon of Monday, June 9, 1930, Jake Lingle—a star journalist for *The Chicago Tribune*—was walking toward Illinois Central Station on Randolph Street, where he was planning to catch the train to Washington Park racetrack in Homewood.

He had a straw boater on his head and a copy of the racing form under his arm, and he waved to some companions in a passing car as he entered a short pedestrian subway that passed under Michigan Avenue.

The tunnel was crowded, so Lingle didn't notice the two men sidling up behind him, or one of them—a tall blond man in silk gloves—pulling out a gun. Lingle was shot in the back of the head. He collapsed forward and hit the floor. His hat rolled off and came to rest a foot away from the body as the crowd scattered. The gunman turned and vaulted away, discarding both gloves and murder weapon at the scene.

The Tribune decried the killing of its own man as a gangland attempt to silence the press—Lingle had been gunned down for telling the truth, it claimed. Its editors collaborated with six other newspapers to raise more than $60,000 in reward money for information leading to an arrest. Lingle had been friendly with Chicago police commissioner William Russell, who poured every resource at his disposal into the investigation—his men made more than six hundred arrests in the following weeks.

But soon after Lingle's funeral—where he was given the full works, with a marching band, police in parade dress, and thousands of mourners—the dark truth about him began to come out. In reality, Lingle was part reporter, part mob fixer.

His job saw him "cavorting with cops and robbers and working his sources in speakeasies"—he was close to politicians, police, and the gangs. Al Capone considered him a "good friend" and once gifted him a diamond-studded belt buckle. And he used the cover of journalism to enrich himself to a staggering extent—he lived a lavish lifestyle in a suite at Hotel Stevens, overlooking Lake Michigan, and an investigation into his finances found that he was pulling in $60,000 a year when his *Tribune* wage was $65 a week.

Lingle's friendship with the police commissioner secured him advance information on raids, which he sold to the gangs who ran the speakeasies. He moved on to charging them for protection—cutting Commissioner Russell in on the money if he agreed not to target particular gambling dens or saloons. But "his head got too big for his hat," as Capone might have said—and according to some reports, the week before Lingle died, the infamous mob boss had found out the journalist had been working for his rivals too, and stopped taking his calls.

Russell was determined to find out who had killed his friend, and he brought the Crime Lab into the investigation to try all its forensic tricks. The first man on the scene had the foresight to handle the gun with a handkerchief so it could be dusted for prints, but the killer had worn gloves. Calvin Goddard—the lab's director and the ballistics expert from the Saint Valentine's Day massacre inquest—fired a bullet from the gun into a waste basket and compared it under a microscope to the one removed from Lingle's brain to prove the gun was the murder weapon.

Then, even though the serial numbers had been filed off, the lab's scientists were able to decipher them by looking at changes to the crystalline structure of the metal underneath and tracing the original buyer to a sporting goods store on the North Side.

During the investigation, Keeler was sitting in his private office at the lab when two "tough-looking gents" sauntered in and shut the door behind them. Keeler looked up. "What can I do for you gentlemen?" he asked. They glared at him.

"We've come to make you an offer," one said.

"We'll pay you $50,000 for the bullet that killed Jake Lingle," said the other.

The projectile was locked in a safe elsewhere in the lab, and Keeler knew it would be a vital piece of evidence in the eventual trial. He tried to stall the men and mumbled something about not knowing the combination to unlock the safe. "Wait here," he said, telling the men he needed to ask his assistant. "I'll be right back."

Heart pounding, Keeler walked quickly between his colleagues in the office outside. "Go back to the shooting range!" he whispered. "Start firing machine guns! Hurry!"

As the puzzled investigators made their way toward the range, Keeler took a deep breath and returned to the office where the men were waiting. He sat back behind his desk and leaned back in his chair. "Sorry, gentlemen, I can't give you the bullet," he said. "It's evidence in a murder case, entrusted to us."

The men had just started advancing on Keeler when the building shook with gunfire. They froze, shared an alarmed glance—Was it the police? A gang war?—and then slunk out of the room and out of the building. A grinning Keeler walked to the shooting range and told his colleagues to hold their fire.

At around the same time, a man named Frank Bell, who had been arrested on suspicion of robbery, told police he knew who had killed Lingle. He singled out Richard Sullivan, who Bell said had been his accomplice in a number of other crimes, including the murder of Greek restaurant owner Chris Patras.

Although the details Bell gave matched those of a real unsolved murder, Sullivan denied all knowledge of this, Lingle's killing, and all the other crimes Bell had implicated him in.

Meanwhile, police were fairly certain they'd found Lingle's real murderer—a mob enforcer from St. Louis called Leo Brothers. But before they could proceed, they needed to rule out Bell's testimony—and they decided to do it with the lie detector.

Keeler ran the first test on his own, but when he showed it to Vollmer and Larson, they disagreed with his interpretation. So, "after some discussion, and there still being a disagreement," it was decided to retest Bell with all three men present.

Although they often corresponded on cases and shared notes afterward, it would be one of the few times all three of them ran a test together. Vollmer asked the questions while Keeler and Larson examined the markings on the scroll of paper as it came off the machine—indicating a spike here or a fall there—and talking in hushed tones as the chief's deep voice reverberated around the quiet room.

This time, the verdict was unanimous. Each time Vollmer asked a question, like "Did Sullivan kill Lingle?" or "Were you with Sullivan when he killed Lingle?," the lines on the chart made their characteristic jumps. Bell was lying—partly to get the reward money, but also to frame Sullivan, who had been chasing after Bell's girlfriend while he was locked away and driving him "frantic with jealousy."

But Bell had made a fatal miscalculation. Leo Brothers was able to lean on his mob connections to get just fourteen years in prison for killing Lingle, but Bell and Sullivan were tried and convicted of murdering Patras, the Greek restaurateur, and sentenced to death in the electric chair in the Cook County Jail.

* * *

The lie detector test on Bell was one of the last times Vollmer, Keeler, and Larson were all together in person, because the chief was struggling. Although his teaching course was getting good reviews, it was taking a toll on his health. He still wasn't fully recovered from his heart attack—he kept a jar of nitroglycerin tablets close at hand to manage his chest pains. He was still trying to run the Berkeley Police Department remotely, and his workload was piling up. Pat was worried about him.

He also found himself mediating frequent disputes between John Larson and Leonarde Keeler, who were starting to have serious disagreements over the lie detector. In the past, Larson had overlooked some of Keeler's transgressions because of their friendship, but his patience was wearing thin.

When a girl fainted while being questioned by Keeler, Larson insisted that a doctor be present for every test. He wrote a preamble that Keeler could use that gave subjects the option to opt out if they wanted to.

He insisted that Keeler avoid vague fishing expeditions like the one in the Mayer case, and he wanted those who confessed to sign a statement confirming that no "rough means" had been used.

But Keeler endlessly disappointed him, and he began to regret ever letting him near the machine back in Berkeley. "Vollmer forced Keeler on me," Larson moaned to a friend years later. "Keeler never did any work."

He accused Keeler of having "no sense of basic values" and placing the lie detector on the same basis as fingerprint evidence. Soon Larson was writing to Vollmer, complaining about how the younger man was talking the polygraph up as infallible and rushing ahead with commercialization before it was ready. He asked the chief to rein Keeler in.

"Caution Keeler whenever you see him to cut out his talk about the infallibility of this because I know it is not infallible," Larson told Vollmer in January 1931. "Tell him to never have it used so that men are discharged because of the interpretation of the record, or legal action of any sort taken. This he has already done on one or two occasions."

In early 1931, Vollmer suffered another heart attack. He and his wife had been spending more time away from the city and were finding it harder to return to cold Chicago each time. Vollmer had already told the university that once his course finished in March 1931, he would not be coming back. He lined up a similar job at the University of California, which he planned to combine with his police chief role at Berkeley.

In his absence, Larson and Keeler's relationship imploded completely.

A MALIGNANT HEART

On November 18, 1935—a few weeks after his original trial date for selling drugs to Max Dent—Joe Rappaport sat in a Cook County courtroom on trial for murdering him.

Chicago was in the midst of a cold snap. The first snows of winter were starting to fall, and by the end of the brief trial, a white blanket had spread across lawns and roofs, dulling the sound of footsteps and the hum of passing cars.

Rappaport, who was wearing a smart gray suit and had his dark hair slicked thickly back, stood to stiff attention as Judge Joseph Burke entered the courtroom and called the trial to order. Burke was in his mid-forties and was just embarking on the longest judicial career in Illinois history (he died in 1990 at the age of 101).

He looked out over the courtroom. Rappaport sat on one side of a long wooden table, opposite his attorney, Simon Herr, who had also represented Morris Rappaport in his manslaughter trial earlier that year.

Max Dent's mother, Annie, was one of the first prosecution witnesses. Her gray hair was tied up in a dark headscarf, and she was wearing a thick, fur-lined coat—but she still shivered, and the folds of skin at her neck trembled as she relayed the harrowing story of how she'd witnessed her son's shooting firsthand.

Rappaport watched impassively, leaning back in his chair or resting his face in his hands, long fingers pressing anxiously at his temples. He showed little emotion as Assistant State Attorney John Boyle, a well-groomed young man with a pocket watch dangling from a silver chain, worked the courtroom into a crescendo.

"Do you see the man who shot your boy in the courtroom?" Boyle asked, and the room shivered with tension.

"I do!" she declared, and her hands were steady—one "unwavering finger" pointed directly at Joe Rappaport.

Federal agents from the narcotics bureau described Dent's work for them and detailed the sting operation on Rappaport that seemed to have instigated his death. Agent Edwin Klein told the court that after he'd been arrested, Rappaport had sworn to "get" Dent.

* * *

Rappaport's defense rested on trying to prove he'd been nowhere near the scene of the crime. Herr's first witness was a businessman who said he'd seen Rappaport outside the Lawndale Theatre, a mile away, not long before the shooting.

Joseph Schufeldt, a twenty-four-year-old handbill distributor, said he'd seen the murder happen and that Rappaport was not the culprit. "The man I saw was short and fat; he wore a dark sweater, dark trousers, and a cap. It was not Joseph Rappaport."

Estelle Cohen, a twenty-one-year-old with short dark hair, backed up this version of events. "The man was stout and rather short," she said. "I did not see anyone else get into the car which drove north. I know Joe Rappaport. I did not see him there that night."

Rappaport took the stand himself and denied everything: he hadn't sold drugs to Dent, hadn't threatened him, didn't murder him. He wasn't even in the neighborhood at the time of the shooting. "I had no reason to kill Dent," he insisted. "He had said he would not testify against me, and that if he did testify, he would tell the truth—that he had framed me for the G-men" (a slang term for government agent, now particularly associated with the FBI).

As Burke called a recess for lunch on November 20, the trial seemed finely balanced—one set of witnesses placed Rappaport at the scene with a clear motive, and the other completely contradicted them. But during the break, his defense fell apart.

Rappaport's attorney, Simon Herr, returned to the courtroom fifteen minutes before the trial was due to resume at two PM and was told that Joseph Schufeldt—who had testified in his client's favor—had been arrested.

At around the same time, Estelle Cohen—the defense's other key witness—was approached by a bailiff, who told her she was wanted on the telephone. Cohen had finished on the stand at eleven thirty and remained in the courtroom before going to lunch with Martha and Rose Rappaport at a restaurant around the corner—she lived close to them on Douglas Boulevard and was a friend of the family.

She stepped out into a public hallway, which had a bank of phone booths on one wall. As soon as Cohen confirmed her identity on the phone, the door of the booth next to her opened, and she was accosted by two men wearing the tan jackets of bailiffs, who arrested her and took her to the state's attorney's office on the second floor of the courthouse. Martha and Rose saw this happening, but when they protested, prosecutor John Boyle ordered them to be arrested too.

Cohen was interrogated by Captain Dan Gilbert, who accused her of lying on the witness stand that morning. He told her she'd go to jail if she didn't confess that she lied. He took her into an office where his colleague Lieutenant Kelly repeated the same trick. They promised, Cohen said, that "they would be real good to her and see that she came to no harm" if she came clean.

When she insisted on the veracity of her story, they turned to the interrogation technique of the day. "Alright," Kelly said. "We will put the serum in your arm and send for the machine. Take a seat in the other room."

But Cohen's refusal to change her story didn't matter in the end, because the other defense witness—Joseph Schufeldt—had quickly caved to similar pressure. He was already telling the courtroom below that his entire testimony had been a lie. In fact, he now said, he hadn't been anywhere near the scene on the night of the shooting.

Herr was dumbfounded. "And you still persisted in lying to me and to this court and jury despite the harm you may have done to the defendant's chances?" he asked.

"I did it as a favor to the family," Schufeldt replied. "I was told to say that."

It looked bad. After he sat down, Herr leaned across to Rappaport and told him he was "in serious difficulty" and that it might be best to change his plea to guilty and "throw himself upon the mercy of the court." But Rappaport refused—he told Herr he was innocent and that under no circumstances would he plead guilty, regardless of how many people came forward to say they'd perjured themselves. He was, however, "taken wholly by surprise and was utterly helpless," Herr wrote.

The revelations proved a killer blow for the defense, which quickly unraveled: the booker from the Lawndale Theatre confirmed the boxing match Rappaport said he'd watched that night hadn't been shown there; Joe Terradesh, who owned a restaurant Rappaport claimed he'd gone to after the movie, said he hadn't seen him there either.

At eight PM that evening, the judge gave his final instructions, reminding the jury that the fact Rappaport had sold drugs did not establish his guilt in a murder trial, that he wasn't the only person with a potential motive for killing Dent, and that a high bar was required for a murder conviction. "Malice shall be implied when no considerable provocation appears and when all the circumstances of the killing show an abandoned and malignant heart," he said. He gave them four options to choose from: not guilty, a prison term of fourteen years or longer, life in prison and death.

Two hours later, the jurors knocked on the door of the jury room. The foreman, Delbert White, stood up and read out the verdict, underneath which he and the other eleven jurors had signed their names.

"We, the jury, find the defendant, Joseph Rappaport, guilty of murder, in manner and form as charged in the indictment, and we fix his punishment at death," he said.

Throughout the short trial, Rappaport had tried to present a "tough guy" image, wrote one reporter, but when the verdict came down, that facade briefly cracked. As his fate was read out, Rappaport stiffened, and the blood drained from his face before he recovered his composure and forced his features into a "sickly smile."

* * *

His family quickly rallied around him. His sisters, Martha and Rose, had, like Estelle Cohen, been held in police cells overnight after their arrest without access to a lawyer. They'd missed the verdict and now faced perjury charges. They were accused of inducing Schufeldt to lie, and the prosecutor, John Boyle, also claimed he'd heard Rose telling Schufeldt to "be careful what you say" when they crossed paths in the state's attorney's office after his arrest. When Martha was taken back to Boyle's office the next day, he seemed to take great pleasure in revealing her brother's fate. "Well, he got the limit, and you will get the limit, too, if you don't come through and tell us what we want to know."

The sisters leant on their father's connections in the Jewish community and scraped together as much money as they could to secure a heavyweight attorney for Rappaport's appeal. William W. Smith was law partner of the famous Clarence Darrow—in May 1924, they'd worked together on the so-called "Trial of the Century," in which Darrow defended Nathan Leopold and Richard Loeb, two students who'd kidnapped and murdered fourteen-year-old Bobby Franks. They'd wanted to showcase their "intellectual superiority" by committing the perfect crime.

By the time the Rappaport trial came around, Darrow was a frail old man of seventy-nine, but he came out of retirement to try and help his former partner get the conviction quashed.

But on December 30, 1935, Smith's motion for a retrial was denied, and Joe Rappaport's execution date was set for February 14, 1936.

Outside the courtroom, Smith—a dour-faced, middle-aged man with round frameless glasses—told reporters that the next step would be to take Rappaport's case to the Illinois Supreme Court.

FRANKENSTEIN'S MONSTER

Shortly after the Wall Street Crash, Leonarde Keeler had an idea that would take the polygraph out of the interview room and into the world of commerce. He wrote an excited letter to August Vollmer, detailing his plans to offer lie detector tests to department stores, which were losing tens of thousands of dollars a year to employee theft.

Staff could, Keeler suggested, be screened every six months or so, and the dishonest ones stamped out. "I believe we would quickly weed out the "lifters" and gangs that I know to be working the store, eliminate these, and put the "fear of the Lord" in the others," he wrote. In 1931, he struck a deal with the insurance conglomerate Lloyds of London to offer banks a 10 percent discount on their premiums if they allowed Keeler to test their employees regularly.

This sort of enterprise infuriated John Larson, who saw it as a "betrayal" of the principles of the lie detector. Since August Vollmer had left Chicago in March 1931, Larson found himself getting more and more frustrated with the way the machine, which he still considered to be his invention, had slipped out of his control.

As well as driving ahead with screening tests, Keeler had started to sell his own devices, under the brand "Keeler Polygraph." Looking back decades later, Larson considered this a turning point. "By shifting the terminology from cardio-pneumo-psychogram to a machine with an owner's name, the emphasis became commercial and purely mechanical," he wrote.

Although he wrote to Keeler, praising the neat design of the younger man's version of the polygraph, privately he disparaged it, telling friends it was identical to his own device in all but minor details and accusing Keeler of being a "copyist" and charlatan who had never had an original idea in his life.

Worse, Keeler was putting the machine not in the hands of scientists, but of anyone who would pay. Larson scolded him, saying that the lie detector test was "not a technique which should be turned loose and used by laymen or even by men who have only been trained superficially for a short time."

"I had this question fairly well controlled until you started putting out machines," he continued. "Because until then this sort of work could only be accessible to university people trained in laboratories. Now anyone who you or your firm release a machine to can go ahead and mess things up."

He worried about untrained laymen running the polygraph on subjects who weren't fit to be tested. "Sooner or later, a death is going to come for which the examiner as a layman will be responsible," he warned.

In fairness, Keeler's approach to commercialization was relatively cautious at first. Given the press he was getting, he could have sold the devices as fast as they could be built, netting $125 in royalties each time, but instead he maintained relatively strict control over who was allowed to buy and operate them, and kept the right to veto each sale.

Deep down, he agreed with Larson—he knew that if put in the hands of the wrong people the reputation of the lie detector could be dealt a blow from which it might never recover. It's just that Larson now considered Keeler—with his lack of qualifications and penchant for bending the rules—to be exactly the wrong kind of person.

He collected examples of Keeler's transgressions: how he'd complicate the test procedure by asking irrelevant questions about homosexuality or masturbation, how he'd once taken advantage of police protection to slap a suspect in the face, how he'd charge women's groups $35 for polygraph demonstrations and then cheat on the card test by using audience reactions rather than reading the chart.

"Unfortunately Leonarde hadn't gone over too well with the scientists because they look on him as a clever technical operator only, but one who has not had sufficient controlled academic training,"

Larson told Vollmer. He felt his own reputation was being tarnished by association.

Larson cast himself in the role of an overworked parent, running around after his inexperienced protégé to "debunk and pull Keeler's chestnuts out of the fire after he has commercialized and charged for what should be a scientific investigation."

He'd been working nights on the task Vollmer had set the two men, of scientifically validating the lie detector, fitting the study in around his day job. But the more research he did and the more he saw of how Keeler and his disciples were using the machine, the more Larson became convinced that the polygraph was not fit for use in criminal investigations. Without an underlying theory of the science of deception—an explanation of why, exactly, lying would show a telltale pattern of physiological activity—the machine was little better than a parlor trick.

There had already been a number of cases where Keeler and Larson had looked at the same record and disagreed in their verdicts. "We have made mistakes and will doubtless continue to make mistakes," Larson told Vollmer. "There is no reason at this time, therefore, to protect such mistakes for evaluation by the jury and afford chances of miscarriage of justice."

The chief was shocked by Larson's sudden change in attitude. He still hoped the lie detector could clean up Chicago, even though he'd left the city himself. "My own opinion is that you cannot throw in the wastebasket all of your labors," he wrote. Larson agreed up to a point—he thought the machine might have a place as a medical tool, to be used only by a fully trained psychiatrist to diagnose mental illness—a stethoscope for the mind. If it happened to solve a crime in the process, then great, but it shouldn't be thought of as a "lie detector."

In May 1931, Keeler tried to get the polygraph into the courtroom again—and asked Larson to join him in testifying on behalf of Virgil Kirkland, a high school football star from Gary, Indiana, who had raped and murdered his girlfriend, Arlene Draves, after a drunken night drinking bootleg spirits. This time, Larson refused to take part. He "thought that a test conducted in a courtroom was scientifically worthless," and he wrote to the judge, who agreed—the test was not allowed to take place in front of a jury.

It had only been a year since their previous joint attempt to get the lie detector admitted in the robbery case in Wisconsin, but Larson's attitude toward the test—and toward Keeler—had flipped completely. "John wouldn't join me, and I'm sure he was quite upset by the whole affair," Keeler admitted.

It was Keeler's lack of discipline that riled Larson the most. He'd worked hard and held several jobs to get his medical degree, and although Keeler had finally gone back to Stanford in the summer of 1930 to complete his undergraduate studies, he showed little inclination to go further.

Larson wrote to Vollmer, urging him to "use whatever influence you have on Leonarde"—he wanted Keeler to finish his medical studies like he'd promised, in the hope that a grounding in fundamental science might change some of his tendencies, particularly "his restlessness and inability to follow a routine piece of work through accurately." (Keeler did apply to a number of medical schools but couldn't get in because of his poor grades.)

Because of Keeler the country had, Larson wrote, "become overrun with unskilled operators and commercial salesmen who obligated the purchase of the 'machine' to expend several hundred dollars to take the course."

Not only had Keeler taken the bulk of the credit for what was Larson's invention, he had "prostituted" the polygraph until it was little more than "a racket" that Larson was determined to stop. "While I spent years in research on psychiatric phases and training, [Keeler] fostered a Frankenstein's monster in the form of a psychological third degree."

Larson's book was another source of anger. It was supposed to be a joint project—Larson had promised to list Keeler as a coauthor. But he'd pressed the younger man for contributions throughout the process and got little back in return—of the book's one thousand pages, Keeler had supplied less than five. Once, when Larson phoned Keeler for an update, his wife, Kay, called back to tell him the couple were going for an outing to the Indiana dunes. "While this work was being done, I didn't get any outings," Larson sulked.

When it was finally published in 1932, he couldn't bring himself to put Keeler's name on it as a coauthor, instead listing him only as a collaborator. Vollmer considered Larson dropping Keeler's name a "breach of faith," particularly when it became clear that the book—a dry tome with full sections lifted from dusty physiology volumes, with a scattering of case studies—was full of barbs and criticisms of Keeler's work. The younger man couldn't fail to notice.

"I received a copy of John Larson's book the other day and rather felt that he outdid himself in knocking me every time he had a chance," Keeler complained. "Instead of coming to me for details and getting a true account of the facts, he published every slanderous thing he could think of about me. Of course, all this was put in after I read the original manuscript. I am sorry that Larson has to resort to publishing his criticisms rather than telling me about them to my face. I feel that I can hardly trust him in future."

Vollmer's patience was running out too. "I want to take this occasion to express my profound regret that Larson took time out of his busy life to criticize your work," he told Keeler. "His book is on my desk, but as yet I have had no opportunity to read the contents. It is my opinion that Larson may be slipping slightly, judging from information in two letters recently received; it is possible that the poor chap is overworked."

Keeler made one last effort to bridge the gap and got a conciliatory reply. "I am glad to hear from you as I feel that we can do rather good work if we keep together," Larson wrote.

But by 1934, they were at each other's throats once more. "Our good friend John Larson is still up to his old tricks," Keeler wrote. "Gosh, I've done my best to be friendly, to give him all the credit due him for his good work, and to cooperate with him whenever possible. He always seems so friendly in my presence, but behind my back that's a different story. To individuals and in public talks and articles, he slams and pokes and tells some of the darndest lies you ever heard."

He'd come to think of Larson as the worst kind of hypocrite. "To one group he said I'm rotten for selling machines to untrained operators and dishonest police departments, and to another group he condemns me for refusing to sell machines to those who want them," he wrote.

Larson's old paranoia had returned—he was convinced Keeler was trying to take his job, a claim the other man dismissed as the "preposterous" fantasy of a fertile brain. Keeler did his best to rise above it.

"I still try to speak kindly of John and of course do in public and try hard to ignore his foolishness," he told Vollmer. "I'm going to arrange one more meeting with him and do my best to iron out difficulties, but after that, if he continues his present form of behavior, he can go to the devil. If I thought we could save him from a complete mental breakdown, I'd give him a half interest in the patents, but I'm afraid even that wouldn't help."

The chief put it down to his upbringing. "John is the victim of his heredity and environment, and it is most unfortunate that his lack of tact causes his friends to desert him," he wrote to one of Larson's colleagues in 1933. "My suggestion is that you retain his friendship, because after you analyze the entire situation, you will discover that he is not devoid of marvelous qualities. Like some bad boys, you want to put him over your knee and spank him, and just about the time you are ready to administer capital punishment, you discover some lovable point that makes you change your mind. He is just different from the run-of-the-mill type of men and, because of that fact, occasionally does things that are worthwhile."

He advised Keeler to simply ignore Larson. "Pay no attention whatever to John's talk," he wrote. "Treat him as kindly as you always have in the past, and say not one word that you wouldn't want him to say about you. You can't cure him, not by anything you or anyone may do. He is what he is by reason of all that has gone before him, and nothing that he or any other person can do will remold him or change his behavior pattern in the slightest degree. Treat his talk as you would a mosquito. It is annoying but you can't do much about it."

Vollmer followed his own advice, too—after receiving a copy of Larson's book, he sent a short thank-you note and then didn't speak to him again for twenty years. He stopped answering his letters and calls, and ascribed Larson's attitude to jealousy. "It is unfortunate that his personality is such that he can never become reconciled to the fact that the spotlight happens to be on Keeler instead of himself," he wrote.

On the North Side of Chicago, Keeler continued to grab the headlines with dramatic cases and train up new operators for the Keeler Polygraph. On the South Side, Larson nursed his grievances. Their once close relationship had devolved into jealousy and hatred. And Keeler had found a new partner in his pursuit of fame and justice.

E. NORMOUS WEALTH

In June 1933, Kay Keeler arrived in the Kentucky hill country, "an isolated territory of hidden stills and bloody feuds," to work a case of her own. Bored with her secretarial duties at the crime lab, she'd taken August Vollmer's criminology class at the University of Chicago and studied handwriting recognition and forensics under Herbert Walter, who'd testified against Al Capone in the gangster's trial for tax evasion.

"Instead of taking dictation, she wanted to dictate, to be an integral part of all that was happening," wrote her sister-in-law Eloise Keeler. Soon, Kay's dabbling in forensics morphed into an investigative career, and after mulling over the various techniques in use at the crime lab, she decided to specialize in handwriting analysis.

Like lie detection, this was scientifically dubious, but it propelled Kay into the public eye—she was soon making almost as many newspaper front pages as her husband and his lie detector.

She first appeared in *The Tribune* in 1931 as a twenty-five-year-old and America's first female handwriting expert. Death threats had been sent to four Chicago high-society newlyweds. Kay matched all four notes to the same typewriter, and police lured the extortioner into a trap.

The newspapers absolutely loved Kay—she posed for photos at the crime lab, with her wavy hair cascading down to her shoulders, peering into a microscope or pointing a pistol down the lens of the camera. She was, one reporter gushed, "entirely too young and pretty to be associated with the grim business of fighting crime." At first, she was jealous of not getting as much recognition as Leonarde; soon

she thought her name was in the papers to a "nauseatingly dispropor-
tionate degree."

Kay's intelligence and bravery made her well suited to detective
work. She was in Kentucky, working her biggest case yet, for the
department store Sears, which had been losing a million dollars a year
to forged checks originating from Breathitt County in the foothills of
the Appalachians, signed with names like "E. Normous Wealth."

At first, Sears blamed rogue postmasters, but Kay's handwriting
analysis indicated the checks had been written by at least forty different individuals. When the company sent private investigators to the
scene—hardened folk used to dealing with Chicago gangsters—they
were marched back to the train station at gunpoint by "poorly clad,
unshaven, suspicious-eyed characters."

But Kay had a plan. After signing a release absolving Sears of any
blame should something go wrong, she and her friend Jane Wilson
traveled to Kentucky, where they posed as doctoral students conducting a survey of "pure-blooded" Americans (the residents of the hill
country being particularly proud of their lineage).

The two women rented horses and spent several days roaming
around the hills. When they were confronted by the "mountain folk" in
their jeans and jackets, with their hands on their pistols, Kay had her
slick cover story ready to go: "We've been told that in this section we'd
find direct descendants of the early Americans—probably the only
people in America untainted by foreign blood."

So, they'd be invited into people's homes to share a meal of corn
bread and string beans, and whenever they spied suspiciously gleaming
cookware or a brand-new sewing machine or a gas range or electric toy
train in a place with no gas or electricity, they'd ask the residents to
fill out their survey and finish it off with a signature. "Otherwise, our
professors will think we've just made all this up."

By the time the locals' suspicions were finally aroused a few weeks
later, Kay Keeler and Jane Wilson had identified the locations of hundreds of items of merchandise and found a hidden printing press that
was churning out counterfeit money orders. They'd also collected hundreds of signatures to compare against the forged checks—their work
helped get more than 150 convictions.

Like her husband, Kay also pitted her wits against Chicago's political machine. In 1934, she helped prove widespread election fraud in Cook County. Kay examined the tally sheets used by the vote counters, and noticed that instead of being marked irregularly, they were all of the same length and angle, "as if ticked off in rapid succession." In one recount, 29 percent of ballots were found to have been falsified.

The Keelers often worked cases together—Kay's forensic expertise backed up by Nard's skill with the lie detector. In 1935, they collaborated to investigate a huge explosion at the Vallier coal mine in southern Illinois, which had been the scene of a fraught dispute between rival unions. There had, Nard estimated, been around three hundred violent incidents between 1933 and 1935. Mines had been bombed, and railroad bridges and trains blown up.

He combed over the site of the latest blast, which had destroyed the mine's engine house—where the heavy machines for lowering men and equipment down the shafts were housed. He found what he assumed were the remains of the bomb's timer: a ruined alarm clock, trailing copper wire, and sticky tape. And he ran polygraph tests on two of the prime suspects—Mitch McDonald and Robbie Robertson from the Progressive Mine Workers, a breakaway union group thought to be behind the bombing.

Robertson displayed a strong reaction both during the test and afterward, when he put his fist through the machine and admitted to having a roll of tape like the one on the alarm clock in a first-aid kit at his house, and to owning copper wire and fishing line of the type that had been used.

But merely possessing such common items wasn't enough to prove his guilt. So, by analyzing the jagged cuts in the tape under a microscope at 529x magnification, Kay matched the thread count and weave of the pieces of tape found on the alarm clock with the roll taken from the first-aid kit at Robertson's house. Others found similar matches for the copper wire and fishing line recovered from the bomb mechanism. The culprits were sentenced to twenty-five years in prison, "the hidden truth laid bare by chemistry, photography, microscopy, and the lie detector."

* * *

In February 1935, Leonarde Keeler finally got the chance to present lie detector evidence to a jury. The Frye precedent barred the polygraph from federal court, but individual states and counties could still allow it. The case involved Tony Grignano and Cecil Loniello, who were accused of killing a police officer while fleeing a pharmacy holdup in Portage, Wisconsin. The judge, Clayton van Pelt, had seen Keeler demonstrating the lie detector before and had been waiting for a case where it might prove useful.

Before the test, Van Pelt got both prosecution and defense to agree that Keeler would be allowed to testify regardless of the outcome. On February 7, Keeler spent three hours explaining the results of the test. The two young men had been untruthful, he said, although he tempered his usual assessment of the machine, saying that it was only 75 percent effective and should not be their sole consideration.

After the jury decided to convict, Keeler quickly bounced back to his usual self. "It means that the findings of the lie detector are as acceptable in court as fingerprint testimony," he told the papers.

If it was up to him, there would have been no jury at all. In 1930, he gave a provocative talk called "The Jury System Should Be Abolished," where he outlined his vision for a justice system run on the polygraph. Jurors were too easily swayed by media coverage, Keeler thought, and ought to be replaced by expert criminologists, with a judge on call to rule on any legal tangles.

Privately, though, Keeler was developing mixed feelings about the publicity garnered by cases like this one. The press fascination with the lie detector had helped make him a rich man, but he was starting to question whether media attention was the boon he'd originally thought.

"I wanted publicity in the past because I thought it would help us in our work," Keeler told his father. "I've wanted to be friendly with everyone, including newspaper men. But now I have an abhorrence for publicity. I fear it because it always brings criticism from the more worthwhile people. I'll be happy if I never see my name in the press again."

* * *

Outwardly, the Keelers seemed on top of the world in their eighteenth-floor apartment on the Gold Coast, with sweeping views over Lake Michigan.

They lived a life full of adventure, accompanied always by their German shepherd Chief (named after Vollmer). When they weren't chasing down leads and pursuing Chicago criminals, they were trekking through remote forests or camping under the stars. Once, Keeler brought home a six-month-old jaguar called Lupe from the Brookfield Zoo—it spent an evening lacerating chairs, drapes, and Kay's legs, and the couple were the first visitors to the zoo the following morning to return it.

They bought a yacht, which they nicknamed the *Walla Walla*, after Kay's Washington hometown. Every day after work they'd go down to the waterfront with Chief and swim at the Lake Shore Athletic Club or motor around the little caves and inlets in their boat.

In August 1936, they spent a month cruising around the Great Lakes—docking each night to camp and cook over an open fire. It was, Eloise wrote, "perhaps the last really happy vacation Kay and Nard had together. From then on problems began to mount."

Their freewheeling lifestyle had a cost. The heart condition Keeler had discovered by accident as a teenager was beginning to manifest, and he suffered from palpitations and dizzy spells.

He smoked and drank heavily. Kay's health was suffering too—she also had dizzy spells and was a regular visitor to the Mayo Clinic as she sought medical help to conceive—the couple used their polygraph tests on patients as cover for their frequent trips. "Whatever happens I know we'll always be mighty happy," Keeler wrote. "She is a wonderful helpmate." But their relationship was breaking down too—and the Rappaport case was about to throw both their lives into turmoil.

AN UNTIMELY END

On January 28, 1936, John Larson heard screams coming from the corridor at Joliet Penitentiary, where he'd continued his work with inmates. Recently, he'd been conducting regular polygraph tests on Richard Loeb—one of the two killers Clarence Darrow had saved from the death penalty in the "Trial of the Century."

Larson had gotten to know both men well during their twelve years in prison and had grown to like Loeb—an affable, intelligent man who was interested in history and detective novels.

So, it was a deep shock when Larson raced out into the corridor to find Loeb staggering out of a bathroom completely naked, dripping wet, and covered in blood. He was the first official on the scene, and he saw Loeb's former cellmate, James Day, standing above the dying man, with a straight razor in his hand, blood and water dripping off his body onto the floor.

Loeb had been slashed more than fifty times—his throat appeared to have been cut from behind, and there were what looked like defensive wounds on his hands and arms. In his office, Larson interrogated Day, who said Loeb had lured him into a private shower room and propositioned him, then threatened to cut him with a razor if he didn't cooperate. Day managed to kick Loeb in the groin, he said, and grab the razor—slashing wildly as hot water and steam obscured his vision.

The dead man was still one of the most famous inmates in the country, and prison officials wanted to avoid a scandal. They ordered Larson not to speak to the press and not to testify in Day's trial. But over the following weeks, Larson was quoted extensively in the

Chicago dailies, denouncing corruption in the penal system and detailing the lavish lifestyle the two murderers had been able to maintain at Joliet—with private bathrooms to which they'd invite "broadminded" convicts in exchange for money and favors.

The story became potent ammunition against Henry Horner. The judge who had overseen the canary murder case and officiated at Leonarde Keeler and Kay Applegate's wedding was now the governor of Illinois, sweeping into power with the slogan "With Horner, we'll turn the corner."

Now, Horner was running for reelection. He was in the midst of a grueling primary battle to retain the Democratic nomination, so he pressured prison administrators to suppress the story.

The incident ended Larson's time in Chicago. He was fired, ostensibly for recommending that Day hire his wife's cousin as his attorney (according to Keeler, Larson had threatened to commit Day to a mental institution "for the rest of his life" if he didn't). "Poor old John," Keeler wrote to Vollmer, in a letter dripping in malice. "Finally stumbled and badly stubbed his toe."

By then, Larson had burned his bridges with Vollmer too. The chief had helped launch his career, but now he'd stopped replying to his letters or returning his phone calls.

Larson had spent a year part-time at the University of Chicago, testing the validity of the lie detector, and claimed Vollmer had stopped speaking to him because he turned in a report at the end of it that pointed out all the potential sources of error with the polygraph—mechanical and psychological.

Vollmer told it differently. "It reached a point where it was necessary to wipe Larson off my correspondence list because of his unprofessional and unethical attitude," he told Keeler's friend Charlie Wilson. "It is my opinion that he should have welcomed all that Leonarde was doing and should have assisted rather than obstructed his efforts to put deception detection upon a solid foundation."

Larson found a new job as an assistant psychiatrist in Detroit and settled down into family life, directing some of his nervous energy toward his newborn son, Bill. He dedicated the rest of his time to "trying to break Keeler's racket"—planning talks and writing papers, and secretly collecting evidence that he planned to use to tell the public "the truth about lie detectors."

Vollmer considered Larson's downfall inevitable. "John was certain to come to an untimely end," he told Keeler. "When men continue to double-cross their friends, as he has in the past, there can only be one result."

* * *

Joseph Rappaport whiled away the first months of 1936 playing pinochle with the guards inside the imposing Cook County Jail, which sprawled out behind the criminal courts at Twenty-Sixth and California in South Lawndale.

When he'd first arrived, it had felt like he was entering a fortress. Bulletproof glass protected the information window at the front of the premises, and from an octagonal steel turret at the center, a guard armed with a "riot-gas gun" could survey the exercise yards and the entrance to each cell block. Fierce dogs were trained to recognize escaping prisoners by their white caps.

The warden, Frank Sain, had the look of an undertaker, with a high, pale forehead; jet-black hair ;and a preference for pin-striped suits. He'd fought with the 331st Machine Gun Battalion in the First World War, and together with Sheriff John Toman—an uptight, bespectacled man who was a stickler for hygiene—he brought a military precision to the jail and ruled with an iron fist.

Death-row inmates like Rappaport were usually housed together until a few days before their execution date, when they were moved to a special death cell in the basement, with a clean gray floor, brick walls that were a sickly yellow, and metal bars painted cream.

From there, Rappaport could hear the whine of saw blades and the clanging of hammers as Charles Johnson, the jail's locksmith and handyman, put the finishing touches on a new, improved version of the electric chair in his basement workshop.

The old chair had been used twenty-seven times since it had replaced hangings in 1927. But it was felt that the process of strapping the condemned man in was too slow. Johnson told reporters that he wanted to "humanize" the execution process. "It is my idea to improve the chair so that there will be as little delay as possible in the execution," he said. "My main idea is to shorten the last few agonizing moments before the current is turned on."

Under the old system of buckles and straps it took more than a minute to get a man ready to die; Johnson's designs had cut that to less than twelve seconds. "In the past it was necessary for the guards to pull the straps tight and then buckle them," he explained. "Often the straps were pulled too tight or were buckled incorrectly, inflicting injuries. It was almost like torture."

* * *

On January 24, 1936, three weeks before Joe Rappaport's appointment with the electric chair, the Illinois Supreme Court agreed to hear his appeal, granting him a stay of execution.

The family was tight on funds—his lawyers had already had to apply for financial relief on several occasions and the legal fees were mounting between Joe's appeal and Martha's perjury charges, for which she had just been released on bond.

Rappaport's brother, Morris, raised cash by selling tickets to a benefit dance, leaning on Joe's criminal connections on the outside to help pay for his defense. But the extra money didn't help.

In June 1936, the Illinois Supreme Court finally handed down its verdict. Justice Warren Orr was unconvinced by Rappaport's alibi and believed the defendant's testimony had been "largely discredited." He set a new execution date: October 23, 1936.

Rappaport's lawyers pressed the Illinois Supreme Court for a further stay of execution, to give them time to appeal for a pardon to Governor Henry Horner or take their case all the way to the US Supreme Court.

Then, on October 9, two weeks before his son was due to be executed, Rabbi Israel Rappaport finally succumbed to ill health and passed away, with the uncertainty over Joe's fate hanging over his death bed like a ghost.

When the state Supreme Court denied another stay of execution on October 16, the family decided not to tell their mother, Etta Rappaport, mindful of her previous mental health difficulties and afraid of how she might react to the prospect of losing both a husband and a son in the space of a few weeks. "A rabbi's widow planned happily today for her next visit to her son at the county jail, not dreaming that one hour after midnight Thursday he is scheduled to die," wrote *The United Press*.

The guards spent the weekend practicing with the new model electric chair—one of them standing in for the prisoner as the others raced to strap him in. By Sunday night, they had their time down to six seconds.

By then, there were three other men on death row with Rappaport. Peter Chrisoulas, a forty-year-old Greek with jet-black hair who had shot dead a theater manager; and Andrew Bogacki and Frank Korczykowski, who had murdered a policeman and then made a sensational dash for freedom during their trial, overpowering the guards and battling their way through the courthouse, slashing at deputy sheriffs with makeshift daggers and batons.

A few minutes after one AM on Tuesday, October 20, two days before his own execution date, Rappaport peered through the cream bars of his cell as two guards "half-led, half-dragged" Korczykowski down the short hallway, through a white metal doorway, and into a rectangle of bright light.

The door clanged shut before he could get a glimpse of the execution chamber. He wouldn't find out what was behind that door until he walked through it himself. Rappaport's fate was now up for review by the state pardon board. His life was in the hands of the governor of Illinois.

THE LAST MILE

There was an understandably grim mood on death row the morning after the executions. The bodies of Frank Korczykowski and Andrew Bogacki still lay in their wicker caskets in an anteroom, waiting for someone to collect them. Peter Chrisoulas sat shivering under blankets, wrapped in a thick overcoat—he could never seem to get warm. The other inmates teased him. "Don't shake and shiver so much," they said. "You're gonna burn. You'll never be cold again."

Joe Rappaport played endless games of cards. He was waiting for news from Springfield, where, on Wednesday, October 21, his attorney, William Smith, was pleading for his sentence to be commuted in front of the Illinois Board of Pardons and Paroles, which would take its recommendation to the governor.

Henry Horner was not a big fan of capital punishment, but 1930s Chicago was not a political environment where you could afford to look soft on crime. Successful politicians had to master the tightrope walk of appearing to crack down on mobsters and vice dens while knowing that if they did too good a job, they'd find it very difficult to get reelected, either because of a lack of funding or because they'd been killed.

Horner seemed temperamentally unsuited to the bruising world of Chicago politics. He had a kind, open face, and by 1937 he had cultivated the air of a scholarly grandfather—he was a well-spoken, genial man in his late fifties, with a round, bare head and a bristling moustache, who was usually found with a pair of pince-nez glasses perched on his round nose and a cigar dangling from his lips.

He'd built a good reputation as a judge before becoming the Democratic governor of Illinois in 1932. As the state's first Jewish governor, he faced extreme prejudice from both the electorate and his political opponents—he responded by pouring all his energy into his work.

Horner took his power of clemency particularly seriously, sometimes staying up all night to read case files before making his decision. "Such cases always forced him to consider the humanity of both sides: the victims and their families, but also the offenders, their families, and the human narratives that explained the tragic positions in which the offenders had come to reside," wrote his biographer Charles J. Masters.

*   *   *

The hearing was the defense's last roll of the dice, and they called a battery of surprise witnesses. Smith's aim was to persuade the parole board that Annie Dent was lying about having seen her son's shooting and that she was determined to pin the crime on Joe Rappaport, with little regard for whether he had actually done it.

Certainly, her version of events didn't seem to chime with her behavior on the night of the shooting. If she'd really seen Max being shot, why had she been so surprised when she lifted the corner of William Fenn's raincoat to reveal him beneath it? And where had she gone in between the shooting and the police arriving at the scene?

Clarence Stachowiak, who'd testified that he'd seen Annie Dent rushing down South Lawndale before the shooting, now said that wasn't true. William Wagner, who lived a few doors down from where Max Dent was shot, said he'd rushed out of his house immediately and hadn't seen Annie Dent there either, and Clara Franson from across the street said the same thing.

Max Shain, who lived at 1863 South Lawndale—from where he could see into the Dents' basement apartment, said he'd been standing on his porch when he heard the gunshots and could see Annie Dent in her home.

Two youths, Lester Siegel and Joseph Sternstein, who'd been among the first on the scene after the shooting, said they hadn't seen Annie Dent until later on. They'd been on the state's witness list at the trial but had never been called.

Now, Siegel recalled a conversation he'd had with Annie Dent in Yiddish four or five minutes after the shooting, as they stood near the body. He concluded that it wasn't "humanly or physically possible" for Annie Dent to have seen it happen.

There were other unanswered questions too—about the motivations of Joe Schufeldt, who'd changed his testimony and then accused Martha Rappaport of asking him to do it; and about why Rappaport would have wanted Dent dead even though he'd promised not to testify against him. There were suspicions that someone higher up the pyramid was pulling the strings—Dent had put six other people in federal prison that year alone.

With seven hours to go until the next round of executions, word came through from Springfield of a reprieve—not for Rappaport, but for Chrisoulas, who was also being represented by Smith. The Greek was granted a sanity hearing, which meant an automatic stay of execution. He wept with joy. "God bless you!" he cried. "God bless you!"

But as the clock in the warden's office ticked on, preparations for Rappaport's death continued. In the room next to his cell, prison staff checked wires and soaked sponges in saline solution for attaching the electrodes. His family arrived—Etta, Martha, and Morris crowded into the cell and huddled around Joe as he sat on the narrow bed, lit by the last rays of weak sunlight coming through the high window.

At six PM, Rappaport was sitting in the warden's office, waiting to have his head shaved, when his younger sister, Rose, rushed in with news from Springfield. He'd been given another stay of execution until December 4, to give the state pardon board and Horner more time to consider the case. It was a stunning last-minute reprieve, as "dramatic as any thriller" as the two doomed men "were snatched from the chair."

Rappaport leaped up, embraced his sister, and shouted for joy.

* * *

The pardon board met again on November 24, and while Smith worked one angle in Springfield, the Rappaport family leaned on their Chicago connections. In the governor's mansion, Horner was bombarded with phone calls from religious leaders pleading for mercy.

But Horner was perhaps uniquely unsuited to lobbying from the Jewish community. He didn't put much emphasis on religion and had always been reluctant to use his influence to further Jewish causes.

In the past, he'd been criticized by the community for not commuting the sentence of a Jewish man scheduled to die on Yom Kippur—the Young Jewish Lawyers Association had refused to endorse his 1936 reelection bid because of this. One rabbi accused him of not being a "real Jew," of being "ashamed" of his ancestry.

On December 1, Horner announced his final decision. Despite his "views" on capital punishment, he told reporters, the parole board had heard nothing that would enable him to intervene. "Joseph Rappaport had a fair trial before an able judge and the Supreme Court of this state has affirmed the judgment of the Criminal Court of Cook County," he said. "I find nothing in the record in this case to justify an interference with the penalty imposed by the court."

With this blow, Rappaport seemed to finally give up hope. His usually cheery demeanor at last turned solemn. He gathered his family at the jail again and asked to talk to a clergyman. On the day of the execution, he ordered his last meal and prepared to walk the "last mile"—seventeen steps from his cell to the execution chamber. The guards started setting up the chair again, for both Rappaport and Chrisoulas, whose jet-black hair had turned gray during his year on death row.

Then, just before the dinner hour, the telephone rang in Frank Sain's office. Horner had changed his mind. "Although I believe Joseph Rappaport had a fair trial, under the circumstance I feel that I am warranted in granting the reprieve so that counsel may be given full opportunity to prepare and present the case to the supreme court of the United States," he said, granting a third stay of execution until January 15, 1937.

In his cell, Rappaport embraced his mother, who had brought the news in with her. They posed for the newspapers, both beaming—he in the white shirt and slim tie he'd planned to die in, her gray hair tied up in a black headscarf. The reversal had come so late in the day that at least one of the next day's papers mistakenly reported Rappaport's death.

* * *

It was only a temporary reprieve—for Rappaport, and for Horner. The US Supreme Court declined to hear the case, and the governor was soon being inundated again with letters, phone calls, and telegrams from hundreds of private citizens, priests, rabbis, and ministers asking him to commute the sentence.

Famed lawyer Clarence Darrow, now "a shaggy man with heavy jowls and tousled hair," reportedly traveled to Springfield to speak on Rappaport's behalf, his voice seldom rising above a low drawl, the pockets of his baggy trousers bulging with papers. It was the final court appearance of a distinguished career, and his first direct involvement in a case since his work on the appeal of Bruno Hauptmann, the German carpenter sentenced to death for the infamous kidnapping of the Lindbergh baby.

"In view of facts now known, there is grave doubt that Rappaport committed the deed," Darrow wrote in a letter to the parole board. He argued that the harsh verdict was a result of the perjury allegations that surfaced during the trial and that without those, Rappaport would never have been sentenced to death. "Rappaport should not be held accountable for what his sister might have done or said, even if she did, in her zealousness to save her brother's life, induce a witness to tell a lie."

But the pardon board had been under fire for its leniency—recently, three Chicago policemen had been killed by criminals out on parole. It denied the appeal for clemency, and on the night of February 18, 1937, the guards again started to prepare the electric chair—testing the equipment and running through the grim choreography of taking prisoner from cell to death chamber.

Visitors filed into the viewing gallery, where they sat on wooden benches facing a glass screen, which had been installed after the first few electrocutions, to stop the smells of death drifting over the crowd. One of the newspapers had paid for a phone line into the building so its reporters could dictate proceedings to the newsroom as they happened.

This time, it was almost nine PM when the phone in the warden's office rang. Smith had been pressing the parole board again, telling them he'd found new evidence attacking the testimony of Annie Dent—more neighbors who placed her at home at the time of the shooting so that she couldn't have witnessed it as she claimed. It was dubious, but enough for Horner—whose reluctance to execute anyone was clear.

He signed an executive order giving Rappaport a one-week stay of execution. Paper copies were rushed to the jail by highway patrolmen. Frank Sain entered the death cell to pass on the news. "Is it official?" asked Rappaport as a look of relief came over his face. "I'm the happiest man in the world."

He had resigned himself to death. "Perhaps there is a God, after all," he cried. "I still have faith I will be vindicated. I am beginning to believe now there is some hope for me."

* * *

A week later, on Thursday, February 25, Rappaport was back in the basement of the Cook County Jail for the fifth time, and it was getting crowded. They were a strange trio, all packed into the death cell: Rappaport, the rabbi's son; Mildred Bolton, a middle-aged White woman who'd shot her husband to death at his office; and Rufo Swain, a Black college athlete from Arkansas, accused of the rape and murder of a twenty-four-year-old woman in a hotel room.

Frank Sain was deeply troubled by this—he didn't like the fact that Bolton had to share her cell with two men. But Rappaport didn't mind the company—he played cards with Swain and struck up an unlikely friendship with Bolton, whose cool demeanor during the trial earned her the tabloid nickname "Marble Mildred."

"I met Joe Rappaport tonight for the first time, and there was a lot of kidding about us being 'unseen sweethearts,'" she told reporters. "You know, I wrote him a letter a little while ago, telling him to keep his chin up."

Now, she tried to comfort him as he paced nervously back and forth in the cell. "Don't lose your courage Joe," she said. "Keep your head in the air. Everybody believes you're innocent, and that ought to be of some comfort to you."

Bolton's own impending death seemed to be causing more stress for Sain than for the condemned women herself—as well as being worried about the sleeping arrangements, the warden had grave concerns about what clothing to put her in for the execution. These were partly practical—electrodes were usually attached to the head and the leg; before death, men's trousers were cut off below the knee to accommodate this.

But the convulsions of those being electrocuted were often violent; once, a man's leg had spasmed so hard that it broke free of its leather straps and sent his slipper flying across the room. "I can't let her go in that short skirt," Sain said. "I'll have to get her a bloomer suit." (Sain's desire for propriety, however, did not stop him looking into filming the executions—he thought the footage would make a "great deterrent.")

Horner had been up until midnight the night before, discussing the cases of Rappaport; Swain; Bolton; and Allen and Minnie Mitchell, a Black couple who had committed murder as part of an insurance collection scheme and who were on death row in Menard, in southern Illinois. "The governor is in a tough spot," Bolton said. "Just think, he has five people now with their lives in his hands. Reprieves and requests for commutation have placed all these lives right in his lap at one time."

As the killing hour approached, the chances of a reprieve faded. The prisoners were served elaborate final meals—although it was actually Rappaport's fifth "last meal"; he'd never eaten so well.

After dinner, Rappaport and Swain played cards and watched the clock. Henry Horner sat alone in his study in the governor's mansion in Springfield, wrestling with the moral dilemma. He emerged just after nine PM. His face looked drawn and tired. "Notwithstanding my own views as to the death penalty as the punishment for murder, it is the law of this state and a law which we are bound to obey," he said. "Upon the recommendation of the pardon board I have declined to grant a pardon or commutation of sentence in the case of Joseph Rappaport."

At the jail, Sheriff Toman interrupted Rappaport's card game and beckoned him to the door of the cell.

"Has the governor come through and commuted my sentence?" Rappaport asked.

"No, I'm afraid not, Joe," Toman replied. "But he did give you a five-day reprieve because of the holiday."

The next day was the start of Purim, a three-day period of feasting for Orthodox Jews. Horner had given Rappaport one last short stay of execution until March 2. He was led back to his old cell block. "By the way, Sheriff, that was a fine steak dinner I had tonight," he joked.

There was also a reprieve for Mildred Bolton, who had already changed into her execution outfit of a "gymnasium suit" and bloomers. But Horner didn't want to become the first governor of Illinois to execute a woman in ninety years, so both Bolton and Minnie Mitchell had their sentences commuted to 199 years in prison. "I would have preferred it the other way," Bolton told Toman. "It's not going to be easy for me to leave here. You've all been so good to me."

Rufo Swain and Allen Mitchell—the two Black men on death row—were not so lucky. They were executed simultaneously at midnight, two hundred miles apart. Two hundred people were packed into the viewing area as Swain was led to the chair—some perched on wooden benches, the rest arranged in a tight circle at the back of the room.

There was a black hood over his face, and five guards marched him from his cell, but he shrugged off their attentions and took his last steps alone.

It was a horrible way to die. The flesh turned red, the bowels opened, the mouth hung wide, and saliva dripped down from under the hood. Wisps of acrid smoke rose from where the electrodes touched the skin.

At twelve minutes past midnight, as three prison doctors confirmed Swain's death, Joe Rappaport was back in his old cell, musing on his latest brush with death and wondering if there was anything left that could save him.

DIVINE INTERVENTION

The 20th Century Limited pulled into Chicago's La Salle Street station in a rush of steam and noise. It was nine AM on Monday, March 1, 1937—a crisp, clear morning—and white clouds billowed around the famous train.

Henry Horner was among the smartly dressed figures who stepped off the service and into the hubbub of the station. He had been in New York, meeting other state governors about the economic crisis and the sharp drop in employment, and was on his way back to Springfield, the state capital.

He looked awful. His health was deteriorating. The grueling 1936 reelection campaign had sapped his strength—he was overweight, bitter, despondent; tired of mind and weak of heart.

But, despite chiding from his doctor, he refused to adopt healthier habits: he smoked, ate late, drank bourbon, worked relentlessly. His mood was badly affected by criticism—a heckler on the street could plunge him into a deep depression for days. He couldn't sleep and took to walking the streets of Springfield in the middle of the night, peering into shop windows and wondering what might have been if he'd chosen a different career.

The state capital offered a nice change of pace from frigid, polluted Chicago, but with just his butler, Clarence, for company in the grand sixteen-room governor's mansion, Horner was lonely. He missed the men's clubs and restaurants, the coziness of his bachelor apartment with his collection of Abraham Lincoln memorabilia. The nonstop clemency hearings in the Rappaport case and others had weighed heavily on him too, and he'd developed a persistent, hacking cough.

Now, as he stepped off the overnight train, looking forward to a few hours rest in a hotel bed before his onward journey, he was accosted by a young woman with short dark hair, pencil-thin eyebrows, and high cheekbones, who was wrapped in an expensive-looking fur coat.

Rose Rappaport, Joe's twenty-year-old sister, had been "exceedingly active" on her brother's behalf, just as she had been four years earlier in trying to secure his early release from Leavenworth with almost daily letters to the warden.

Throughout the trial and his various reprieves, she set up meetings with prominent businessmen and harangued visiting rabbis, pressing them to write messages of support. With her brother finally set to die at midnight, she still refused to give up.

That morning, Rose had lain in wait with Rappaport's attorney, William Smith, among the crowds welcoming Horner at La Salle Street station. Smith was armed with sheaves of new affidavits discrediting Annie Dent's testimony and was hopeful the governor would finally commute the sentence. "It is our position that there is at least a strong probability of Rappaport's innocence," he said. "The sole issue before the parole board in its hearings was whether or not Annie Dent had actually seen the shooting. For some reason or other, she has never been personally produced and examined."

As Horner made his way through the station, Rose broke from the crowd and grabbed his arm. "Please, Governor, please listen to me," she pleaded. But the flustered governor ignored her cries and kept his gaze fixed stubbornly ahead as he brushed the woman aside. She shouted a Yiddish curse.

Horner's party moved toward the taxi rank for a cab to take them two blocks to the Congress Hotel, but Rose and Smith followed—keeping Horner's white hat in view as he moved through the crowd, Rose's heels clacking on the station's hard floor. They waited outside his room at the hotel until the governor finally relented and agreed to see them.

"Nothing has occurred to change my mind," he said. Horner had spent many hours agonizing over the decision not to commute Rappaport's sentence, and while he listened to Rose's story with sympathy—tears formed in the corners of his eyes—he offered her no encouragement. "I can't afford to be a sentimentalist in this job," he said later.

Rose was distraught. "If they murder my brother at midnight, they'll be murdering his family, because I'll go, too," she threatened. Horner tried clumsily to console her. Then, as they got up to leave— Rose's shoulders slumped, eyes red with tears—Horner offered just a glimmer of hope.

Smith had pulled him to one side and they spoke in hushed tones. "Governor, I believe these witnesses," said the attorney.

"Mr. Smith," replied Horner, "I think you are wholly sincere in the matter, but I cannot see eye to eye with you. You have exhausted every legal remedy at your command. I have only one other suggestion."

"What is that?"

"Have you thought of submitting this man to a lie detector test?"

* * *

Horner's appreciation for the machine had only grown since 1930, when it helped him solve the canary murder case. When he became governor, he continued to send many of the city's criminal cases to Northwestern's Scientific Crime Detection Lab, which was now headed up by his friend Leonarde Keeler. They had just agreed a deal to work more closely together, with the state providing the lab with $25,000 a year in funding. Horner hoped a test on the lie detector would remove any lingering doubts he had about sending Rappaport to his death.

"Do you advise or recommend it?" Smith asked Horner.

"No. That is up to you. But if you get me a report from such a test, I will consider it."

Horner continued: "I am a great believer in the lie detector. If Rappaport takes the test between now and midnight, and the test shows he is telling the truth when he denies killing Dent, I might grant another reprieve. I will be at the executive mansion in Springfield before midnight."

It was an astonishing thing for Horner to do. The Frye case had set a precedent that meant lie detectors could not be used in the courtroom, but Horner was willing to circumvent the Illinois Supreme Court and his own parole board to try and put his mind at ease. "Never in the history of Chicago—probably never anywhere—had such a move been made to save any murderer," wrote *The Tribune*.

For William Smith and Rose Rappaport, it offered the small chance they'd been looking for. Smith rushed back to his office to try and track down Leonarde Keeler and ask him to conduct the polygraph test.

The first part was relatively easy. Keeler was initially reluctant, but despite what he'd once told his father, he was never one to shy away from a case that could earn him some publicity. He felt he was doing his friend Horner a favor.

But Smith hit a snag at the Cook County Jail, where Sheriff Toman was reluctant to cooperate. Five times he'd set up the chair for Rappaport, moved him down to the death cell, organized a last meal. "He was admittedly in no mood for a sixth fizzle."

Toman refused to allow the lie detector test to go ahead without a signed court order, but it was getting late, and Smith couldn't find a court that was in session. He and his men raced around the city until just after six PM, when they finally reached Chief Justice McKinley, who agreed to hold a special court session in his home in the Edgewater Beach apartments on the shore of Lake Michigan.

McKinley signed the order at the bureau in his residence, with his bailiff and court clerk, who had been hastily summoned, peering over his shoulder at this unique moment in legal history.

IT IS HEREBY ORDERED that the jailor at the County Jail of Cook County permit a test to be made upon the defendant Joseph Rappaport in the presence of a representative of the States Attorney's office and William W. Smith, attorney for said defendant, on this the first day of March 1937, said test to consist of application of a certain machine or contraption commonly known and spoken of as the lie detector.

As McKinley read over the letter, Smith looked anxiously at his watch. There were five hours left.

In Springfield, Horner was sitting by the phone in the governor's mansion, waiting for a call. Rose was with her sister and mother at the Rappaport's home, praying once more for divine intervention.

It was past eight PM by the time Smith picked up Keeler and turned toward the Cook County Jail. The sun had set behind the city as the pair sped south along Lake Shore Drive on their desperate mission, past Wrigley Field and through the Loop. The lake to their left shone like glass, and on their right the silhouettes of skyscrapers rose and fell, like the lines of a polygraph chart, as they carried Joe Rappaport's fate along with them in a small, dark box.

JUDGE AND JURY

It was just after nine PM when Leonarde Keeler and William Smith arrived at the Cook County Jail—passing the vast facade of the courthouse shining bone-white against the dark blue sky. A cordon of guards was waiting by the high barbed-wire fence, and Sheriff Toman stormed out to greet the new arrivals. He seemed to resent this unwanted sideshow to the execution of Joseph Rappaport. "Let Smith in and get this over with," he said.

Keeler, dressed for the weather in a thick double-breasted coat, maneuvered his long frame out of the car. He was thirty-three now—the lithe youth replaced by a thick, solid man—"well coated, well hatted, beautifully shod."

His once wild hair was neatly trimmed, and his face looked puffy and tired. He was drinking too much. Three weeks earlier, he'd blacked out while boarding a train home from Boston. "The connections of my sympathetic nervous system got tangled up, giving me a rare thrill that I hope comes only once in a lifetime," he told Vollmer. "I have had several attacks since, but each one a little less severe than the last."

But he was under strain again—a few days earlier, his father, Charles, had broken his leg in a freak accident—tripping over a small dog while turning to wave goodbye to his grandchildren. He was due to go into surgery, and Keeler was anxiously waiting for news.

There was a wider malaise too. Keeler was constantly grappling with his warring impulses: he wanted to do good work in pursuit of justice, to be respected by the scientists and thinkers he admired. But he was also hungry for fame and for money—he'd grown accustomed to its trappings. "It was his job to expose guilt, but he recognized with growing anguish that there was an immensity of twisted and overlapping impulses beyond what he exposed," wrote Agnes de Mille. The big answers lay beyond his reach—forever the domain of the doctor, the psychiatrist—the kind of man he'd wanted to be but couldn't.

Keeler bent to retrieve the lie detector in its heavy walnut box, and then he and Smith followed Toman through the gates of the jail, across the dusty courtyard, and down into the basement, where Rappaport was waiting.

The prisoner had spent the day in a state of apparently serene confidence. He'd cheated death five times and was sure he could do it again. "Justice won't allow me to die," he'd said the previous night, even as he ordered his latest last meal and the guards moved him back down to the death cell. "I'll think of death when I am old—eighty or ninety."

Rappaport didn't look like he'd been incarcerated for a year—his hair was freshly cut, and he was wearing a shirt and tie, a dark sweater, and stylish checked trousers. He was halfway through eating when he heard a key grating in the lock of his cell, and he looked up sharply—expecting perhaps to see his sister Rose or the warden with news of another reprieve.

Instead, it was Keeler and his entourage, carrying with them the machine that would decide whether Rappaport lived or died. Suddenly, the food was like ashes in his mouth—the prisoner pushed his plate to one side and agreed to forgo his latest last meal for a shot at proving his innocence. There were three hours left.

Keeler laid the lie detector on a table in the cell. It was a world away from John Larson's initial contraption—elegant and sleek, it resembled a wireless radio with dials and switches on the front, and carefully milled holes for the tubes and wires to pass through. The words "Keeler Polygraph" were etched on the case in neat white letters.

Rappaport squashed down his inner turmoil and turned to Keeler with an easy smile. "It will show," he said, "that I am telling the truth."

More men filed into the corridor outside the cell: Sheriff Toman; Warden Sain; Rappaport's attorney, William Smith; prosecutors John Boyle and Marshall Kearney from the state's attorney's office; jail physician Konstantine Theodore; and T. P. Sullivan, the head of the parole board, who would report the results of the test back to Governor Henry Horner.

They peered through the bars with interest as Keeler set up the lie detector. He opened the hinged flap at the top of the box, revealing the hidden machinery within—the accordion-like tambours driving the movement of the pens, the clockwork apparatus to turn the paper roll at just the right speed.

Rappaport pulled off his sweater and rolled up his shirt sleeves. Keeler wrapped a quarter-inch tube filled with mercury around his upper arm and attached a stiff rubber sack to pump it up. The black belt of the pneumograph was wound around Rappaport's chest.

Keeler adjusted the thin ribbon of paper—marked with a faint grid—and turned on the power. All eyes were on the delicate lines that traced the subject's inner life. "Rappaport himself seemed unimportant in this strange show," reported *The New York Times*.

In 1930, Keeler had designed a preamble intended to put suspects at ease and create an appropriate sense of respect for the test. It was a tacit admission that the polygraph ran on fear.

"This machine to which you are connected has been used for some years on criminal suspects and so far has proved a very reliable means of detecting the innocence or guilt of a man, and I'm sure we will not fail in your case," he would say. "Now sit as quietly as possible and answer my questions just 'yes' or 'no.'"

Keeler started the test the same way he'd started hundreds before it, the same way he'd begun his flirtatious interrogation of Kay Applegate years earlier—using the skills he'd honed as a teenager messing around with his friends in the basement of Berkeley's City Hall. The stakes were so much higher now.

The electric light cast sharp shadows on the cell's brick walls. Keeler took a pack of playing cards from his pocket, selected one, and held it in front of Rappaport's dark eyes.

"When I ask you if this is a card, say 'no,'" he said.

"All right," Rappaport grunted.

"Is this a card?"

"No."

Keeler's gaze flicked from suspect to the machine, where "a jagged peak an inch high sprawled on the slowly moving paper tape."

He lifted the card again.

"Is this a card?"

"No."

After repeating this question another ten times, Keeler was satisfied that he had a baseline reading for Rappaport's physiological response when telling a deliberate lie. He straightened the cards and put them back in his pocket. It was time for the prisoner's final judgment.

"Your name is Rappaport?" Keeler asked.

"Yes," came the gruff reply.

"Your home is in Cook County?"

"Yes."

The pens traced an even path.

"Were you in Leavenworth?"

"Yes."

"Do you know who shot Max Dent?"

"No."

Rappaport sat perfectly still between questions. He seemed unchanged. His eyes roved around the room as if scanning for clues. But on the chart, the little vertical lines "broke and jumped."

Keeler asked more questions, moving his focus between subject and chart—judging by feel when to ask a control question and when to put the pressure on and shift gear.

"Did you shoot Dent?"

"No."

"Have you been in jail this time more than six months?"

"Yes."

"Did you ever threaten to kill Dent?"

"No."

"Have you had something to eat today?"

"Yes."

"Did you shoot him yourself?"

"No."

Keeler lifted one edge of the chart with his finger and quickly spooled back through it before he continued.

"Were you present when Dent was shot?"

"No."

"Did you shoot Dent yourself?"

"No."

"Did you ever sell narcotics?"

"Yes."

"Did Dent make a buy from you once?"

"No."

"Did Dent ever buy any narcotics from you?"

"No."

"Were you present when Dent was shot?"

"No."

The styluses danced, tracing rising peaks that looked like cresting waves. They "quivered, flickering jagging lines on the tape—mute lines that sealed a murderer's fate."

The lights in the cell flickered too—in the next room, the electric chair was being tested. Sain had spent the day checking and rechecking the straps and clamps that would hold Rappaport in place if he failed the test, and now the guards were preparing the saline solution that the electrode pads would be soaked in to ensure a good contact with his skin.

Keeler asked a third and final round of questions covering Rappaport's alibi and the perjured witness testimony from the trial. Then he stood up and began wordlessly packing up the lie detector, detaching the instruments from the subject, and packing them into the storage cavity he'd built into the device.

Rappaport looked from Keeler to Smith, trying to read the results of the polygraph in their faces, still protesting his innocence. He'd shown an "iron nerve" during the test, but he was scared now and panicking.

Keeler tore the paper record off the machine and followed the other men as they filtered away from the cell. The steel door slammed shut behind him. Rappaport's attorney looked grim. "It's the end," he said.

* * *

In 1934, Keeler had carefully laid out the conditions for a valid lie detector test. Like Larson, he'd criticized the press for portraying the polygraph too simply—as if a light turned on or a bell rang with every deception. "There is no such thing as a lie detector," he wrote— making the point that the machine was nothing if it was used incorrectly. "There are no instruments recording bodily changes, such as blood-pressure, pulse, respiration, or galvanic reflex, that deserve the name "lie detector" any more than a stethoscope, a clinical thermometer, or a blood count apparatus with a microscope can be called an "appendicitis detector.'"

Privately, he put more weight on his personal abilities than on science, but it meant that what had just happened was all on him. He'd conducted thousands of polygraph exams and relished gently ramping up the pressure to extract a confession—there was something of the joy of a magic trick about it, a combination of skill and subterfuge.

But this felt different. The consequences were tangible and close at hand. Keeler was, wrote one paper, "both judge and jury," and the electric chair was in the next room.

The Rappaport test broke every rule Keeler had laid out. The room had not been dark, empty, and silent. It was crowded with lawyers and witnesses and journalists hanging around outside. "The whole atmosphere was like a circus," Keeler admitted later.

Rappaport should have been shielded from external influences— but the lights of the cell were flickering as they tested the machine that would kill him if he failed. He should have gone without food for a few hours before the test—not been halfway through his last meal on earth.

When John Larson conducted a polygraph test, it took several hours, as he repeated each question several times in a preset order, leaving a solid minute between each one to allow the subject's body to return to baseline. This is still the accepted protocol today. But with

Rappaport, Keeler had been rushing to meet a literal deadline. The whole test took less than an hour.

* * *

In the warden's office, where portraits of the electric chair's previous victims hung on the walls, Keeler unrolled the eight-foot scroll of paper along a glass table to examine it more closely.

Toman sat next to him, pressing a finger down on one end of the chart to keep it flat as Keeler indicated the lines he'd come to think of as the telltale signs of deception: the sharp drops in blood pressure, the cramped "n" shapes made by the breathing line.

"The test shows conclusively that Joseph Rappaport was lying when he told me he was not present when Max Dent was killed and when he said he knew nothing about the murder," Keeler said. "This is my finding, and I consider it as true as any scientific laboratory test."

At 10:05 PM, T. P. Sullivan from the parole board made a long-distance call from the warden's office to the governor's mansion in Springfield, where Henry Horner was waiting by the phone. He passed the mouthpiece to Keeler. "On the basis of my findings, Rappaport is guilty," Keeler told Horner. "From the nature of these tests, I would not interfere with the law."

Horner had taken to conducting his affairs from bed because of his ailing health—he often fell asleep surrounded by stacks of paper, pen dropping from his hand as he drifted off. He accepted the news from the jail without comment, placed the receiver back on its hook, and then sat back for a moment, lost in thought.

In the death cell, Rappaport perched on the table and lit a cigar with shaking hands. Lights out in the rest of the prison was ten PM, but rumors filtered up through the tiers, whispered from inmate to inmate. "Someone's going to burn tonight. Someone is going to the hot seat."

A guard came and sat with Rappaport, instructed to "ease the final hours as much as possible." "He fits himself into the mood of the doomed man," according to an account of executions at the Cook County Jail published in 1946. "Some condemned men prefer to talk or play cards, some spend their time in prayer, others sit in silence."

The jail chaplain, a Catholic called Father Otto Ernst, came to the cell to sit with Rappaport while preparations continued in the room next door. The prisoner sent one last letter to his mother. "I hope the federal men are satisfied now," he wrote, bitterly protesting his innocence until the last.

Rappaport's head was shaved. Dark curls fell to the floor of the cell. His checked trousers were cut off at the knees and his shirt was unbuttoned and opened to the throat.

Just before midnight, Ernst left the cell and two guards in blue shirts entered. They slipped a black silk hood over Rappaport's head, plunging him into a darkness from which he would never escape.

He felt himself being lifted roughly to his feet and led the seventeen steps to the death chamber—Sain walking in front of him with the key, the chaplain behind him, muttering quiet prayers.

Some men tried to fight the guards and escape this grim procession: an inmate called J. C. Scott had ripped off his mask and backed away from the chair in horror; Rappaport's one-time cellmate Rufo Swain had wrestled free so he could step into the room alone. Rappaport was calm. He marched in with his back straight and his head held high.

As he was led through the massive iron door of the death chamber, Rappaport could sense a change in brightness from beneath his hood. A sturdy black chair had been erected on a raised platform, which was lit up like a stage. Its wooden arms "seemed to reach out for its victim." There were three more guards standing behind it.

The big clock on the wall had its own eerie spotlight and its hands read 12:04. The room was warm from the lights and the tests they'd been running on the chair. A drop of sweat rolled down Rappaport's neck.

More than 125 spectators had gathered on the other side of a thick pane of one-way glass. The crowd had watched the guards at work—seen Sain whipping the white dust cover off the electric chair with a magician's flourish. Now they squeezed onto wooden benches or stood together at the back of the room for the finale.

It took less than ten seconds for the five guards to transfer Rappaport into the chair. Two held him down, and three others pinned his arms and legs and snapped the U-shaped clamps into place. He could feel the cold metal of the restraints against his bare shins. A thick black belt was buckled across his chest.

"Rappaport's fists were clenched as he entered the chamber," wrote one reporter. "His face was hidden by the mask. He clenched his hands again as he was strapped in the chair."

A guard pressed an electrode against Rappaport's right leg. Another slipped a rough hand under his hood to attach one to his shaved head. Saline solution dripped down his face and made his eyes sting.

Sain made a final check and then signaled the man at the control panel, which was located behind a metal door in the wall. This would be the last electrocution in Cook County where the burden of responsibility fell on one man: afterward, Sain rigged up a system where four men pressed four buttons simultaneously, so only he would know who had actually done the killing.

At five minutes past midnight, the executioner placed his hand on a polished black handle in the control panel. He pulled the switch. "Its copper blades drew flashes of electric blue."

Rappaport heaved forward as nineteen hundred volts of electricity surged through him. The thick belt across his chest snapped taut. The death chamber filled with the smell of burning flesh.

There were three rounds of shocks: seven seconds, five seconds, five seconds. Sain had his dark eyes fixed on the clock. "These are the times," he said later, "when two minutes can be a long, long time."

Rappaport's body slumped in the chair. Wisps of smoke rose from his reddened skin.

Three doctors emerged from a room at the rear. They pressed their stethoscopes against his chest to check for a pulse.

EPILOGUE

A century on from John Larson, Leonarde Keeler, and August Volmer's first, fumbling experiments, the lie detector refuses to die. There are still millions of tests conducted in the United States each year, and elsewhere its use continues to grow.

In the United Kingdom, the government already uses the machine to assess whether sex offenders have breached their parole conditions, and in January 2020 British authorities announced plans to conduct polygraph tests on convicted terrorists and domestic abusers.

But the polygraph doesn't work. There is no way for an examiner to be sure whether a change in blood pressure is due to fear of getting caught or anxiety about being falsely accused. There is no single telltale sign of deception that holds true for everyone—no Pinocchio's nose. "That's seen as the holy grail of lie detection," says Sophie van der Zee, a legal psychologist at Erasmus University in Rotterdam. "So far no one has found it."

As early as 1941, magazines were writing articles about "countermeasures" that could be used to beat the test by exaggerating the body's response to control questions, for instance, by biting the tongue or stepping on a pin hidden in the shoe.

Scientists have two main criteria for assessing any test. The first is reliability—does it give you the same answer every time you measure the same thing? The second is validity—does it measure the thing it claims to?

The polygraph fails on both counts. Different examiners rating the same charts can get contradictory results, and there are huge discrepancies in outcome, depending on location, race, and gender.

Yes, lie detectors have been used to get confessions from some of the worst criminals, but they've also perpetrated grave miscarriages of justice and allowed murderers and rapists to walk free. The Henry Wilkens and Joe Rappaport cases were among the first in a long, dark history of failure, power imbalance, and human rights violations.

The National Registry of Exonerations lists more than two hundred people who were wrongly imprisoned after failed polygraph tests. And those are just the ones whose convictions were overturned—the real numbers are potentially much higher. In one infamous case in Connecticut in 1973, eighteen-year-old Peter Reilly confessed to the horrific murder of his mother during a polygraph exam, when he'd actually been several miles away at the time. It took two years to clear his name.

Gary Ridgway, a prolific serial killer in Washington state in the 1980s and 1990s, was questioned in 1983 but released after passing a polygraph. He went on to kill at least seven more women. Aldrich Ames, a double agent who funded a lavish lifestyle by selling secrets to the Russians at the height of the Cold War, passed two polygraphs while working for the CIA, and now mocks the test from prison. "Like most junk science that just won't die (graphology, astrology, and homeopathy come to mind), because of the usefulness or profit their practitioners enjoy, the polygraph stays with us," he has said.

The polygraph endures not because it works, but because people think it does. Leonarde Keeler was one of the first to realize that the mere prospect of a "truth machine" was often enough to get confessions. By the 1980s, police officers were extracting admissions of guilt by placing a suspect's hand on a photocopier and getting it to spit out paper with the phrase "He's Lying" preprinted on it.

John Larson wanted to end the third degree, but he ended up creating a psychological form of torture—a nightstick that doesn't leave visible bruises. But by the time he realized this, it was too late. Both he and Keeler approached their invention with pure intentions, but they were corrupted by its power. They thought they could control the lie detector, but it escaped their grasp and destroyed their lives.

* * *

The fallout from the Rappaport case piled the pressure on Keeler. It was condemned as an "affront to justice" in newspapers as far afield as New Zealand. "What man's blood pressure would not mount on facing such a test, knowing that a mechanism of which he had no knowledge was sitting in final judgment on his fate?" pondered *The Press Democrat*.

Keeler found the experience "hideous and unforgettable," wrote his friend Agnes de Mille. "It was excruciating to him to have it thrown repeatedly in his face. Leonarde did always what he believed was just, but he skirted raw suffering, [and] neither his nerve nor his heart could stand up to the strain."

For years afterward, Rose Rappaport bombarded Keeler with venomous letters, cursing his name and detailing the horrors that would befall him for what he'd done to her brother: he'd be rendered mute, she promised, or paralyzed. Every time Keeler read one of these screeds, his blood pressure inched up. His friends begged him to ignore the letters, and he even went to the authorities to stop Rose from contacting him, but "month after month, year after year, the sinister predictions kept coming."

John Larson was "incensed." He'd had to officiate at electrocutions in some of his prison jobs and considered them a "barbarous procedure." He was horrified by what Keeler had done. "He has no brakes," he wrote. Larson collected newspaper clippings on the case and added it to his long list of grievances. "Because of . . . the lack of psychiatric skill and other factors, Rappaport died regardless of his innocence or guilt," he wrote.

In 1938, both Leonarde and Kay Keeler lost their jobs at the Scientific Crime Detection Lab when it was sold to the city of Chicago. Kay, tired of being viewed as the magician's assistant, set up her own detective agency—an all-female operation that was an immediate hit. Keeler founded his own polygraph company, but he was eclipsed by his wife, who was soon making far more money than they had previously earned together.

Her success drove a wedge between the couple. They fought more viciously and more often. They argued about work and politics and how Kay spent her every free moment taking flying lessons. Keeler had built his career on distrust, and he was heartbroken when he arranged to have his wife followed by a private investigator, who discovered that she had been "constantly unfaithful."

They separated in April 1940. Without her, Keeler's life went slowly off the rails. He descended into alcoholism, and in December of that year he "cracked up" during an investigation and spent four months in the hospital. In 1941, when a man he was testing hurled himself out of the eighth-floor window of his office, Keeler was distraught. He spent two weeks "recovering" with the aid of the bottle.

Where he once commanded the attention of a room, now he stumbled and wavered. "His certainty was rotted away," wrote de Mille. He was haunted by the ghosts of cases old and new. The letters from Rose kept coming.

* * *

Kay remarried Rene Dussaq—a boxer, Olympic rower, Hollywood stuntman, and deep-sea diver who matched her taste for adventure. He could speak six languages, had overthrown governments in South America, and had fought in two duels. A 2016 book suggests he was a Cuban double agent who was responsible for the Kennedy assassination.

They moved to Washington, where Kay signed up for the Women's Auxiliary Service Pilots, civilians who took on noncombat missions to free men up for service in the Second World War. Keeler wanted to serve too but failed the medical because of his high blood pressure, his failing eyesight, his history of ulcers, and his propensity to faint.

Instead, he helped his country in his own way by doing polygraph jobs for the US Army—the start of the military's long and ongoing relationship with lie detection. He tested prisoners of war and employees at the Oak Ridge nuclear facility. After the war, it was suggested that he travel to Europe to use the lie detector to investigate Hitler's death.

But mainly, while Kay ferried planes from factory to base and towed targets for training exercises, Keeler spent the war years drinking and carousing with a succession of young women, who wrote him sickly sweet love letters and fawning poems.

He was deeply depressed and filled with self-loathing. When de Mille visited him in Chicago on New Year's Eve 1943, she was shocked by her glimpse into his life. He'd been drinking for forty-eight hours straight and alternated between sobbing over Kay and a kind of wild mania. When de Mille hid his liquor, Keeler called her a bitch and smashed his fist into the door. "He was the greatest detective in America, and he couldn't find his own bottles of whiskey right under the sink," she wrote. He left the party on a stretcher and spent the next three weeks in the hospital.

Eleven months later, Kay was killed in a fiery plane crash when she ran out of fuel over Ohio during a routine supply run and was forced to attempt an emergency night landing in dense fog. Keeler was devastated.

By 1948, he was in a sanatorium in California, being treated for high blood pressure. He had double vision and blood in his urine. August Vollmer offered him a lifeline—an easy job as a criminology professor back in Berkeley, but Keeler declined.

Instead, he courted wider fame: He played himself in Hollywood movie *Call Northside 777*, about a man wrongly accused of killing a cop; in 1949 he cofounded "The Court of Last Resort," which promised to help those wronged by the system fight for justice and which started the long tradition of lie detection as entertainment with a spin-off TV show.

But behind the scenes, his business was struggling. Sales of his polygraph were stagnant. The market had been flooded with competitor devices, and Keeler seemed unable to do the basics—consumed by his demons and his vices and the monster that he had unleashed.

His doctors told him to rest. After seven weeks in the hospital in the summer of 1949, he vowed to take a yearlong break from the polygraph. But on September 7, he suffered a major stroke. For two weeks, he was unable to move or speak—just as Rose Rappaport had predicted twelve years earlier.

He never recovered. Leonarde Keeler died in the hospital on September 20, 1949. He was forty-five years old. His ashes were placed at the Chapel of the Chimes in Oakland, the urn engraved with a simple inscription:

"Ye Shall Know the Truth."

* * *

August Vollmer was devastated by Keeler's early death. "I regarded him with the affection that a father would a son, and I am certain that he had a feeling of loyalty to me that is only found in father-and-son relationships," he wrote. "I shared with him all of his joys and sorrows; I was his leaning post when he felt too weak to stand alone."

Vollmer was seventy-three and had his own slate of medical issues; a few weeks after Keeler's death, he had major surgery to remove a tumor in his intestines. "Not a pleasant experience, and not to be recommended to your friends as a substitute for golf or any other outdoor pleasure," he wrote.

After his wife, Pat, died in May 1946, Vollmer's life of travel and police surveys in cities all over the world shrunk to the small house he'd shared with her on Euclid Avenue in Berkeley.

He spent his time corresponding with the like-minded police chiefs he'd seeded across the country. Soon, even letter writing became difficult. In 1950, he was diagnosed with Parkinson's disease. He approached the condition with good humor, joking to a friend over cocktails in his home that although the affliction made pouring ingredients difficult, it had given him "the best stirring action" he'd ever had.

He kept writing, as best he could, hunting and pecking on his Royal typewriter. Interviewers came to his house to write books and profiles on the father of modern policing. But Vollmer's legacy is muddled by a controversial belief in eugenics that he developed in later years and the current backlash against the system of law enforcement he helped to bring about. In 2020, there were calls for Vollmer Peak— the highest point in the Berkeley hills—to be renamed.

As his health got worse, he spent more time in his garden, thoughts far from policing or polygraphs. There were more operations on his throat and stomach, his thyroid and eyelid. His behavior became erratic and sometimes violent. He was terrified of losing his sight and being unable to read.

In his lucid moments, he was making plans. "There comes a time when it is necessary to call a halt . . . I have seen too many men hold on too long, and make perfect idiots of themselves, not to profit by their mistakes," he wrote.

In 1955, he started organizing his files—he donated his criminology library to the Berkeley Police Department, and reams of correspondence to the Bancroft Library at the university. On the morning of November 4, he ate breakfast, helped his housekeeper change the bedding, and then went down to his study and took the gun out of his desk drawer. It had been a gift from his deputy marshals—the holster had the word "Chief" written on it.

As he walked out into the garden, he called up to his housekeeper, who was carrying the sheets downstairs. "Call the police, because I am going to shoot myself."

The morning sun beat down on the flowerbeds. The gun was in his right hand. August Vollmer turned his back to the house, put the barrel against his head and pulled the trigger.

* * *

After leaving Chicago in disgrace, John Larson spent the rest of his life bouncing around the country from job to job, burning bridges wherever he went. Unable to serve in the war because of his age and health issues (eyesight, arthritis, ulcers, kidney stones), he took jobs at a psychiatric clinic in Seattle, a rehab facility in Connecticut, as director of a state asylum in New Mexico and medical director of a mental hospital in Arizona.

He was as dedicated as ever. In 1947, doctors found cancerous growths on his left ankle and amputated his leg below the knee. He was back at work two days later with a wooden prosthetic in place. From 1949, he spent eight years as medical director of Indiana State mental facility in Logansport before he was fired for uncovering fraud—from there he went to Tennessee, Montana, Iowa, and South Dakota.

All the while, he spent thousands of dollars of his own money collating material and documenting the spread of the lie detector. He obsessively tracked Keeler—cursing his success and taking special pleasure in his failures, gloating over rumors of his descent into alcoholism.

Larson's few remaining friends sent him reports on Keeler's misdeeds, and he returned his scathing assessments. "Your tip to me, to take it easy that he will hang himself, is working out," Larson told one former colleague. "The top psychologists look upon him as a plagiarist and pseudo-scientist."

He said Keeler had been forced into his research by August Vollmer, and because of this "high school boy in short pants," the science behind the lie detector had been left to wither. "I originally hoped that instrumental lie detection would become a legitimate part of professional police science. It is little more than a racket," Larson said in one interview. "The lie detector, as used in many places, is nothing more than a psychological third degree aimed at extorting confessions as the old physical beatings were. At times I'm sorry I ever had any part in its development."

Larson devoted his time to trying to stop the spread of the machine. He supported anti-polygraph laws, lobbying politicians and unions with long letters. He sent thousands of surveys to polygraph operators all over the country, quizzing them on their experience and techniques, but received only a handful of replies. In the 1950s, he formed a "Society to save the lie detector" to try and "take the blinders off the deluded public" and destroy the myth of infallibility. But he was, as Keeler's former boss Calvin Goddard once told him, just "a lone prophet crying in the wilderness." He was fighting an unstoppable tide.

By then, the lie detector had become a fixture of popular culture— appearing in comics, television shows, and advertisements. William Marston, whose blood pressure work had inspired Larson's original device, spent much of the 1920s and 1930s running salacious "experiments" for the tabloids, usually involving young women.

After failing to get lie detector evidence admitted in court in the Frye case, Marston directed his efforts toward marketing instead of justice. "The Lie Detector charts the emotional reactions produced by shaving," read one full-page newspaper advert based on an experiment Marston ran. "In one case after another, the shaver's involuntary reactions, as automatically recorded by the Lie Detector, prove Gillette's outstanding superiority."

Marston was a relentless self-publicist, and he went on to find greater fame under a pseudonym: Charles Moulton. In 1940, he was working as psychological consultant for the entertainment industry when he was interviewed by Olive Byrne, a former student who was in an unusual three-way relationship with Marston and his wife. The piece caught the eye of Max Charles Gaines, the publisher of DC Comics.

Gaines hired Marston as a consultant to promote the positive side of comics, which were the scapegoat of the times for parents all over America. He came up with the idea of a superhero whose character would be based not on brute strength, but on subtler themes—emotions like love and kindness.

Wonder Woman appeared for the first time the following year, her appearance said to be inspired by the two female figures in Marston's domestic life. In an echo of Marston's research decades earlier, instead of a sword, she carried the "lasso of truth"—a loop of golden thread that compelled anyone who touched it to honesty.

* * *

John Larson's wife, Margaret, passed away in 1960, and he was lost without her. In his records, he still had the lie detector record from that first test at College Hall almost forty years earlier.

By then, he was "much diminished"—a one-legged, cantankerous sixty-eight-year-old who looked and behaved like he was in his eighties. He retired in 1963 and settled in Nashville, Tennessee, where he lived off social security and a small pension. He planned to finally sift through the reams of polygraph material he'd been carting around the country, to write his magnum opus and settle some scores. But he never finished the book. In September 1965, he was sorting through manuscript pages when he suffered a sudden heart attack and died, aged seventy-four.

Larson had hoped that Leonarde Keeler's demise might slow the momentum of the lie detector. But in the last years of his life, he came to realize the horrible truth. "The machine had outlived Keeler, outlived Vollmer, would outlive them all," writes Alder. "Where there had once been a single Keeler, now there were hundreds, each touting his own device. The machine had begun to breed, proliferate, mutate."

Of course, Larson blamed Keeler for this, but he was not without fault. Both men were drawn in by the power of the polygraph—yes, Keeler had used it as a party trick and cheapened its scientific foundations by running rushed tests under the glare of the media spotlight, like the one on Joe Rappaport.

But Larson had used it to seduce Margaret Taylor, and he'd jettisoned scientific impartiality by inserting himself into the Henry Wilkens case. He disdained Keeler's fondness for publicity but courted the newspapers himself. At one time or another, he considered all of the things he chastised Keeler for—advertising work, employee screening, a television series. He loathed the machine but wanted the credit for inventing it.

Not long before he died, a defeated Larson summed up his decades-long battle with the lie detector. "Beyond my expectations, thru uncontrollable factors, this scientific investigation became for practical purposes a Frankenstein's monster, which I have spent over forty years in combatting."

In the same year, the US Committee on Government Operations issued one of many official rebuttals of the polygraph. "People have been deceived by a myth that a metal box in the hands of an investigator can detect truth or falsehood."

But the voices of scientific alarm have been drowned out and disregarded. And today, a new wave of lie detection technologies are coming to market, powered by brain scans and artificial intelligence. They're being greedily adopted by police forces and governments, drawn in by the false promise of a machine that tells the truth.

CODA

In June 2015, Ricky Smith—a large White man with close-cropped dark hair and a mournful expression—walked into a shabby hotel conference room in Florida to relive something he'd spent thirty years trying to forget.

Inside, sitting at a laptop in a crisp blue shirt and tie was Dr. Larry Farwell, the inventor of a lie detection technology he calls "brain fingerprinting."

Farwell, a Harvard graduate with boyish blond hair and faraway blue eyes, is in his seventies, but refused to reveal his precise age for security reasons. "I have some powerful, motivated, and resourceful enemies," he wrote in an email when I asked. "I am an existential threat to some very bad people."

He first became interested in lie detection in the late 1980s, as a graduate student at the University of Illinois. A local doctor contacted Farwell's supervisor, Emanuel Donchin, about a patient who had fallen from a grain silo and broken his neck, leaving him paralyzed "from the eyeballs down."

Together, Farwell and Donchin designed a system that enabled the boy to spell out words with only his thoughts, using electroencephalography (EEG), a now common neuroscience tool where noninvasive electrodes are attached to the scalp to measure brain activity.

Farwell thought EEG had more to offer, and he spent the next few years developing an algorithm that he claims can detect knowledge hidden in the brain with 99.9 percent accuracy. Brain fingerprinting looks for a specific pattern of neural activity called the "P300-MERMER" response, which Farwell says is displayed when a person sees something significant—something they might have seen before.

He uses it to run guilty knowledge tests. Just as Leonarde Keeler would run through different murder weapons, looking for the one that elicited the greatest response on a polygraph, Farwell presents suspects with lists of words associated with a crime that only the culprit would know were significant, in the hope that their brain's recognition response will give them away.

He earnestly believes brain fingerprinting could have prevented 9/11. "These people were already on watch lists, they were already suspected of terrorist activities, but we didn't have sufficient evidence," he said. "Brain fingerprinting could have provided the evidence we needed to bring the perpetrators to justice before they actually committed the crime."

For more than twenty years, Farwell has been working on the case of Danny Harris, who claims he was wrongly convicted of the 1986 murder of Kristina Nelson in Council Bluffs, Iowa.

In 2015, Farwell tracked down Ricky Smith, who was a potential witness, living under an assumed name in Florida. "I talked my way into his house and I persuaded him to take a brain fingerprinting test," he said. It reminded me of John Larson and how he'd stepped over the line to befriend Henry Wilkens in his desire to crack the case.

Smith was a teenager when Nelson was murdered and was now in his late forties. He was wearing glasses and a striped polo shirt and had a goatee. He sat down opposite Farwell, in front of a large monitor. He was nervous. He said the real murderers had threatened to kill him if he talked.

Farwell placed a sleek headset on Smith's head—it looked like a pair of headphones with an extra strut; the white plastic stood out against his brown hair. In the brain fingerprinting version of the guilty knowledge test, subjects see three types of stimuli: probes, which are details about a crime only the perpetrator would know; irrelevants, which are equally plausible alternatives; and targets, which are details of the crime already widely known to everyone.

If the murder weapon was a baseball bat, for instance, the suspect could be presented with the words "baseball bat" along with "lead pipe," "candlestick" and "spanner." "When we present those items on the screen, the individual who knows what the murder weapon was, his brain will say "Aha" when that comes up," Farwell explained. "He'll notice it."

Farwell pressed a button on his keyboard. Smith looked at the monitor, where a small white "x" appeared against a blue background, interspersed with phrases like "burn clothes" and "bloody overalls," each one repeating several times. On Farwell's laptop, the readings from the various scalp electrodes spooled out like the lines of a polygraph—peaks and troughs in blue, pink, and green, representing different frequency brain waves.

At the end of the test, Farwell pulled up a graph of Smith's average responses to each stimulus on his laptop. It said: "Brain Fingerprinting Results," and then in red: "Information Present, Statistical Confidence 99.9%."

"From the information stored in your brain," Farwell told Smith, "you have a clear record of who committed the crime, and what you did with the perpetrators afterward to help them cover up the crime."

Smith looked shaken. Farwell pressed home his advantage. By the end of their conversation, which felt more like an interrogation than a scientific test, Smith had agreed to testify in court against the real murderers. He had seen them entering a party with their overalls covered in blood, and although he denied all knowledge of the murder, he admitted to helping them get rid of their clothes by suggesting they burn them. In February 2018, Smith signed an affidavit supporting Danny Harris in his ongoing appeal.

* * *

Brain fingerprinting is just one of dozens of new lie detection technologies that have been developed since John Larson's death. The polygraph lives on, and it has spawned many imitators. Each new breakthrough in technology has come with an associated attempt to detect deception.

In the 1960s, the US Department of Defense responded to criticism of the polygraph from civil rights groups by investing in more subtle alternatives. Abandoned projects from this time include the "wiggle chair," which covertly tracked movement and body temperature during interrogation, and an elaborate system for measuring breathing rate with an infrared laser aimed at the lips through a hidden hole in the wall.

In 1970, two former Army officers began promoting voice stress analysis, which it was claimed could detect deception even over the phone. Like the polygraph, this technology has been repeatedly debunked, but it also refuses to die: it was used during the interrogation of George Zimmerman, who shot teenager Trayvon Martin in 2012; and in a 2007 pilot scheme in London that tried to catch benefit cheats over the phone.

More recently, focus has shifted to the brain. In the mid-2000s, two companies—Cephos and NoLieMRI—started selling lie detection based on fMRI brain scanning. It drew on the notion of "cognitive load"—the idea that our minds have to work harder when we're lying and that this can be detected in patterns of blood flow to different areas of the brain. Cephos claimed 95 percent accuracy but failed in its attempts to get fMRI lie detection admitted as evidence in court.

In 2008, the Brain Electrical Oscillations Signature test, invented by Indian neuroscientist Champadi Raman Mukundan (and based on EEG, like Farwell's brain fingerprinting) made global headlines when it was used to sentence a woman to death, in a grim echo of the Rappaport case (her murder conviction was eventually overturned).

Since 9/11, funding has kicked into a higher gear, and the border has become the new testing ground for the latest generation of lie detectors. In 2014, travelers at Bucharest airport in Hungary were greeted by AVATAR, a digital border guard that combines multiple methods of deception detection into a single unit, much like John Larson did with the polygraph in the 1920s. But this time, artificial intelligence has been added to the mix.

AI and machine learning are accelerating deception research by spotting previously unseen patterns in reams of data. Bharat Singh and colleagues at the University of Maryland have developed software that they claim can detect deception from footage of courtroom witnesses with 88 percent accuracy, for instance.

Another technology called Silent Talker uses an AI model to analyze more than forty different types of micro-gestures in the face and head. In 2019, I visited the company's office in central Manchester while reporting a story for *The Guardian*. I was shown video footage of a young man lying about taking money from a box during a mock-crime experiment, while in the corner of the screen a dial swung from green to yellow, to red.

The technology only needs a camera and an internet connection to function. In theory it could be run on a smartphone or used on live television footage—perhaps during political debates—although cofounder James O'Shea said the company doesn't want to go down that route. Like Keeler, he's targeting law enforcement and insurance.

Far from learning the lessons from the dark history of the polygraph, we're replacing the subjective scoring of a human examiner with something that might be even worse—the black box of an algorithm. "We don't know how it works," O'Shea said of Silent Talker. "The AI system learned how to do it by itself."

* * *

On a bright day in February 2019, I took the train to Grays, in Essex, to meet Terry Mullins, one of about thirty private polygraph examiners working in the United Kingdom. Mullins is in his late sixties—short and broad-shouldered, with a warm, no-nonsense demeanor. He worked as a mechanical engineer until spinal problems forced him to take a desk job, and got interested in lie detection after meeting Guy Heseltine, the long-time examiner for daytime television program *The Jeremy Kyle Show* (which was canceled not long after our meeting, following the suicide of a guest who had failed a lie detector test on the show).

Soon afterward, Mullins signed up for the ten-week, $6,000 training course offered by the American Polygraph Association, and became a certified examiner. The machine has given his career a fascinating third act.

In his first-floor office in Grays town center, opposite a derelict 1930s cinema called The State, Mullins pulled the tools of his latest trade from a large leather case. The basic equipment has barely changed in a century, but it now feeds into a £9,000 ($11,385) processor that converts the body's signals into lines on a computer: red for blood pressure, blue for breathing, green for skin conductivity, pink for movement. He showed me how the heart rate hitches when a subject lies, and how some people hold their breath to try and interfere with the test.

Over the last fifty years, he's traveled to fifty-three countries, testing corrupt politicians, convicted murderers, and pedophile priests. He has interrogated disgraced members of military dictatorships, Olympic athletes accused of doping, and a woman who claimed to have been abducted by aliens.

Between 2010 and 2012, he worked in Nigeria, screening more than two thousand police officers suspected of links to the terrorist group Boko Haram. He prefers criminal cases, but every January he takes part in the annual glut of work from suspicious spouses—the private examiner's bread and butter.

Now, though, he's moving on from the polygraph. In the corner of Mullins's office there was a small monitor with a webcam on top, and a thin, translucent black bar fixed to the bottom—an eye tracker.

The EyeDetect test is based on the research of John Kircher, a University of Utah academic who spent years developing objective digital scoring algorithms for polygraph tests, only to find that examiners didn't want them. They preferred to read the charts by feel.

In 2002, Kircher drove to Washington State to climb Mount Rainier with his colleague Doug Hacker, an expert in the psychology of reading. During the long drive, they came up with the idea of detecting deception by monitoring eye movements during a reading test—looking for signs of increased cognitive load. It's well known, for instance, that our pupils dilate slightly when we're thinking hard about something.

They recruited Ann Cook, an eye-tracking expert, and Dan Woltz, who studies cognitive load, and together the quartet developed the "oculomotor deception test." By mid-2005, they had something that was as accurate as the polygraph in a mock crime.

In 2013, a spin-out company called Converus (the name comes from the Latin for "with truth") launched the EyeDetect test for

employee screening, claiming an accuracy of 86 percent and immunity
to countermeasures. "This involuntary response that occurs in the eyes
is something that you can't control; in fact, you can't even feel that it's
happening," said the company's president and CEO, Todd Mickelsen.

To demonstrate EyeDetect at trade shows, Converus designed a
directed lie test, like the card test Leonarde Keeler used to show off the
power of the polygraph.

Mullins, who licenses the technology and offers it to companies,
handed me a business card and asked me to write down a number
between two and nine on it, without letting him see. I wrote the number seven on the card in blue pen, circled it, and slipped it into my
pocket.

I sat down in front of the screen and placed my head on an adjust-
able chin rest as Mullins moved the display back and forth until the
eye tracker was exactly 60 centimeters away from my face. In drop-
down menus, I selected my age, gender, reading ability and the fact
that I wear glasses. A few clicks later, and the tracker had locked onto
my eyes, which appeared on the display as lurid green ovals, moving
around inside a small black box.

The test started with an explanation, and then a series of statements appeared on the screen. They were simple and repetitive: "My
number was two," "The number that I chose was not six," and so on.

I had to answer as quickly and accurately as possible, clicking the
left button on the mouse for true and right for false, and lying on questions about the number I'd written down. Frequent double negatives
in the prompts made it hard to just mindlessly click through—people
doing that are flagged as uncooperative and fail the test.

As I read, the eye tracker recorded where I looked, when I started
reading each sentence, whether I fixated on any particular words,
and for how long. It measured my pupil diameter, accurate to a
hundred-thousandth of a millimeter, up to sixty times a second. By com-
bining that information with data on response times and blink rates, the
EyeDetect algorithm creates an estimate of cognitive load and converts
it into a score of 1 to 100. Anything over 50 indicates you're telling the
truth—but why take a risk on someone who scored a 55?

EyeDetect has thrived as a cheap and quick alternative to the polygraph. My numbers test took just over six minutes, and a full screening test can usually be done in under half an hour. Mullins charges £65 ($85) + tax for a single EyeDetect test, compared to upward of £500 ($656) for a polygraph exam. Tens of thousands of tests are now being conducted each year in more than forty countries.

The test has been used by FedEx in Panama and Uber in Mexico to test drivers, and by the credit ratings agency Experian with staff in Colombia. In the United Kingdom, there's a pilot study in progress to test sex offenders, who are often "the vanguard of technology in criminology," according to Andy Balmer, author of *Lie Detection and the Law*. Other customers have included the government of Afghanistan, McDonald's, and dozens of local police departments in the United States.

In May 2018, EyeDetect was accepted as evidence in a district court in New Mexico, during the trial of a former high school coach accused of raping a young girl. The coach, a war veteran with PTSD and a heart condition that made him ineligible for the polygraph, passed the test with a score in the 90s. There were more admissibility hearings on the way. "The interest has come about because there is now a viable tool that is not as intrusive and can't be bribed," Mickelsen said.

After a couple of days training, anyone can run the test.

* * *

It's been a hundred years since the first polygraph test, and there's still no such thing as a lie detector. We haven't made a scientific breakthrough or discovered the root of deception in the brain.

But lie detection endures. Amid rising division and border panic, we're turning to science in a desperate search for truth. New techniques are, as Ken Alder predicted in 2007, slipping into the role that the polygraph once played, while the original machine enjoys an unexpected, undeserved renaissance.

That's a problem. Because all too often, lie detectors get aimed at the most vulnerable in society—women in the 1920s, suspected dissidents and homosexuals in the 1960s, benefit claimants in the 2000s, asylum seekers and migrants today. "Scientists don't think much about who is going to use these methods," said Giorgio Ganis, who studies countermeasures against new forms of lie detection. "I always feel that people should be aware of the implications."

History serves as a warning. John Larson wanted to end the third degree but just ended up giving corrupt police officers a new tool of coercion. Leonarde Keeler courted fame and fortune but died a bitter, lonely man, haunted by the demons of the men he'd condemned. Henry Wilkens evaded justice for his role in his wife's death, and Joe Rappaport's fate was ultimately decided not by trial, but by theater.

At the end of my EyeDetect test, Terry Mullins pulled up my results on his computer. On the desk in front of the truth machine sat a mouse mat with an image of a woman's eye and a slogan that could be from the future or the past. "In God We Trust," it read. "All others get verified with EyeDetect."

Mullins peered at the screen through his glasses. There was a chart of my responses to each of the digits from two to nine. One column listed my average pupil diameter during statements about each number, accurate to six decimal places. A graph displayed the algorithm's best guess at the number I had written down on the card in my pocket. It felt like a magic trick.

It was late afternoon, and the sun cast prison stripes on the wall through the blinds. Mullins looked up and grinned.

"Any confessions?"

ACKNOWLEDGMENTS

Reporting a book set on the other side of the Atlantic during a global pandemic was challenging and would have been impossible without the help and support of dozens of people.

While the world fretted about variants and R numbers, I was lucky to be able to disappear into the newspaper archives for nights at a time—an unusual form of escapism, but one I'd highly recommend. I found stories about government corruption and disease control, about geopolitical turmoil and the rising price of fuel. The 1920s and 1930s were wild, but familiar.

Huge thanks to Richard Pike, my brilliant agent at C&W, for making this happen and for (again) holding my hand through the process of proposal to publication and shaping this book into what it is with thoughtful feedback and advice. Thank you also to Luke Speed at C&W, and Kristine Dahl and Tamara Kawar at ICM.

I'm so grateful to my editor, Joel Simons, for taking this book on and for his enthusiasm for the project from day one. Thanks also to everyone else at Mudlark/HarperCollins, including Sarah Hammond, Simon Armstrong, Fiona Greenway, and Alan Cracknell, plus Steve Leard and Jo Ireson. Thank you to Rebecca Nelson and all at Crooked Lane Books.

Thank you to all those who helped me access documents remotely, including Ginger Frere at Information Diggers; Marisa Louie Lee; Nailah Holmes at the New York Public Library; and Ken Alder, who kindly shared some excerpts of John Larson's correspondence with me and whose book was a big influence on this one.

When I was finally able to travel, I stood on the spot in Chicago where Max Dent was gunned down, and retraced Henry Wilkens's mad dash to the hospital on the night of his wife's murder. At the Bancroft Library, I pored over the personal effects of August Vollmer, Leonarde Keeler, and John Larson—reams of correspondence, degree certificates, fingerprints, and photos. Thank you to Susan McElrath and all the other archivists at the Bancroft for their help—the material I accessed there was vital and illuminating, and the people who left it behind were complicated and flawed and fascinating. I hope I've done their stories justice.

Thank you to my friends and family, especially my early readers: Edd Pickering; Sophie Hines; Tom Fenton-Anwyll; my sister, Lina; my dad, Jaldeep; and my mum, Alka, for helping me trim down and polish my sprawling first draft. And most of all, thank you to my wife, Sara, for being an inexhaustible well of love, support, patience, and truth.

A NOTE ON SOURCES

This book was born backward. I first got interested in lie detection after I saw Dr. Larry Farwell conducting a brain fingerprinting test on the Netflix show *Making a Murderer*. I spent the next year reporting a story for *The Guardian* on some of the new forms of lie detection technology based on brain scans and artificial intelligence.

It was during that research that I first came across the stories of John Larson, August Vollmer, and Leonarde Keeler—and the two gripping, dramatic cases of Henry Wilkens and Joe Rappaport in John Larson's 1932 book *Lying and Its Detection* and in *The Lie Detectors* by Ken Alder.

I've tried to reconstruct the cases as vividly as possible while sticking to the facts—my primary sources included thousands of newspaper reports; hundreds of books, academic journals, and magazines; and thousands of pages of court documents, prison records, and the personal correspondence and personal effects of Keeler, Larson, and Vollmer, and their acquaintances, much of it held at the Bancroft Library at University of California, Berkeley.

It was a privilege to read through their letters and documents, and get a sense of their personalities from their files: Larson's chaotic but obsessively focused, Vollmer's rigidly organized, Keeler's running the gamut from snake handling to murder investigations.

Following is a list of sources that proved particularly useful during my research—whether for direct accounts of various cases, background information on characters, or just to get a sense of what San Francisco and Chicago were like in the 1920s and 1930s. There are fuller notes on each chapter and sources for quotes in the references section below.

SELECTED BIBLIOGRAPHY

Adams, Charles F. *Murder by the Bay*. Sanger, CA: Word Dancer, 2005.

Alder, Ken. *The Lie Detectors: The History of an American Obsession*. New York: Free Press, 2007.

Balmer, Andy. *Lie Detection and the Law: Torture, Technology and Truth*. New York: Routledge, 2019.

Baumann, Ed. *May God Have Mercy on Your Soul: The Story of the Rope and the Thunderbolt*. Chicago: Bonus Books, 1993.

Block, Eugene B. *Lie Detectors: Their History and Use*. New York: D. McKay, 1977.

Bunn, Geoffrey C. *The Truth Machine: A Social History of the Lie Detector*. Baltimore: Johns Hopkins University Press, 2012.

Cutler, Irving. *The Jews of Chicago: From Shtetl to Suburb*. Urbana: University of Illinois Press, 1996.

Ekman, Paul. *Telling Lies; Clues to Deceit in the Marketplace, Politics, and Marriage*. New York: W. W. Norton, 2009.

Flamm, Jerry. *Good Life in Hard Times: San Francisco's "20s and "30s*. San Francisco: Chronicle Books, 1977.

Halperin, James L. *The Truth Machine*. New York: Del Ray Books, 1997.

Hammett, Dashiell. *The Maltese Falcon*. New York: Alfred A. Knopf, 1930.

Jackson, Joseph Henry. (ed.). *San Francisco Murders*. New York: Bantam, 1948.

Keeler, Eloise. *The Lie Detector Man: The Career and Cases of Leonarde Keeler*. Boston: Telshare, 1983.

Larson, Erik. *The Devil in the White City*. London: Bantam, 2004.

Larson, John A. *Lying and Its Detection*. Chicago: University of Chicago Press, 1932.

Lee, Clarence D., and V. A. Leonard. *The Instrumental Detection of Deception: The Lie Test*. Springfield, MA: Charles C. Thomas, 1953.

Lykken, David T. *A Tremor in the Blood: Uses and Abuses of the Lie Detector*. New York: McGraw-Hill, 1980.

Masters, Charles J. *Governor Henry Horner, Chicago Politics and the Great Depression*. Carbondale, IL: Southern Illinois University Press, 2007.

Meyer, Pamela. *Liespotting*. New York: St. Martin's Griffin, 2011.

Marston, William Moulton. *The Lie Detector Test*. New York: Richard R. Smith, 1938.

Oliver, Willard M. *August Vollmer: The Father of American Policing*. Durham, NC: Carolina Academic Press, 2017.

Pacyga, Dominic A. *Chicago: A Biography*. Chicago: University of Chicago Press, 2011.

Parker, Alfred E. *Crime Fighter: August Vollmer*. New York: Macmillan, 1961.

Parker, Alfred E. *The Berkeley Police Story*. Springfield: Charles C. Thomas, 1972.

Pettit, Michael. *The Science of Deception: Psychology and Commerce in America*. Chicago: University of Chicago Press, 2013.

Samors, Neal, and Michael Williams. *The Old Chicago Neighborhood: Remembering Life in the 1940s*. Chicago: Chicago's Neighborhoods, 2003.

Sinclair, Mick. *San Francisco: A Cultural and Literary History*. Oxford: Signal Books, 2004.

Sinclair, Upton. *The Jungle*. New York: Doubleday, Page, 1906.

Smith, James R., and W. Lane Rogers. *The California Snatch Racket: Kidnappings During the Prohibition and Depression Eras*. Fresno, CA: Linden, 2010.

Summerscale, Kate. *The Suspicions of Mr. Whicher: Or the Murder at Road Hill House*. London: Bloomsbury, 2009.

Vollmer, August, and Alfred E. Parker. *Crime, Crooks and Cops*. New York: Funk & Wagnalls, 1937.

Winkler Dawson, Kate. *American Sherlock: Murder, Forensics and the Birth of American CSI*. New York: Putnam, 2020.

Wright, Richard. *Native Son*. London: Vintage Classics, 2000.

ARCHIVAL SOURCES

California Digital Newspaper Collection at cdnc.ucr.edu.

Court records on Joe Rappaport case—case file 76623, People v. Rappaport, Circuit Court of Cook County Archives, and case file 18385 from Chicago NARA.

John Larson Papers (Bancroft Library at UC Berkeley—BANC MSS 78/160 cz).

Leonarde Keeler Papers (Bancroft BANC MSS 76/40 c).

August Vollmer Papers (Bancroft BANC MSS C-B 403).

Berkeley Police Department Papers (Bancroft BANC MSS 72/227 c).

Charles Keeler Papers (Bancroft BANC MSS C-H 105).

Leavenworth Prison files on Joe Rappaport, prisoner #32147 from Kansas City, NARA.

Agnes de Mille Papers (New York Public Library—(S) *MGZMC-Res. 27).

Various genealogical records including birth and death certificates, military draft cards, census records and passenger manifests accessed via ancestry.co.uk.

REFERENCES

PART ONE

THE SUNSET DISTRICT

PAGES 3–13

The murder of Anna Wilkens and the subsequent police investigation have been reconstructed largely from newspaper reports from *The San Francisco Examiner, The Chronicle*, and *The Call*—all around the time of the incident and from reports of witness testimony during the trial.

The San Francisco Call 112: 90 (October 19, 1922).
Details of Anna and Henry's family history come from genealogical records, including birth and death certificates and passenger manifests. Images of her prayer book were provided by a relative.
Oakland Tribune (June 4, 1922).
Oakland Tribune (June 6, 1922).
San Francisco Call 111, no. 125 (May 31, 1922).
San Francisco Call 111, no. 129 (June 5, 1922).
San Francisco Call 112, no. 9 (July 17, 1922).
San Francisco Call 112, no. 93 (October 23, 1922).
San Francisco Call 112.no. 95 (October 25, 1922).
San Francisco Chronicle (May 31, 1922).
San Francisco Examiner (March 6, 1923).
San Francisco Examiner (June 1, 1922).
Santa Ana Register (May 31, 1922).

Stefanie E. Williams, "The Rise and Decline of the German-Speaking Community in San Francisco, 1850–1924," *Argonaut* 31, no. 1 (Summer 2020).

Woodland Daily Democrat (May 31, 1922).

WRITTEN IN BLOOD
PAGES 14–20

Background on the Castor brothers comes from genealogical records and newspaper reports.

San Francisco Call 112. no. 13 (July 21, 1922).

San Francisco Call (August 5, 1913).

San Francisco Call 112, no. 77 (October 4, 1922).

San Francisco Chronicle (August 4, 1922).

San Francisco Chronicle (October 26, 1922).

San Francisco Examiner (March 12, 1922).

Oakland Tribune (August 3, 1922).

ARGUMENTS AND ALIBIS
PAGES 21–27

Charles F. Adams, *Murder by the Bay* (Sanger: Word Dancer, 2005), 153.

Kate Winkler Dawson, *American Sherlock: Murder, Forensics and the Birth of American CSI* (New York: Putnam, 2020), 103.

San Francisco Call 111, no. 127 (June 2, 1922).

San Francisco Call 111, no. 128 (June 3, 1922).

San Francisco Call 112, no. 27 (August 7, 1922).

San Francisco Call 112, no. 73 (September 29, 1922).

San Francisco Call 112, no. 87 (October 16, 1922).

San Francisco Examiner (February 10, 1923).

San Francisco Examiner (June 4, 1922).

San Francisco Examiner (June 5, 1922).

San Francisco Examiner (June 7, 1922).

San Francisco Examiner (June 9, 1922).

San Francisco Examiner (July 19, 1922).

PART TWO

THE TOWN MARSHAL

PAGES 31–40

Background on August Vollmer comes from a number of biographies written by him and others, noted in the bibliography.

Gene E. Carte and Elaine H. Carte, *Police Reform in the United States: The Era of August Vollmer, 1905–1932* (Berkeley: University of California Press, 1975).

Berkeley Record (June 13, 1906), quoted by Ken Alder in *The Lie Detectors: The History of an American Obsession* (New York: Free Press, 2007).

Gene E. Carte and Elaine H. Carte, *Police Reform in the United States— The Era of August Vollmer, 1905–1932* (Berkeley: University of California Press, 1975), quoted by Willard M. Oliver in *August Vollmer: The Father of American Policing* (Durham, NC: Carolina Academic Press, 2017).

Frederick L. Collins, "The Professor Who Cleaned Up a City," *Collier's* magazine (November 8, 1924), https://babel.hathitrust.org/cgi/pt?id=mdp.39015056079406.

Willard M. Oliver, *August Vollmer: The Father of American Policing* (Durham, NC: Carolina Academic Press, 2017), 272.

Alfred E. Parker, *Crime Fighter: August Vollmer* (New York: Macmillan, 1961), 22, 38, 41.

Robert Shaw, "Forty Fighting Years: The Story of August Vollmer," *Oakland Post Enquirer*, 1938, quoted by Willard M. Oliver in *August Vollmer: The Father of American Policing* (Durham, NC: Carolina Academic Press, 2017).

Vollmer, August, and Albert Schneider, "School for Police as Planned at Berkeley," *Journal of Criminal Law and Criminology* 7, no. 6, article 10 (1917).

O. W. Wilson, O. W. "August Vollmer," *Journal of Criminal Law and Criminology* 44, no. 1, article 10 (1953): 91–103.

COLLEGE COPS

PAGES 41–45

Daily Californian (October 17, 1918), quoted by Rex W. Adams in "The 1918 Spanish Influenza," Berkeley's Quinta Columna, *Oakland Tribune,* https://cshe.berkeley.edu/sites/default/files/chron1_excerpt_adams.pdf.

Albert Deutsch, "America's Greatest Cop," *Collier's* magazine (February 3, 1951).

Hans Gross, 1905–1911, *Criminal Psychology: A Manual for Judges, Practitioners, and Students* (Boston: Little, Brown), quoted by Susanne Weber in *The Hidden Truth: A Sociological History of Lie Detection* (London: London School of Economics and Political Science, 2008).

Robert Shaw, "Forty Fighting Years: The Story of August Vollmer," *Oakland Post Enquirer,* 1938)—quoted by Willard M. Oliver in *August Vollmer: The Father of American Policing* (Durham, NC: Carolina Academic Press, 2017), 215, 236.

Alfred E. Parker, *The Berkeley Police Story* (Springfield, MA: Charles C. Thomas, 1972), 33.

Alfred E. Parker, *Crime Fighter: August* Vollmer (New York: The Macmillan Co., 1961), 100

August Vollmer and Alfred E. Parker, *Crime, Crooks & Cops* (New York: Funk & Wagnalls, 1937), 224.

THE ROOKIE

PAGES 46–51

Background on John Larson comes from his personal papers and correspondence at the Bancroft Library in UC Berkeley; his 1932 book,

Lying and Its Detection (Chicago: University of Chicago Press, 1932); and Ken Alder, *The Lie Detectors: The History of an American Obsession* (New York: Free Press, 2007).

Alder, *The Lie Detectors*, 4, 24.
"Faked Hold Up"—John Larson Papers, Bancroft Library, carton 1, folder 9.
Oakland Tribune (January 6, 1921).
San Francisco Chronicle (May 23, 1920).

THE APPARATUS

PAGES 52–60

This version of events is based on August Vollmer's account as published in various biographies. John Larson disputes this—in his private papers he says he was ill at home when Bill Wiltberger came to his house with news of the College Hall case and Marston's paper.

August Vollmer to John Larson, January 21, 1924—John Larson Papers, Bancroft Library, box 1, folder 18.
Daniel Defoe, *An Effectual Scheme for the Immediate Preventing of Street Robberies and Suppressing All Other Disorders of the Night* (1731).
"Faked Hold Up"—John Larson Papers, Bancroft Library, carton 1, folder 9.
William M. Marston, "Psychological Possibilities in the Deception Tests," *Journal of the American Institute of Criminal Law and Criminology* 11, no. 4 (February 1921): 551–570.
W. M. Marston, "Systolic Blood Pressure Symptoms of Deception," *Journal of Experimental Psychology* 2, no. 2 (1917): 117–163, https://doi.org/10.1037/h0073583.
Alfred E. Parker, *The Berkeley Police Story* (Springfield: Charles C. Thomas Publishing, 1972), 69, 70, 71.

San Francisco Examiner (June 10, 1922).

Alfred E. Parker, *Crime Fighter: August Vollmer* (New York: The Macmillan Co., 1961), 108, 109.

SECRETS OF THE SOUL

PAGES 61–69

There are several conflicting accounts of the College Hall case—not helped by the fact that it was the first of several different sorority thefts the lie detector was used to investigate. This version is based on Ken Alder's account, as well as those in Vollmer's biographies and the John Larson Papers. Vollmer and Larson disagree on exactly what happened to Helen Graham after her test.

Ken Alder, *The Lie Detectors: The History of an American Obsession* (New York: Free Press, 2007), 7, 12.

John A. Larson, *Lying and Its Detection* (Chicago: University of Chicago Press, 1932), 339, 341.

Larson's police report (May 7, 1921), quoted by Ken Alder in *The Lie Detectors: The History of an American Obsession* (New York: Free Press, 2007).

Alfred E. Parker, *Crime Fighter: August Vollmer* (New York: The Macmillan Co., 1961), 110, 113.

David Redstone, "The Case of the Dormitory Thefts," *Reader's Digest* (December 1947): 19.

San Francisco Examiner (August 9, 1922).

THE MAGICIAN

PAGES 70–78

Leonarde Keeler's early life is based on *The Lie Detector Man: The Career and Cases of Leonarde Keeler* (Telshare, 1983), the biography by his sister Eloise Keeler; personal letters and other effects at the Bancroft Library; and an obituary published in the journal *Polygraph*; as well as the sources quoted.

Biographical sketch of Leonarde Keeler in Agnes de Mille Papers, New York Public Library, 94.

Charles Keeler, *An Epitome of Cosmic Religion* (Berkeley, CA: Sign of the Live Oak, 1925), quoted by Ken Alder in *The Lie Detectors: The History of an American Obsession* (New York: Free Press, 2007).

Charles Keeler, "Friends Bearing Torches," essay, Charles Keeler Papers, Bancroft Library, carton 5, folder 38.

Charles Keeler to Leonarde Keeler (August 17, 1930) (quoted by Ken Alder in *The Lie Detectors: The History of an American Obsession* (New York: Free Press, 2007).

Charles Keeler to Leonarde Keeler (January 29, 1936), Charles Keeler Papers, Bancroft Library, box 3.

Eloise Keeler, *The Lie Detector Man: The Career and Cases of Leonarde Keeler* (Boston: Telshare, 1983), 2, 4, 9, 13.

Leonarde Keeler, "The Lie Detector," *Cub Tracks* magazine (April 1926).

Letter, August Vollmer to Viola Stevens (April 21, 1950), Leonarde Keeler Papers, Bancroft Library, carton 2, folder 10.

"A Tribute to Leonarde Keeler"—Leonarde Keeler Papers, Bancroft Library, carton 2, folder 21.

THE BAKER AND THE PRIEST

PAGES 79–86

This account is based on John Bruce, "The Flapjack Murders," in *San Francisco Murders*, ed. *Joseph Henry Jackson* (New York: Bantam, 1948); Kate Winkler Dawson, *American Sherlock: Murder, Forensics and the Birth of American CSI* (New York: Putnam, 2020); Charles F. Adams, *Murder by the Bay* (Sanger, CA: Word Dancer, 2005); and contemporary newspaper reports, particularly from *The Examiner* and *The Post*.

Bruce, "The Flapjack Murder," 185, 193, 194, 196.
Dawson, *American Sherlock*, 44, 56, 62, 63.

James R. Smith and W. Lane Rogers, *The California Snatch Racket: Kidnappings During the Prohibition and Depression Eras* (Fresno, CA: Linden, 2010), 189.

Los Angeles Evening Express (August 11, 1921).

San Francisco Examiner (August 11, 1921).

THE INFERNAL MACHINE

PAGES 87–92

The press scramble for access to Hightower is detailed in *Lie Detectors: Their History and Use* (New York: D. McKay, 1977) by Eugene Block, who at the time was city editor of *The Call-Bulletin, The Examiner*'s sister paper.

Eugene B. Block, *Lie Detectors: Their History and Use* (New York: D. McKay, 1977), 133, 134.

Kate Winkler Dawson, *American Sherlock: Murder, Forensics and the Birth of American CSI* (New York: Putnam, 2020), 66.

John A. Larson, *Lying and Its Detection* (Chicago: University of Chicago Press, 1932), 371.

San Francisco Call 110, no. 35 (August 17, 1921).

San Francisco Chronicle (August 12, 1921).

James R. Smith and W. Lane Rogers, *The California Snatch Racket: Kidnappings During the Prohibition and Depression Eras* (Fresno, CA: Linden, 2010), 238.

PART THREE

PACIFIC HEIGHTS

PAGES 95–104

Ken Alder, *The Lie Detectors: The History of an American Obsession* (New York: Free Press, 2007), 93.

Hanford Sentinel (June 10, 1922).

John A. Larson, *Lying and Its Detection* (Chicago: University of Chicago Press, 1932), 380.

Letter, John Larson to August Vollmer (April 20, 1927), Berkeley Police Department records, Bancroft Library, box 10.

Oakland Tribune (June 9, 1922).

Oakland Tribune (October 9, 1922).

Petaluma Daily Morning Courier (June 10, 1922).

San Francisco Call 111, no. 133 (June 9, 1922).

San Francisco Chronicle (June 25, 1922).

San Francisco Examiner (June 10, 1922).

Santa Ana Register (June 10, 1922).

SAP AND SAWDUST
PAGES 105–110

Sacramento Bee (August 4, 1922).

San Francisco Examiner (June 18, 1922).

Santa Rosa Republican (May 23, 1922).

IMPS AND DEMONS
PAGES 111–114

San Francisco Call 112, no. 12 (July 20, 1922).

San Francisco Call 112. no. 77 (October 4, 1922).

Santa Rosa Republican (October 18, 1922).

THE THIRD DEGREE
PAGES 115–121

John A. Larson, *Lying and Its Detection* (Chicago: University of Chicago Press, 1932), 96.

San Bernardino County Sun (October 27, 1922).

San Francisco Chronicle (July 15, 1922).

San Francisco Call 112, no. 10 (July 8, 1922).
San Francisco Call 112, no. 12 (July 20, 1922).
Santa Cruz Evening News (July 17, 1922).

A WILD SORT OF COUNTRY
PAGES 122–129

San Francisco Call 112:25 (August 4, 1922).
San Francisco Chronicle (August 4, 1922).
San Francisco Chronicle (August 5,1922).
San Francisco Examiner (August 5, 1922).
Oakland Tribune (August 3, 1922).
Oakland Tribune (August 4, 1922).

WHOLESALE SLAUGHTER
PAGES 130–136

Oakland Tribune (August 3, 1922).
Sacramento Bee (August 4, 1922).
Sacramento Bee (August 8, 1922).
San Francisco Call (August 3, 1922).
San Francisco Call 112, no. 25 (August 4, 1922).
San Francisco Chronicle (August 4, 1922).
San Francisco Examiner (August 4, 1922).
San Francisco Examiner (August 5, 1922).
San Francisco Examiner (August 9, 1922).

CHICKEN DINNERS
PAGES 137–143

Oakland Tribune (August 7, 1922).
Oakland Tribune (October 25, 1922).
San Francisco Call 112, no. 27 (August 7, 1922).
San Francisco Call 112, no. 34 (August 15, 1922).

San Francisco Call 112, no. 38 (August 19, 1922).
San Francisco Chronicle 112:38 (August 19, 1922).
San Francisco Examiner (August 15, 1922).
Santa Rosa Republican (October 10, 1922).

AN AID TO THE STORK
PAGES 144–148

San Francisco Call 112, no. 54 (September 7, 1922).
San Francisco Call 112, no. 69 (September 25, 1922).
San Francisco Call 112, no. 71 (September 27, 1922).
San Francisco Call 112, no 72 (September 28, 1922).
San Francisco Call 106, no. 86 (October 16, 1919).
San Francisco Examiner (September 2, 1922).
Stockton Daily Evening Record (September 25, 1922).

THE RISING TIDE
PAGES 149–155

Bakersfield Morning Echo (October 4, 1922).
San Francisco Call 112, no. 76 (October 3, 1922).
San Francisco Call 112, no. 77 (October 4, 1922).
San Francisco Call 112, no. 78 (October 5, 1922).
San Francisco Chronicle (October 5, 1922).
San Francisco Examiner (October 4, 1922).
San Francisco Examiner (October 14, 1922).

THE TWILIGHT ZONE
PAGES 156–159

A detailed account of Marston's involvement in the Frye trial was written by Jill Lepore, "On Evidence: Proving Frye as a Matter of Law, Science, and History, *Yale Law Journal* 124, no. 4 (2015): 1092–1158.

Court transcript of *Frye v. United States* (D.C. Cir 1923).

THE CASE FOR THE DEFENSE
PAGES 160–167

Oakland Tribune (October 24, 1922).
Sacramento Bee (October 23, 1922).
San Francisco Call 112, no. 87 (October 16, 1922).
San Francisco Call 112, no. 94 (October 24, 1922).
San Francisco Call 112, no. 95 (October 25, 1922).
San Francisco Chronicle (October 24, 1922).
San Francisco Examiner (October 24, 1922).
San Francisco Examiner (October 25, 1922).
Santa Ana Register (October 25, 1922).

A TRUE MARINER
PAGES 168–174

Oakland Tribune (November 1, 1922).
Oakland Tribune (November 2, 1922).
San Francisco Call 112, no. 96 (October 26, 1922).
San Francisco Call 112. no. 101 (November 1, 1922).
San Francisco Call 112, no. 102 (November 2, 1922).
San Francisco Chronicle (November 4, 1922).
San Francisco Chronicle (November 5, 1922).
San Francisco Examiner (October 30, 1922).
San Francisco Examiner (November 1, 1922).
San Francisco Examiner (November 4, 1922).

BRIDGE OF SIGHS
PAGES 175–179

San Francisco Call 112, no. 108 (November 9, 1922).
San Francisco Call 112, no. 115 (November 17, 1922).

San Francisco Chronicle (March 17, 1923).

San Francisco Examiner (March 14, 1923).

San Francisco Examiner (March 16, 1923).

TRUTH SERUM

PAGES 180–186

Details of John Larson and August Vollmer's contact with Henry Wilkens after his trials are drawn from correspondence kept in the Bancroft Library.

Berkeley Gazette (June 26, 1923), quoted by Ken Alder in *The Lie Detectors: The History of an American Obsession* (New York: Free Press, 2007), 36.

Robert E. House, "The Use of Scopolamine in Criminology," *American Journal of Police Science* 2, no. 4 (July–August 1931): 328–336.

John A. Larson, *Lying and Its Detection* (Chicago: University of Chicago Press, 1932), 380, 381.

Letter John Larson to Henry Wilkens (March 27, 1923), Berkeley Police Department records, box 10.

Los Angeles Evening Express (March 23, 1923).

Los Angeles Times (June 27, 1923).

"The Making of "Truth Serum," *Bulletin of the History of Medicine* 79, no. 3 (Fall 2005): 500–533.

San Francisco Examiner (March 18, 1923).

San Francisco Examiner (March 19, 1923).

John Larson to August Vollmer (April 20, 1927), Berkeley Police Department records, Bancroft Library, box 10.

John Larson to August Vollmer (July 27, 1927), Berkeley Police Department records, Bancroft Library, box 10.

August Vollmer to John Larson (October 16, 1928), Berkeley Police Department records, Bancroft Library, box 38.

John Larson to August Vollmer (October 29, 1928), Berkeley Police Department records, Bancroft Library, box 10.

FIRE AND VENOM
PAGES 187–199

Biographical sketch, Agnes de Mille Papers, New York Public Library.

Cub Tracks (April 1926): 106.

"The Day That Berkeley Burned," *California* (spring 2019).

Charles Keeler to Dean Charles F. Rieber (September 9, 1924), Charles Keeler Papers, Bancroft Library, box 3.

Eloise Keeler, *The Lie Detector Man: The Career and Cases of Leonarde Keeler* (Boston: Telshare, 1983), 14, 15, 24, 116.

Leonarde Keeler to Charles Keeler (March 28, 1923), Charles Keeler Papers, Bancroft Library, box 7.

Leonarde Keeler to Charles Keeler (March 12, 1924), Charles Keeler Papers, Bancroft Library, box 7.

Leonarde Keeler to John Larson (April 29, 1924), John Larson Papers, Bancroft Library, box 1, folder 9.

John A. Larson, *Lying and Its Detection* (Chicago: University of Chicago Press, 1932), 389.

John Larson to Leonarde Keeler (May 5, 1924), John Larson Papers, Bancroft Library, box 1, folder 9.

John Larson to Don Kooken (April 18, 1933), John Larson Papers, Bancroft Library, box 1, folder 10.

Los Angeles Times (July 22, 1924) quoted by Ken Alder in *The Lie Detectors: The History of an American Obsession* (New York: Free Press, 2007), 162.

Willard M. Oliver, *August Vollmer: The Father of American Policing* (Durham, NC: Carolina Academic Press, 2017), 383.

Charles Sloan to John Larson (June 26, 1924), John Larson Papers, Bancroft Library, box 1, folder 16.

Willard M. Oliver, *August Vollmer: The Father of American Policing* (Durham, NC: Carolina Academic Press, 2017), 393.

Ken Alder, *The Lie Detectors: The History of an American Obsession* (New York: Free Press, 2007), 82.

Kay Applegate to her parents, quoted by Ken Alder in *The Lie Detectors: The History of an American Obsession* (New York: Free Press, 2007), 83.

Leonarde Keeler to Charles Keeler (March 5, 1933), quoted by Ken Alder in *The Lie Detectors: The History of an American Obsession* (New York: Free Press, 2007).

Leonarde Keeler to John Larson, John Larson Papers, Bancroft Library, folder 9.

Leonarde Keeler to John Larson (April 1, 1927), John Larson Papers, Bancroft Library, box 1.

John Larson to Leonarde Keeler (March 23, 1925), John Larson Papers, Bancroft Library, box 1, folder 9.

John Larson to Leonarde Keeler (June 6, 1925), John Larson Papers, Bancroft Library, box 1, folder 9.

Leonarde Keeler to August Vollmer (May 25, 1925), Berkeley Police Department records, Bancroft Library, box 10.

August Vollmer to Leonarde Keeler (May 18, 1925), Charles Keeler Papers, Bancroft Library, box 11.

PART FOUR

STOOL PIGEON

PAGES 203–212

The Rappaport case was covered by the Chicago papers. Details of the police investigation and its aftermath come from *Official Detective Stories* magazine (January 1945), *Crime Detective* magazine (October 1938), and *Front Page Detective* magazine (August 1937). Background on Max Dent is from genealogical records.

Irving Cutler, *The Jews of Chicago: From Shtetl to Suburb* (Champaign: University of Illinois Press, 1996), 225.

A. J. Liebling, "Second City," *The New Yorker* (January 12, 1952).

John Martin, "He Passed Up Jail for the Chair," *Official Detective Stories* (January 1945).

Charles J. Masters, *Governor Henry Horner, Chicago Politics and the Great Depression* (Carbondale: Southern Illinois University Press, 2007), 98.

PRISONER #32147

PAGES 213–220

From Leavenworth Prison, I obtained Rappaport's prisoner file, which was full of detailed biographical information. I cross-referenced this with newspaper reports and genealogical records.

Chicago Tribune (March 2, 1937).
Letter, H. I. Davis to Warden Tom White, January 30, 1931, Leavenworth Prison files.
Letter, Rose Rappaport to Warden Tom White, November 27, 1930, Leavenworth Prison files.
Letter, Rose Rappaport to Warden Tom White, May 7, 1930, Leavenworth Prison files.
Letter, Warden Tom White to Rose Rappaport, November 29, 1930, Leavenworth Prison files.
Chicago Tribune (October 9, 1935).
John Martin, "He Passed Up Jail for the Chair," *Official Detective Stories* magazine (January 1945).
"Stoolie!," *Front Page Detective* magazine (August 1937).
Telegram from correspondence kept in Rappaport's Leavenworth Prison file.

AN UNPOLISHED DIAMOND

PAGES 221–225

The dream sequence is from Alfred E. Parker, *The Berkeley Police Story* (Springfield, MA: Charles C. Thomas, 1972). Background on the Crime Detection Lab is from Eloise Keeler, *The Lie Detector Man: The Career and Cases of Leonarde Keeler* (Boston: Telshare, 1983), and various papers and documents at the Bancroft Library at UC Berkeley.

Ken Alder, *The Lie Detectors: The History of an American Obsession* (New York: Free Press, 2007), 90.

John Larson to August Vollmer (August 1, 1924), Berkeley Police Department records, Bancroft Library, folder 10.

John Larson to August Vollmer (April 1, 1926), Berkeley Police Department records, Bancroft Library, folder 10.

John Larson to August Vollmer (June 14, 1926), John Larson Papers, Bancroft Library, folders 10, 18.

Leonarde Keeler, "A Method for Detecting Deception," *American Journal of Police Science* 1, no. 1 (January–February 1930): 38–52.

Alfred E. Parker, *The Berkeley Police Story* (Springfield, MA: Charles C. Thomas, 1972), 19.

August Vollmer to John Larson (June 7, 1926), John Larson Papers, Bancroft Library, box 1, folder 18.

August Vollmer to John Larson (June 19, 1926), John Larson Papers, Bancroft Library, box 1, folder 18.

A PAINTED SPARROW

PAGES 226–235

Susanna Calkins, "The Real Canary Murder Case of 1929," *Criminal Element* (May 2, 2019), https://www.criminalelement.com/the-real-canary-murder-case-of-1929/.

Chicago Tribune (November 2, 1929).

Leonarde Keeler to Charles Keeler (July 13, 1929), Charles Keeler Papers, Bancroft Library, box 7.

Leonarde Keeler to August Vollmer (April 17, 1930), Berkeley Police Department records, Bancroft Library, box 10.

Eloise Keeler, *The Lie Detector Man: The Career and Cases of Leonarde Keeler* (Boston: Telshare, 1983), 24, 25, 43, 45, 60.

John A. Larson, *Lying and Its Detection* (Chicago: University of Chicago Press, 1932), 383.

John Larson Papers, Bancroft Library, carton 1, folder 7.

Letter, John Larson to Leonarde Keeler (April 10, 1932), John Larson Papers, Bancroft Library, box 1, folder 9

National Commission on Law Observance and Enforcement (Wickersham Commission), 151.

Willard M. Oliver, *August Vollmer: The Father of American Policing* (Durham, NC: Carolina Academic Press, 2017), 438.

Michael Pettit, *The Science of Deception: Psychology and Commerce in America* (Chicago: University of Chicago Press, 2013).

August Vollmer and Alfred E. Parker, *Crime, Crooks & Cops* (New York: Funk & Wagnalls, 1937), 104.

August Vollmer to Leonarde Keeler (August 26, 1930), Charles Keeler Papers, Bancroft Library, box 11.

THE REPORTER

PAGES 236–240

Ken Alder, *The Lie Detectors: The History of an American Obsession* (New York: Free Press, 2007), 121.

Chicago Tribune (June 12, 1997), https://www.chicagotribune.com/news/ct-xpm-1997-06-12-9706120389-story.html.

Chicago Tribune (October 2, 2011) https://www.chicagotribune.com/news/ct-per-flash-jakelingle-1002-20111002-story.html.

Eloise Keeler, *The Lie Detector Man: The Career and Cases of Leonarde Keeler* (Boston: Telshare, 1983), 42.

John A. Larson, *Lying and Its Detection* (Chicago: University of Chicago Press, 1932), 376.

My Al Capone Museum, http://www.myalcaponemuseum.com/id34.htm

John Larson to John A. Greening (February 28, 1935), John Larson Papers, Bancroft Library, box 1, folder 3.

John Larson to Robert Borkenstein (June 18, 1952), Beulah Graham Papers, courtesy of Ken Alder.

John Larson to August Vollmer (January 5, 1930), August Vollmer Papers, Bancroft Library, box 18.

A MALIGNANT HEART
PAGES 241–245

I obtained the court files from the Rappaport case, which detailed the judge's instructions to the jury, as well as various motions and affidavits raised during the trial.

Courier-Post (November 21, 1935).

"Stoolie!," *Front Page Detective* magazine (August 1937).

FRANKENSTEIN'S MONSTER
PAGES 246–252

This section is based on correspondence kept in the Bancroft Library, but Ken Alder's book *The Lie Detectors: The History of an American Obsession* (New York: Free Press, 2007) was particularly helpful for piecing together the timeline.

Ken Alder, *The Lie Detectors: The History of an American Obsession* (New York: Free Press, 2007).

Leonarde Keeler to August Vollmer (December 17, 1929), Charles Keeler Papers, Bancroft Library, box 7.

John A. Larson, *Lying and Its Detection* (Chicago: University of Chicago Press, 1932), 413.

John Larson Papers, Bancroft Library, carton 1, folder 9 (undated).

John Larson to Leonarde Keeler (December 21, 1931), John Larson Papers, Bancroft Library, carton 1, folder 9.

John Larson to Don Kooken (April 18, 1933), John Larson Papers, Bancroft Library, box 1, folder 10.

John Larson to Thomas Johnson (August 13, 1961), John Larson Papers, Bancroft Library, box 2, folder 13.

John Larson to August Vollmer (April 28, 1931), John Larson Papers, Bancroft Library, box 1, folder 18.

John Larson to August Vollmer (October 9, 1931), John Larson Papers, Bancroft Library, folder 18.

Leonarde Keeler to August Vollmer (May 26, 1931), Berkeley Police Department records, Bancroft Library, box 10.

John Larson to Leonarde Keeler (October 27, 1932), Leonarde Keeler Papers, Bancroft Library, carton 1, folder 17.

John Larson to August Vollmer (April 28, 1931), Berkeley Police Department records, Bancroft Library, box 10.

John Larson Papers, Bancroft Library, carton 1, folders 3 & 7.

John Larson to August Vollmer (August 19, 1932), John Larson Papers, Bancroft Library, box 1, folder 18.

Leonarde Keeler to George Haney (March 1, 1934), Leonarde Keeler Papers, Bancroft Library, carton 1, folder 12.

Leonarde Keeler to August Vollmer (March 19, 1934), August Vollmer Papers, Bancroft Library, box 17.

Leonarde Keeler to August Vollmer (September 19, 1932), August Vollmer Papers, Bancroft Library, box 17.

Leonarde Keeler to August Vollmer (March 19, 1934), August Vollmer Papers, Bancroft Library, box 17.

August Vollmer to George Haney (July 12, 1933), August Vollmer Papers, Bancroft Library, box 42.

August Vollmer to Leonarde Keeler (October 4, 1932), August Vollmer Papers, Bancroft Library, box 42.

August Vollmer to Leonarde Keeler (April 4, 1934), August Vollmer Papers, Bancroft Library, box 43.

August Vollmer to John Larson (June 16, 1931), John Larson Papers, Bancroft Library, box 1, folder 18.

August Vollmer to Charlie Wilson (March 1, 1934), August Vollmer Papers, Bancroft Library, box 43.

E. NORMOUS WEALTH
PAGES 253–257

Ken Alder, *The Lie Detectors: The History of an American Obsession* (New York: Free Press, 2007).

Eloise Keeler, *The Lie Detector Man: The Career and Cases of Leonarde Keeler* (Boston: Telshare, 1983), 43, 88, 89, 102.

Leonarde Keeler to Charles Keeler (February 14, 1936), Charles Keeler Papers, Bancroft Library, box 7.

Leonarde Keeler to Charles Keeler, quoted by Ken Alder in *The Lie Detectors: The History of an American Obsession* (New York: Free Press, 2007).

AN UNTIMELY END

PAGES 258–262

Background on executions and the Cook County Jail are from "The Death Watch" in *True Detective* magazine (September 1946) and Ed Baumann, *May God Have Mercy on Your Soul: The Story of the Rope and the Thunderbolt* (Los Angeles: Bonus Books, 1993).

Ed Baumann, *May God Have Mercy on Your Soul: The Story of the Rope and the Thunderbolt* (Los Angeles: Bonus Books, 1993), 328.

Belvedere Daily Republican (June 17, 1936).

Chicago Eagle (May 20, 1937).

Chicago Tribune (February 23, 1936).

Irving Cutler, *The Jews of Chicago: From Shtetl to Suburb* (Champaign: University of Illinois Press, 1996), 129.

Leonarde Keeler to August Vollmer (March 25, 1936), August Vollmer Papers, Bancroft Library, box 17.

Oshkosh Northwestern (October 20, 1936).

August Vollmer to Leonarde Keeler (April 8, 1946), August Vollmer Papers, Bancroft Library, box 44.

August Vollmer to Charlie Wilson (March 1, 1934), August Vollmer Papers, Bancroft Library, box 43.

THE LAST MILE

PAGES 263–270

Associated Press (December 2, 1936).

Austin American Statesman (October 24, 1936).

Ed Baumann, *May God Have Mercy on Your Soul: The Story of the Rope and the Thunderbolt* (Los Angeles: Bonus Books, 1993), 332, 343.

Belvedere Daily Republican (February 15, 1937).

Chicago Tribune (October 23, 1936; December 2, 1936; February 19, 1937; February 25, 1937).

Court records

Decatur Daily Review (December 4, 1936).

Leader-Telegram (October 24, 1936).

Charles J. Masters, *Governor Henry Horner, Chicago Politics and the Great Depression* (Champaign: Southern Illinois University Press, 2007), 109, 206.

Pharos-Tribune (Logansport, Indiana) (March 14, 1938).

Pittsburgh Press (February 26, 1937).

Times (Hammond, Indiana) (February 19, 1937).

Times (Munster, Indiana) (February 26, 1937).

DIVINE INTERVENTION
PAGES 271–275

Chicago Tribune (March 1, 1937).

Court records.

Kansas City Star (March 3, 1937).

Thomas B. Littlewood, *Horner of Illinois* (Evanston: Northwestern University Press, 1969).

United Press (March 1, 1937).

"Stoolie!," *Front Page Detective* magazine (August 1937).

JUDGE AND JURY
PAGES 276–284

Associated Press (March 1, 1937; March 2, 1937).

Ed Baumann, *May God Have Mercy on Your Soul: The Story of the Rope and the Thunderbolt* (Los Angeles: Bonus Books, 1993).

Biographical sketch of Leonarde Keeler, Agnes de Mille Papers, New York Public Library.

Chicago Tribune (March 2, 1937; March 2, 1947).

"The Death Watch," *True Detective* magazine (September 1946).

Indianapolis News (March 2, 1937).

Kansas City Star (March 3, 1937).

Eloise Keeler, *The Lie Detector Man: The Career and Cases of Leonarde Keeler* (Boston: Telshare, 1983), 116.

Leonarde Keeler, "A Method for Detecting Deception," *American Journal of Police Science* 1:1 (January–February 1930), 38–52.

Leonarde Keeler, "Problems in the Use of the "Lie Detector," reprinted in *Polygraph* 23:2 (1994), 174–180.

Leonarde Keeler to August Vollmer (February 26, 1937), August Vollmer Papers, Bancroft Library, Box 17.

Literary Digest (March 13, 1937).

New York Times (March 2, 1937).

San Francisco Examiner (March 3, 1937).

Star Tribune (June 6, 1937).

United Press (March 2, 1937).

EPILOGUE

PAGES 285–294

Ken Alder, *The Lie Detectors: The History of an American Obsession* (New York: Free Press, 2007).

"Aldrich Ames Speaks Out on Polygraph Testing," FAS Project on Government Secrecy (November 30, 2000), https://sgp.fas.org/news/secrecy/2000/11/113000.html.

Biographical sketch of Leonarde Keeler, Agnes de Mille Papers, New York Public Library.

Eloise Keeler, *The Lie Detector Man: The Career and Cases of Leonarde Keeler* (Boston: Telshare, 1983), 117.

Interview with Amit Katwala.

John Larson Papers, Bancroft Library, and box 1, folder 2; box 1, folder 4, Biographical sketch of Leonarde Keeler, Agnes de Mille Papers, New York Public Library; and box 1, folder 8.

Letter, John Larson to J. A. Greening (December 10, 1938), John Larson Papers, Bancroft Library, box 2, folder 4.

Letter, John Larson to August Vollmer (June 2, 1951), John Larson Papers, Bancroft Library, box 1, folder 18.

Letter, August Vollmer to Viola Stevens (April 21, 1950), Leonarde Keeler Papers, Bancroft Library, carton 2, folder 10.

Willard M. Oliver, *August Vollmer: The Father of American Policing* (Durham, NC: Carolina Academic Press, 2017), 540, 541, 542.

The Press Democrat (March 4, 1937).

"Use of Polygraphs as Lie Detectors by the Federal Government," House Report No. 198 (March 22, 1965), Tenth Report by the Committee on Government Operations.

CODA

PAGES 295–303

This section draws partly on reporting originally conducted for a piece for *The Guardian* "long read." That piece, published in September 2019, is available online: https://www.theguardian.com/technology/2019/sep/05/the-race-to-create-a-perfect-lie-detector-and-the-dangers-of-succeeding.

Email from Dr. Larry Farwell to Amit Katwala, April 2, 2019

Phone interview with Larry Farwell, January 22, 2019

Video of brain fingerprinting test on Ricky Smith provided to the author by Farwell

PICTURE CREDITS